MACHINE TRACTABLE DICTIONARIES: DESIGN AND CONSTRUCTION

Printed in the United States of America

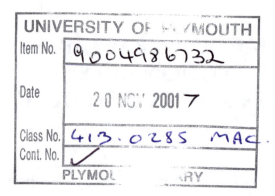

Library of Congress Cataloging-in-Publication Data

Machine-tractable dictionaries : design and construction / [edited by] Cheng-ming Guo.
p. cm. – (Ablex series in computational science)
Includes bibliographical references and indexes.
ISBN 0-89391-853-9
1. Lexicography–Data processing. 2. Machine translating. 3. Artificial intelligence. I. Guo, Cheng-ming. II. Series.
P327.M25 1994 94-355
CIP

Ablex Publishing Corporation
355 Chestnut Street
Norwood, New Jersey 07648

To my mother, and
to the memory of my father

CONTENTS

CONTRIBUTORS

Robert A. Amsler
The MITRE Corporation
Mclean, Virginia, USA

B. T. S. Atkins
Oxford University Press
11 South Street
Lewes, Sussex BN7 2BT, England

Nicoletta Calzolari
Istituto di Linguistica
Computazionale del CNR – Pisa
Dipartimento di Linguistica –
Università di Pisa
Via della Faggiola 32
I 56100 Pisa, Italy

Arthur Cater
Department of Computer Science
University College Dublin
Belfield, DUBLIN 4, Ireland

Paul A. Day
Department of Computer Science
University of Exter
Exeter, Devon, U.K.

Pim van der Eijk
Research Institute for Language and Speech
State University of Utrecht
Trans 10
3512 JK Utrecht, The Netherlands

Martha W. Evens
Computer Science Department
Illinois Institute of Technology
Chicago, IL 60616 USA

Edward A. Fox
Department of Computer Science
Virginia Polytechnic Institute and State University
Blacksburg, VA 24061 USA

Lynette Hirschman
Spoken Language Group
MIT Laboratory for Computer Science
545 Technology Square
Cambridge, MA 02139 USA

Makoto Nagao
Department of Electrical Engineering
Kyoto University
Kyoto, Japan

Sergei Nirenburg
Center for Machine Translation
Carnegie Mellon University
Pittsburgh, PA, USA

J. Terry Nutter
Department of Computer Science
Virginia Polytechnic Institute and State University
Blacksburg, VA 24061 USA

James Pustejovsky
Computer Science Department
Brandeis University
Waltham, MA 02254 USA

Allan Ramsay
Department of Computer Science
University College Dublin
Belfield, DUBLIN 4, Ireland

Amanda J. C. Sharkey
Department of Computer Science
University of Exeter
Exeter, Devon, U. K.

Noel E. Sharkey
Department of Computer Science
University of Exeter
Exeter, Devon, U. K.

Brian Slator
The Institute for the Learning Sciences
Northwestern University
1890 Maple St.
Evanston, IL 60201 USA

Yorick Wilks
Computing Research Laboratory
New Mexico State University
Las Cruces, New Mexico 88003 USA

Toshio Yokoi
Japan Electronic Dictionary Research Institute, Ltd.
Mita Kokusai Building Annex, 4-28,
Mita 1-Chome
Minato-ku, Tokyo 108 Japan

PREFACE

It is universally acknowledged that an adequate computer system that processes natural language is in want of an adequate natural language dictionary. These words are truer today than ever before.

Owing to the challenge of the Fifth Generation Computing Technology Drive in Japan, which had as part of its goal to become the "biggest information peddler of the next century," more and more researchers have become increasingly interested in processing general unrestricted text, particularly in knowledge acquisition from general unrestricted text. Demonstration programs with toy lexicons in natural language processing (NLP) in general and knowledge acquisition in particular are shying away from the scene, but reluctantly. Replacing them are efforts at large knowledge acquisition systems with very large lexicons.

Researchers who are currently involved in this information adventure, as well as those who would like to join in, are faced with one ultimate research question: how to house the pearls of wisdom of the entire human civilization—past, present, and future—in computer files that are easily retrieved?

One sensible approach to coping with this challenge is to construct a very large lexicon, and use it as the core of a knowledge acquisition system that automatically acquires new information from machine-readable sources. Each time a piece of new information is acquired, it will be used to enrich the lexicon. The ever-growing lexicon facilitates a never-ending process of knowledge acquisition from general unrestricted text. Thus the lexicon, which is part and parcel of the NLP system, evolves over time to become a wonderful product of the future with commercial value.

Lexicons of this breed are named machine-tractable dictionaries, or MTDs for short. In essence, MTDs are isomorphic to what are called electronic dictionaries in Japan, and lexical systems at IBM, Yorktown Heights. This book is intended as a contribution to what is hopefully a wealth of ideas on the applications of machine-readable dictionaries (MRDs) and the design and construction of MTDs heading toward lexical knowledge bases.

Over the last 15 years or so, intensified interest has been witnessed in the study of MRDs. Conferences and workshops have been held in Europe, the United States, and Japan to discuss issues of concern in automating the lexicon. The year 1990 alone witnessed five major workshops on the lexicon held worldwide. A lexical resource center has already been set up at the Computing Research Laboratory of New Mexico State University with funding from the American government. A special interest group in lexical research within the area of computational linguistics, called the *SIGLEX*, has also been set up, with James Pustejovsky of Brandeis University as the chairman. In January 1987, an entire panel session at the Third Conference on Theoretical Issues in Natural Language Processing (henceforth TINLAP-3) held at New Mexico State University was devoted to the study of "Words and World Representations," a TINLAP-3 label for MRD-related research.

According to Don Walker, chairman of the panel session on "Words and World Representations," the surge of interest in MRDs was not accidental. Motivations were at work both on the theoretical and the applicational levels. In terms of theories, a wide variety of grammars were becoming increasingly lexicalist. These theories increasingly assume that much grammatical knowledge resides in the lexicon itself, and that many grammatical structures follow from constraints on the use of particular lexical items. Examples of such grammars are Lexical-Functional Grammar (Kaplan & Bresnan, 1982), Generalized Phrase Structure Grammar (Gazdar & Pullum, 1985), and Categorial Grammar (Lewis, 1971). MRDs have been found to be of substantial use in the context of analyzing natural language texts within the framework of those linguistic theories. In terms of applications, the development of production systems, human/machine interfaces, and expert systems have generated pressing and practical demands for automating the lexicon.

It is not surprising at all that researchers expect the information contained in MRDs to be ready for use on their systems. Unfortunately, such expectations are not warranted. The so-called "machine-readable" dictionaries are just electronic versions of conventional dictionaries designed and made for human use. The design and construction of MTDs from MRDs and other machine-readable sources involves major efforts, the scale of which unfolds as your travel through the book continues.

This book consists of two parts—an edited part (Part One) and an authored part (Part Two). I am both the editor and the author of the book.

In the latter half of 1990, a special forum on the design and construction of MTDs was conducted via electronic mail among a group of top-notch researchers from Europe, Japan, and the United States. Edited versions of their contributions appear in Part One of this book. Part Two of this book, which represents my own contribution to the forum, comprises the gist of my doctoral dissertation completed in Summer 1989 under the advisorship of Dr. Yorick Wilks, Director of the Computing Research Laboratory (CRL) of New Mexico State University. The bibliography given at the end of this book was built upon a generous contribution from Dr. Martha Evens, who compiled the original bibliography on National Science Foundation grant IRI - 8704619 to Illinois Institute of Technology.

I am deeply indebted to all contributors of Part One for their honest opinions on the design and construction of MTDs.

The research presented in Part Two of this book was conducted over a period of 3 years from September 1986 to August 1989 in the exciting and challenging surroundings of New Mexico State University in Las Cruces, New Mexico. It is meant to be a detailed account of an attempt at MTDs. The research was partially funded by the American National Science Foundation.

I thank Yorick Wilks for being a constant guide in the completion of this research. He has been an excellent promoter of the research on LDOCE. Thanks are also due to Derek Partridge, my major academic advisor before he left for work at the University of Exeter in England. I thank my professors at New Mexico State University for providing interesting discussions and arguments on my research. Ken Paap, David Martin, Don Dearholt, and John Barden are certainly to be commended for doing that.

The research has been scrutinized by the Natural Language Group at the CRL on many occasions. Members of that group, including Yorick Wilks, Jerry Ball, Afzal Ballim, David Farwell, Tony Plate, Paul Mc Kevitt, Xiuming Huang, Li Chen, Min Liu, Brian Slator and Sylvia Cand. De Ram, have constituted a stimulating environment during the pursuit of this research. Special thanks are due to Dan Fass, who helped to iron out some of the worst wrinkles in my description of the construction processes. Roger Schvaneveldt and Jim MacDonald from the Cognitive Science Group of the CRL made very useful comments and suggestions when the work was presented to them.

I would like to express my gratitude to Robert A. Amsler for generating one of the first two critiques of the book, the unabridged version of which appears as the introduction. I admire him for his honesty in passing judgments on others' research as well as his courage in lending his judgments to be judged. Owing to the special nature of the introduction, the reader might experience some unusual "cold," as it were, at the beginning, which, in the author's humble opinion, suggests nothing short of a long, warming shower to follow.

Finally, I would like to express my heartfelt thanks to Professor Frank Anderson, head of the Department of Computer Science, University College, Dublin, for his support in the preparation of this book.

Cheng-ming Guo

INTRODUCTION

Dr. Robert A. Amsler
The MITRE Corporation
McLean, Virginia

The work is intended to review the state of the art in our understanding of machine-readable dictionaries (MRDs) and consider both whether and how one can develop the next level of tool, which Cheng-ming Guo and the New Mexico School of machine-readable dictionary research have named "the machine-*tractable* dictionary." The essence of "tractability" in this regard is that such a work comprises a computational representation of the contents of a machine-readable dictionary that embodies both the computer science understanding of a database and the computational linguistic understanding of a parsed and semantically disambiguated text. This level of lexical tool is thus the precursor to the still more advanced *lexical knowledge base,* as Amsler and Calzolari have defined it, in which all the contents of the original dictionary would be replaced by relationships between concepts in a knowledge-based representation system.

Because lexical knowledge base construction continues to elude us at this stage, the machine-tractable dictionary (a.k.a. dictionary database) may constitute a necessary intermediate step and considerations of what we can do to cover the ground from our present understanding of MRDs to reach MTDs constitute a useful evaluation.

The book is divided into two major sections, the first of which is a series of solicited essays from those both directly involved with MRD research and by others whose computational linguistic agendas would be directly affected by the existence of MTDs. As such, one gets a bit of a jolt between essays that cover the ground all the way from detailed reports on the nuts and bolts assembly of a MTD to nearly pure philosophical speculation about whether in principle such a thing as an MTD can be constructed at all. It very much has the air of a survey of the research community to gauge their degree of acceptance of the notion of MTDs, rather than what the title more directly suggests—a work about their design and construction. However, given that the field is rather more art than engineering at this stage, the skepticism probably is most healthy and the overall impression is that of a series of thought-provoking essays exploring what MTDs are and could (or could not) be.

The second portion of the book is Cheng-ming Guo's thesis on the specific effort to build a MTD at New Mexico State University and includes three rather appealing surveys of the history and development of MRD research, semantic primitives, and human and machine learning (Chapter 17). The last is included because the approach to MTD construction taken borrows insights from learning theory.

The actual exposition of the technique employed to create an MTD out of the *Longman Dictionary of Contemporary English* (LDOCE) focuses on the automatic disambiguation of sense meanings in LDOCE through the use of the limited defining vocabulary of this particular dictionary. I suspect that much more authoritativeness is being imparted to definitions and defining vocabulary of the creators of LDOCE than they would feel comfortable accepting (Sue Atkins' essay in the first part of the book supports this view that lexicographers in general feel uneasy when their work falls under the computational lexicologist's unblinking eye), but the exposition is carried through with appropriate experimental methodology.

The end product, however, leaves one feeling a little less than completely satisfied. The problem lies not so much with any flaw in the work performed, but in the inescapable conclusion that the study of any one dictionary leads more toward conclusions about that book than about the real target of the research—the concepts of meaning in the English language itself. Not only is the work on LDOCE as yet inconclusive, but in order for work of such a nature to be conclusive it would have to be paralleled by work on additional MRDs and a comparison of the results.

James Pustejovsky's chapter, "Polysemy and Word Meaning," clearly places him in the camp of concerned overseer to the busy industry of the MTD mechanics attempting to disassemble, tag, and reassemble their MRDs into MTDs. He presents a framework much more oriented toward what I would characterize as *contextual lexical semantics* rather than *dictionary lexical semantics*, but the representational issues of both areas are similar. When he presents examples employing *fast* in various sentences, my impression is not of a need for specific dictionary senses to cover such usage, but of the need for a specific semantic extension of parsing capabilities. Thus, examples such as *a fast motorway* or *a fast garage* do not make me question the inadequacy of the senses of *fast* recorded in good dictionaries, but more the need for the expansion of these elliptical compounds into more explicit forms such as:

a motorway on which cars can travel fast
a motorway over which travel takes place quickly
a motorway on which the average speed of travel is fast
a garage at which workers perform their work quickly

Thus, this is not a dictionary problem, it is a problem of contextual meaning. The ambiguity of the textual occurrences of *fast* does not require the dictionary to expand its sense discriminations, but that the computational linguist clarify their understanding of the ellipsis involved using what may be an even harder commodity to obtain—world knowledge.

However, lest I seem negative on this point, Pustejovsky's recognition of the qualia *structure* of word meaning clearly reflects a real phenomenon. The constitutive, formal, *telic* and *agentive* roles for words in context are real. What I question is whether it is the lexicon that bears the responsibility for containing the explicative power to disambiguate these elliptical constructions. There doesn't seem to me to be anything missing in the lexicon. The missing information is in the world knowledge that imparts the understanding of what purpose something such as a *motorway* or a *garage* has, who the agents of the events that take place on or in such places are, and only then is it appropriate to call upon the lexicon to answer the question as to what *fast* means.

This raises a particular point about dictionaries that is often discussed: Where does lexical knowledge leave off and world knowledge begin? The answer typically given is that encyclopedias embody world knowledge, whereas dictionaries contain only lexical knowledge. However, the dilemma is not that simply resolved. I would contend that the dictionary includes world knowledge in the texts of its definitions. To be sure, some of what appears in the definition can be expressed in the more restricted relationships of taxonomies and part-whole relationships, but whenever text is employed to explain something, the tendency for world knowledge to creep in with the information being imparted is nearly irresistible. MRDs contain small but quite significant bits of world knowledge in their textual components. It may well be that what eludes researchers in their efforts to construct both world knowledge bases and lexical knowledge bases is the inability to separate these two tasks without a loss of, respectively, required capacity or required capabilities.

Lynette Hirschman's chapter continues to explore the relationship between world knowledge and lexical knowledge. She debates the question of whether it makes sense to believe in the semiautomatic construction of a lexical knowledge base acquisition system starting with MTDs. She notes that by using sublanguages and bootstrapping from these, one ought to be able to reach an impressive range of lexical knowledge base coverage. More specifically, she outlines a plan:

> That is, we use an MTD to parse sentences, use the parses to derive syntactic patterns, then use the syntactic patterns and string relations to identify substitution classes and from there, semantic classes. These in turn, can provide sublanguage-specific co-occurrence patterns, which will reveal the basic sublanguage relations. Also, given a good description of words and structures in the general language, it should be possible to describe patterns of specialization from the general language to the sublanguage, which can facilitate training procedures for new sublanguages or support recovery strategies for handling unknown words or constructs or concepts in a sublanguage. (p. xx)

What Hirschman identifies is the tension existing today between the knowledge base engineers who correctly perceive the NLP problem as being soluble with access to ample amounts of world knowledge, but then cannot propose any method to use existing knowledge-base acquisition methods developed for expert systems to build such a massive lexical knowledge base, and the pure empiricists who are exploring the reach of the application of statistical methods to text study, but cannot offer any proof that such techniques can derive the specific knowledge needed for given applications of NLP. The answer seems to lie in the MTD serving an intermediate role to both groups. The knowledge engineers can explore how to represent its contents, somewhat formal to begin with, in terms of valid knowledge base structures, and the empiricists can explore how to extract the information that the MTD displays from texts directly.

Arthur Cater's chapter also attempts to work backward from the needs of a natural language processing system to reach toward what an MRD must contain. He offers an inventory of what lexical knowledge comprises, but he does not address the more pressing problem of how this information can be obtained in the quantities prescribed. There is not a great deal about whether MRDs provide this data nor how MTDs should represent it. However, he concludes, once again, that world knowledge is essential and reinforces the sense of a seamless transition from knowledge about words and knowledge about concepts in the world as being the requirement needed to solve the natural language problem.

Nicoletta Calzolari offers a tantalizing outline of what MRDs can provide, as well as what they lack. The outline, however, is not expanded sufficiently to explain how one can obtain these results. We thus have something of a "wish list" of potential resources and expertise that is seen as relevant, but no further elaboration as to how these sources can be used.

To some degree Calzolari compliments the Cater chapter by explaining that MRDs do contain many of the prerequisites, but we are still left wondering whether there is a practical means of assembling all these resources.

Pim van der Eijk first explains the concept of a neutral dictionary. In essence, the idea is that the critical element of neutrality is that it does not select winners or losers between competing linguistic theories. Instead it will represent all perspectives. This is contrasted with standardization, in which competing theories will be considered and either a winner will be selected or some consensus formed from components of all the theories.

The dilemma here is probably not between neutrality and standardization, but instead over the amount of knowledge available for consideration. I believe what is really involved is that there are nothing but incomplete representations of lexical data and that the task is one of fitting together these portions of incomplete representations. Because each representation was based on only part of the portrait of a lexical concept as explained in some incomplete lexical or linguistic theory, they cannot be fitted together into a single whole.

The situation is analogous to getting several subsets of the pieces to an unknown number of jigsaw puzzles and being asked to fit the pieces together into whole puzzles. It is worse because the images portrayed on the completed puzzles are in fact of the *same* scenes in many cases. Not only can one not tell exactly how many puzzles are represented by the pieces, but one also cannot tell whether any two pieces are part of the same puzzle or not. Standardization would be making a claim that all the pieces could be forced to make up one puzzle for each scene. This cannot be done because each puzzle is cut somewhat differently and there are two issues involved for each piece. First, what scene does this piece relate to and second, of which puzzle about that scene is it a part?

So, we are left with the task of attempting to sort out what the jumble of puzzle pieces shows of the scenes. Van der Eijk suggests that we can minimize the representation of this situation by a process of *normalization*, forming a sort of lowest common denominator for all the portions of the puzzle scenes that are shared between two or more puzzles. I believe there may be a flaw in this belief in that it is possible for MRDs to contain inconsistent information. In the jigsaw puzzle analogy, it would be as though certain clues one might rely on, such as the shape of the puzzle pieces, were in fact not constant even within one puzzle. The puzzles were hand-cut rather than cut out by machine, and each puzzle piece may be of a unique shape.

What appears to be the actual domain of this *neutral dictionary* is that of a logic-based lexicon to be constructed rather than a format into which existing MRDs can be placed. The goals of forming the union of existing representations, acquiring properties by inheritance, and not enforcing conformance seem to exclude the existence of contradictions that if present would create havoc in such a system.

Allan Ramsay offers arguments against a neutral dictionary being possible. However, there are two anomalies in Ramsey's chapter. In the segment on morphology, he concludes that neutrality and storage efficiency are contrary goals for morphological information, yet this seems to be reaching beyond the intention of lexical representation to drag in an outside problem in order to defeat the premise. Why would storage efficiency be necessary for the existence of a neutral lexicon? This is to say that the *existence* of a neutral lexicon does not depend on it simultaneously being storage efficient any more than the convergence of a mathematical summation series requires that it converge fast enough to be computationally useful for approximating the sum.

Then, in the section on syntax, he notes that existing dictionaries do not select any linguistic theory and have little syntactic information of use. This seems a mixed argument; that is, if existing lexicons have achieved neutrality because of their limited syntactic information, then they do exist already and he has defeated his own argument that dictionaries cannot be neutral.

In all, what Ramsey seems to be claiming is that no *useful* neutral lexicon can exist, where usefulness simultaneously implies storage efficiency and syntactic relevance. I can sympathize with the view that neutrality may not be a panacea for dictionaries, in that to be neutral they would have to abandon being maximally useful, but it is not the same thing as claiming that no neutral dictionary can exist. And certainly the concept of neutrality does not have to carry the extra baggage of being most computationally efficient.

Brian Slator's very short chapter keynotes some fallacies that often confuse novices to the MRD field. The first is in assuming that all dictionaries are of equal quality. This can often be heard in comments such as, "I looked up the word 'x' in *the* dictionary and the definition was inadequate," or "I tried using a dictionary once and its definition was quite poorly done." This would be equivalent to saying, "I don't consider English literature very good because I read a novel written in English that was really badly written."

Amore subtle refinement of this argument may be given in the form, "I think the dictionary was a Webster's." It turns out that the name "Webster" is no more specific to only quality dictionaries than the term "authorized" is a guarantee of quality for a biography. Noah Webster's original dictionaries have long since passed into the public domain, and although the *Merriam-Webster* company is a direct descendant of the original products, the name itself can be used by anyone who chooses to claim the heritage.

The second fallacy is that of confusing what logic has to say about meaning and what the dictionary offers as an explication of *usage*. Thus, for example, the reason the verb *to be* has many senses in a conventional dictionary, whereas it has but two "useful sense distinctions" in AI, is that the dictionary's entry is attempting to cover all the usages of *be* in text, many of which are not at all synonymous with either of the logician's senses. Words often acquire highly specialized meanings due to a variety of quirks of history, language origin, or metaphoric extension. When one reads a dictionary entry for a closed class word, such as the verb *to be*, one must be prepared for an enumeration of data about the word, rather than merely the specification of what the verb's necessary role is in logic. *Red* may be either a color or a descriptor of someone believing in communism, but neither explains its meaning in "I caught him red-handed," or "It's a red herring." I suppose a logician would declare these two instances to refer to the color of the hands or the herring, because red can only have two referents. However, a natural language system doing so would have missed the point entirely.

J. Terry Nutter's chapter takes us deep into the world of practicing computational lexicologists. It deals with the realities of computation over megabytes of MRD data and immediately contrasts with the speculative essays before it that tend to see an all-or-nothing utility to using machine-readable dictionary data to build a lexicon. As is often the case when considering experimental reality vs. theory, the reality is always much messier than the theory and simultaneously more rewarding and more frustrating than can easily be imagined by those who limit their investigations to theoretical work.

MRDs are large and very messy typographic bodies of data. Not unlike an archaeological dig, they require exceptional attention to detail in their excavation to reveal things properly. If this book had been about machine-tractable archaeological data, rather than machine-tractable dictionaries, there would have been some understanding from the start that the data involved literally came out of the ground. As it is, we have entertained the fiction that dictionaries are somehow pure works of logic, perhaps written down by unskilled ancient scribes, and can be studied for their wisdom independent of how we came to possess these works.

In actuality, MRDs require careful processing to yield their secrets. They are the constructs of groups of lexicographers sharing some perhaps limiting perspective on how to describe lexical information. As such they are no better than any other manmade artifact. They contain mistakes, inconsistencies, and as always, do not come with sufficient instructions for their complete explication. What suffices for a guide to the use of the dictionary for the human reader is only the barest set of heuristics to the computational lexicologist seeking to tease apart font codes and arcane abbreviations into transitional states for a transduction of the dictionary into separate components.

Thus, it is perhaps not surprising that in Nutter's chapter the concerns are almost all requirements for successful lexical excavation, rather than higher goals of philosophical import. Praise be for those with shovels who clear off the debris so that we may all consider the evidence, rather than just sit back comfortably in our easy chairs and debate what the state of the world is or should be.

From the detailed business end of machine-readable dictionaries we turn now to the applications to which an MTD may be expected to be applied. The next series of chapters views MTDs not as linguistic repositories in and of themselves, but as the resource that specific applications expect to turn to in order to solve their problems in natural language computation. The range of applications is quite broad, from machine translation to information retrieval.

Toshio Yokio describes the EDR electronic dictionary project of Japan. What is most intriguing about his chapter is the lack of moralizing over the theory on which the EDR project is based. In the West, this has often been seen as dooming the project to failure because without adequate theoretical premises, it is nevertheless proceeding to create a very large body of data.

I tend to feel the truth is in between. There is ample evidence in the rest of the book that the debate over what should (or even could) be in an MTD is not over. If the West were to have to finish this debate before any MRDs were prepared we would not have any at all. The basis for MRD research has been existing data that contained an unknown amount of computationally useful orthographic, phonetic, syntactic, semantic, and pragmatic information. To the degree that the EDR project produces another body of such data, it will have succeeded in creating a new source of information worthy of study. To the degree that it limits what it places in the EDR electronic dictionary to incontrovertable data it could fall into Ramsey's category of a *useless* but consistent neutral lexicon.

This chapter shows that the image of an MTD as a large computer-oriented work based on existing MRDs (and hence the print products they represent) is well understood. What remains is to determine whether this image alone is enough to carry the day and produce a useful product for computational linguistics or whether this effort was premature. There is no clear answer from any quarter. The frustrations of J. Terry Nutter in excavating existing MRDs does not give us enough data to determine whether there is a sufficient body of understanding yet available to tell us the best representation of MRD data. The theorists clearly offer no resolution as to what data is needed, other than that it is massive and not entirely available in any existing source of which they know.

It is easy to be pessimistic, but it is less clear that the utility of the result won't itself be one of the critical parts of the puzzle required before a better answer can be created. The best MTD may require some experimentation with MTDs we can build today. This is architecture without architects. There is no discipline of MTD design and construction to guide us, so we must build structures to see if they stand up.

Edward A. Fox and J. Terry Nutter offer a glimpse into what is expected of the applications of an MTD. The CODER system has been under development at VPI & SU since 1985 to explore the use of the lexicon for information retrieval (IR). The basic premise is that one can expand the limited information offered in a user query to an IR system using knowledge derived from a suitably organized MTD with explicit semantic relations added to make clear the meanings of the definitions or other lexical linkages in the dictionary.

The results seem as yet to be inconclusive; that is, as the authors state it, "it is quite likely that the effectiveness of information retrieval systems can be significantly improved through the use of a lexicon server." This shows, especially because this research is now 8 years old, how difficult it is to make a significant improvement in information retrieval. It also highlights that MTDs may well exist before we know what they are good for.

Makoto Nagao presents a clear view of the requirements that machine translation researchers have for MTDs. The data is especially significant because up until this point most of the book has focused on monolingual dictionaries in which the point of language representation was always to understand the original lexical concepts in context by selecting from all their possible meanings represented in an out-of-context dictionary. In MTDs the problem is a little more complex because there are two languages involved and at least one dictionary is bilingual. Thus, not only is there the issue of which of the possible meanings offered does this lexical element have in one language, but what should this element become if its meaning were to be translated into a second language.

The initial dilemma is that context may be much broader for an MT application than it is in a monolingual application. Knowing how to deal with meaning across languages is a significant problem in that the multiplication of the senses required from a monolingual dictionary to a bilingual dictionary may be considerable.

To play is an adequate verb for use in English with most musical instruments, yet if this is to be translated to Japanese, the original definition must be mapped to different forms for pianos, flutes, guitars, and many others. The dilemma is simply that although we know you do not do the same thing to *play* a piano (i.e., sit quietly on a stool and depress keys) that we do when we *play* a flute (i.e., blow through a tube while controlling the output of air through variously arranged holes along the side of the tube), the language in question may or may not have decided to recognize these distinctions in its lexical forms. I can say "I tickled the ivory," for playing the piano, but not for the flute. The potential for the distinction is there. We just look the other way in some languages and ignore it.

This result is especially significant when we consider that monolingual dictionaries often contain much more information about other aspects of words than their bilingual cousins. Thus, you do not find etymologies, or especially good treatments of definitions in bilingual dictionaries although they do enumerate many more phrases in which a word may appear.

Thus an MTD is not a monolithic creation. If MT is one of its functions then it will have to deal with the distinctions significant to MT. If it is to serve both monolingual and bilingual applications, then it will need to reconcile the multiplicity of sense discriminations according to the language pairs it is built to handle and find a place for the monolingual material it contains that reflects these perhaps finer or phrasal supplementary values.

Nagao concludes with the patient warning of someone who has seen the problem well and needs to caution the impetuous new lexicologist from assuming that the book they hold in their hand is the book they need.

Sergei Nirenburg's contribution brings us full circle again, back to the original observation that MTDs are but the stepping stone to a lexical knowledge base. Knowledge-Based Machine Translation (KBMT) may be a reasonable representational format in which to address the concerns Nagao raised about what dictionaries need to know in order to perform well for MT systems. Bearing an interesting relationship to research papers on knowledge representation systems, the issues in Nirenberg's chapter are those of inheritance ("We try to be consistent in the names of ontological concepts going down a subtree"), primitives ("Wherever possible, we use scientific, rather than lay terms," and "Consistently throughout the ontology, we use English words in one sense only as names of ontological concepts"), and quantification ("For example, the meaning of the English word *old* may refer to the range (> 0.8) of the AGE attribute"). These concepts, whereas implicit in dictionaries, are much more a part of knowledge base design than MTDs.

Neural networks and connectionism are powerful ideologies in contemporary computing. In many areas the computing capacity required is still a few orders of magnitude too large for our current computers to handle, but because computing capacity is the least limiting factor in the future of computing, it is worth pondering as soon as possible what one could do if one could compute far better than is currently possible.

The Sharkey, Day, and Sharkey chapter is in just such a context. The principle is that if we represented a connectionist network of, for example, nouns or adjectives and then input members of the other classes, noting which values were appropriately toggled on/off (or numerically weighted), we could represent words as connectionist responses. Some subset of the adjectives, such as colors, tastes, or textures, could be used and then guesses made as to the others. Such a system could better model semantics than much of what we have so far been able to do with symbolic values. Adjectives especially do not seem comfortable within noncontinuously scaled ranges, and have a definite sense of being much more highly correlated with each other in their values than other more denotatively organized information.

There is, of course, an enormous literature on the modeling of lexical information in the human mind. It was psycholinguistics' founding premise and today occupies a large group of cognitive psychologists. Thus, in this context, the discussion of connectionism here is but the tip of an enormous mountain of other research that perhaps needs to be considered before one can make a rational review of this chapter.Why is this chapter here? I would suppose the answer is that we understand so little how to build the right MTD at this point that we are still forced to consider whether an MTD might have to await the arrival of the connectionist's computing hardware many years from now before its contents can be produced.

That is, do we have any idea how to build a *tractable* semantic representation of meaning? It would appear the answer is no. We do not know how to represent such information, how to extract it from MRDs, or even what needs to be included in order to meet the needs of NL programs. There are nothing but interesting experiments being performed at relatively small scales. Admittedly the scale seems to be even smaller for connectionist experimentation than for symbolic, but that may only be because we measure the size of the results by how much data we can amass, rather than how close they get us to the required amount of data that needs to be amassed. Put another way, the issue is whether we are climbing to the top of the tallest tree in order to get closer to the moon. The thought that perhaps instead of looking for tall trees we should contemplate a wholly new technology for amassing such data could be more correct than we want to believe. If one had been asked to propose technologies for reaching the moon in the 17th century, the very idea of turning to alchemy for the development of burnable liquids and explosive solids would have been ludicrous next to using more sensible methods such as balloons or flocks of geese. So, connectionist MTDs might basically just be a 21st-century perspective that we cannot find reasonable today.

Sue Atkins presents a unique perspective of a professional career lexicographer viewing the current intense interest of computational linguists in the contents of MRDs. She begins appropriately enough with two cautions: (a) that natural language processing is attributing entirely too much logical consistency to dictionaries intended solely for human readers, and (b) that natural language processing is attributing entirely too little attention to the prerequisite skills required for professional lexicographers to become masters of their discipline.

Despite the apparent contradiction in these-that the print dictionaries are entirely less accurate than computer professionals think them to be, and that the task of constructing a dictionary entry requires far more skill than computer professionals are willing to believe is needed-there is a common element behind both cautions. It is that publishers, who could easily become villains here, deliberately enforce nonintellectual criteria on the print products they produce that must be the cause of the trouble. That is, both because dictionaries are smaller and less detailed than the lexicographer's original understanding of the words and because lexicographers have never been offered the chance by anyone to produce products unfettered by limitations of size, there is a lexicography gap in current lexical descriptions available in print products.

The issue of size is a very real one. Publishers count the characters in their printed books very carefully and would appear to publish dictionaries according to preset size limitations that have nothing to do with whether within such a size limitation one can do justice to the material to be covered. There are *vest pocket, pocket,* and *collegiate* dictionaries whose individual editions are carefully sized according to how large the competitor's products are, much more than whether they have met certain standards of scholarship. One suspects the production of such a work is a matter of hiring and producing a product and then trimming it to fit. Even in the *unabridged* category, one suspects that cost of production dictates the decision of much information and that the degree of detail is dictated not by the data available to the lexicographic staff, but the desire for a certain uniformity in the level of coverage.

The answer to all of this, of course, is that lexicographers should be paid to produce a dictionary for computational linguists rather than to produce one just for human readers. Such a dictionary, presumably primarily an electronic product, would not have size limitations because its primary means of reproduction, through the electronic copying, costs a negligible amount compared to the cost of discovering and recording the data. Second, the basis for such a lexicon should be established as one more akin to what computational linguists are concerned about—coverage of the vocabulary of contemporary texts that people expect to be processing by computer.

The soundness of this advice, or at least its novelty, can be seen as probably the most influential force in funding for natural language research today. The Japanese EDR project clearly had this as its objective and regardless of whether the criteria for the creation of their resulting dictionary were sufficiently deliberated within the computational linguistic community, the funding and intentional creation of an electronic dictionary are clearly directed at meeting just such a goal. The British National Corpus Project can thus be seen as a British response to the same concerns, and the ACL's Data Collection Initiative and now DARPA Linguistic Data Consortium being funded at a multimillion dollar level are clear recognitions that text data may be the key to the future of NL research. Thus, it is perhaps appropriate that Sue Atkins' paper ends the contributed paper section of the MTD book because it is the prologue to the future.

the head being modified. Typically, a lexicon requires an enumeration of different senses for such words, in order to account for the ambiguity illustrated below.

1. *a fast little boat:* Ambiguous: a boat driven quickly / one that is inherently fast
2. *a fast typist* : the person performs the act of typing quickly
3. *a fast game* : the motions involved in the game are rapid and swift
4. *a fast book* : one that can be read in a short time
5. *a fast driver* : one who drives quickly
6. *a fast and difficult decision* : a process that takes a short amount of time

These examples involve at least three distinct word senses for the word *fast*: (a) to move quickly, (b) to perform some act quickly, and (c) to do something that takes little time. But in fact, any finite enumeration of word senses will be unable to account for creative application of this word, as in the phrases *a fast motorway* and *a fast garage*. The adjective *fast* in the first phrase refers to the ability of vehicles on the motorway to sustain high speed, whereas in the latter phrase it refers to the length of time needed for a repair. As novel uses of *fast*, we are looking at new senses that are not covered by the enumeration given above.

2. PERMEABILITY OF WORD SENSES

Part of my argument for a different organization of the lexicon is based on a claim that the boundaries between the word senses in the analysis of *fast*above are too rigid. Still, even if we assume that enumeration is adequate as a descriptive mechanism, it is not always obvious how to select the correct word sense in any given context. Consider the systematic ambiguity of verbs like *bake* (discussed by Atkins, Kegl, & Levin, 1988), that require discrimination with respect to *change-of-state* versus *create* readings:

7. *John baked the potatoes for 40 minutes.*
8. *Mary baked a cake.*

The problem here is that there is too much overlap in the core semantic components of the different readings. Hence, it is not possible to guarantee correct word sense selection on the basis of selectional restrictions alone. Furthermore, as language evolves, partial overlaps of core and peripheral components of different word meanings make the traditional notion of word sense, as implemented in current dictionaries, inadequate (see Atkins, forthcoming IJL paper, for a critique of the flat, linear enumeration-based organization of dictionary entries). The only feasible approach would be to employ considerably more refined distinctions in the semantic content of the complement than is conventionally provided by the mechanism of selectional restrictions.

3. DIFFERENCE IN SYNTACTIC FORMS

It is equally arbitrary to create separate word senses for a lexical item just because it can participate in distinct syntactic realizations–and yet this has been the only approach open to computational lexicons that assume the ambiguity resolution framework outlined earlier. A striking example of this is provided by verbs such as *believe* and *forget*. Observe in examples 9-12 that the syntactic realization of the complement determines which word sense for the verb is chosen (see, for example, Grimshaw, 1979).

9. Mary believes that John is in Boston.
10. Mary believes the rumor.
11. Mary believes the headlines.
12. Mary believes John.

Although the complements are distinct, an explanatory lexicon should be able to relate the senses being used here. That is, that when Mary believes a headline, it is the *proposition* that it denotes that is believed. Similarly, when Mary believes John, she believes something (a proposition) that John *said*.

4. AMBIGUITY AND COMPOSITIONALITY

To overcome these shortcomings in current lexicon design, the richer structure for the lexical entry proposed here takes to an extreme the established notions of *predicate- argument structure, primitive decomposition* and *conceptual organization* . These are then viewed as defining a space of possible contexts in which a word can be used. Rather than committing to an enumeration of a predetermined number of different word senses, a lexical entry for a word now encodes a range of deeper aspects of lexical meaning. Looking at a word in isolation, these meaning components simply denote the semantic boundaries appropriate to its use. Viewing a word in the context of other words, mutually compatible aspects in the respective lexical decompositions become more prominent, thus forcing a specific interpretation of each individual word. It is important to realize that this is a generative process that goes well beyond the simple matching of features. On the contrary, such a framework requires, in addition to a flexible notation for expressing semantic generalizations at the lexical level, a mechanism for composing these individual entries on the phrasal level.

To get a better understanding of how the distinctions in lexical meaning manifest themselves, it is important to study and define the role that *all* lexical types play in contributing to the overall meaning of a phrase. This is not just a methodological point. Crucial to the processes of semantic interpretation that the lexicon is targeted for is the notion of *compositionality*, necessarily different from the more conventional pairing of verbs (as functions) and nouns (as arguments). As we indicated earlier, if the semantic load in the lexicon is entirely spread among the verb entries—as many existing computational systems assume—differences like those exemplified in examples 7-12 can only be accounted for by treating *bake*, *believe*, and so forth as polysemous verbs. If, on the other hand, elaborate lexical meanings of verbs and adjectives could be made sensitive to components of equally elaborate decompositions of nouns, the notion of spreading the semantic load evenly across the lexicon becomes the key organizing principle in expressing the knowledge necessary for disambiguation (cf. Pustejovsky, in press; Pustejovsky & Anick, 1988).

Briefly, this can be done by allowing nouns a relational structure as rich as that assumed for verbs. I will refer to this as the *qualia structure* of a word. This specifies four aspects of a word's meaning: (a) the relation between an object and its constituent parts, (b) that which distinguishes it within a larger domain, (c) its purpose and function, and (d) factors involved in its origin or "bringing it about."

These aspects of a word's meaning are called its *constitutive role*, *formal role*, *telic role*, and *agentive role*, respectively (for details, see Pustejovsky, in press). The motivation for positing such characterizations of word meaning is that by enriching the semantic descriptions of nominal types, we will be able to spread the semantic load more evenly through the lexicon, while accounting for novel word senses arising in syntactic composition.

To illustrate how this might be useful, let me return to the ambiguities discussed earlier in my discussion, namely, the example with *fast*. We can capture the general behavior of how such adjectives predicate by making reference to the richer internal structure for nominals suggested above. That is, we can view *fast* as always predicating of the *telic*role of a nominal. For example, consider the qualia structure for a noun such as *car*:

car(*x*)
[Const: ıbody, engine,...ß]
[Form: car-shape(*x*)]
[Telic: move(P,*x*), drive(P,y,*x*)]
[Agent: artifact(*x*)]

Notice that the telic role specifies the purpose and function of the noun. In the phrase, a *fast car,* it is the relation specified there (see as an event, namely, a process, *P*) that is modified by the adjective as being fast. Similarly, for the nouns *typist, waltz, book,* and *reader,* it is their telic role that is interpreted as being fast (without going into details, we note here the telic role of *typist* determines the activity being performed, namely typing; similarly for *waltz,* its telic role refers to dancing). Hence, the interpretations of *fast* in examples 1-5 earlier can all be derived from a single word sense, and there is no need for enumerating the different senses (cf. Pustejovsky, in press). The lexical semantics for this adjective will indicate that it acts as an event predicate, modifying the telic role of the noun, as illustrated in the minimal lexical semantic structure for *fast* below:

$$fast(*x*) \;=>\; (telic\text{: } \lambda P \quad E\ [fast(E) \wedge P(E,\ *x*)])$$

Notice that, in addition to obviating the need for separate senses, we can generate the novel use of *fast* mentioned previously in the phrase a *fast motorway,* because the telic role of *motorway* specifies its purpose, and it is this activity that is interpreted as fast:

$$[telic\text{:}travel(P,cars) \wedge on\ (P,*x*)].$$

The composition of the expression defining *fast* with the lexical aspect it specifies as its target—the telic role of its argument (*motorway*)—results in an interpretation corresponding to a use of the word when referring to a road, one that allows for fast travel by cars.

In this chapter I have sketched an approach to lexical semantic research that I believe overcomes the problem of polysemy and lexical ambiguity. By concentrating on generative operations in the lexicon, which create new senses, rather than fixed meanings, we can account for the creative use of words within a finite vocabulary.

CHAPTER 3

MACHINE TRACTABLE DICTIONARIES AND OPEN SUBLANGUAGES

Lynette Hirschman
Spoken Language Group
MIT Laboratory for Computer Science

Language is inherently open and it changes in many different dimensions simultaneously. Dictionaries are closed, in that they capture a finite subset of language at a given time in history, often for a specific purpose. What happens when we try to describe language in the inherently closed framework of a dictionary? More specifically, can we use the notion of sublanguage to close off language in order to better describe it via a closed medium such as an MTD? If so, how can we automate the building of specialized systems, and specifically MTDs, to support cost-effective, robust natural language understanding systems for specific applications?

1. OPENNESS AND (SUB)LANGUAGE

First, what do we mean by openness? Historical change in language has long been of interest to linguists. A very different dimension of openness lies in the distinction between competence and performance. Traditional computational linguistics has modeled competence, but to handle spontaneous spoken language, as well as certain kinds of written language, computational techniques must be developed to handle performance, including the kind of errors and corrections that characterize spontaneous speech.

Researchers have frequently described sublanguages, rather than the full language, in order to close or limit language. We define sublanguage here as the specialized use of language for communication, generated by a restricted community, concerned with a particular subject matter, (e.g., weather reports, medical records, stock market reports, etc.). However, sublanguages turn out to be open, too. In fact, they are more open than the full language. At first glance, talking about the openness of sublanguage appears to be a contradiction. Computational linguists have focused on sublanguage precisely to escape the problems of handling the full, open language. To the extent that computational linguists have been able to build working systems, this has been done by limiting the application domain and by exploiting the fact that people use a subset of the general language (e.g., a sublanguage) when performing a limited task in a specific domain.

Sublanguages are open because the border between a sublanguage and the general language is fuzzy. The general language is always available to the user of a sublanguage. Sublanguage is also open in the way that language in general is open. It contains metalinguistic and discourse constructs that permit the introduction of new terminology and new relations between entities. This is connected to so-called historical change, which in a sublanguage may occur at a much faster rate than in the language at large, as the field changes (e.g., the phrases genetic engineering and *gene-splicing* are relatively recent terms, reflecting the rapid advances in molecular biology).

Despite these issues, restriction to specific sublanguages has proved productive because it does help to control the size of the vocabulary and the range of syntactic constructions and semantic relations used. It also limits the context in which the communication takes place, and perhaps most importantly of all, it limits the amount of domain knowledge needed in order for the natural language system to understand or process input text in a particular domain. It is, of course, the vocabulary and the domain knowledge that are essential to building a machine tractable dictionary (MTD), particularly one that will support automated language understanding.

Even when we attempt to limit the amount of domain knowledge required to understand language in a limited domain, we still face a formidable task, namely the knowledge engineering bottleneck. In order to understand an input text, the system must have a model of the entities in the domain and their possible relationships to each other. Simple lexical knowledge (e.g., part of speech information) is useful, but not sufficient. For example, the following sentence is quite unintelligible, even though we may be able to identify dwarf, cordon, and whip as nouns: " For training a dwarf as a cordon, buy 1-year old whips." This is a sentence describing how to grow a fruit tree. To understand it, we need to know that dwarf, cordon, and whip all refer to fruit trees or root stock for fruit trees. The knowledge engineering bottleneck is a major obstacle to acquiring a domain model. To date, there is no automated methodology for acquiring this kind of information, although this is a very active area of current research.

2. SUBLANGUAGE-SPECIFIC SYSTEMS

If we commit to using sublanguage to limit both vocabulary and the amount of domain-specific knowledge to be acquired, how do we address the issue of building sublanguage-specific systems quickly (and automatically)?

Approaches to collecting the knowledge required to understand language input range from the knowledge engineering, expertise-intensive approach discussed earlier to the purely stochastic approach. The knowledge engineering approach (the intuitionist approach) uses the basic AI knowledge engineering paradigm: Find a human expert and elicit knowledge of words, objects, and relations in the domain. This approach suffers from all the problems of knowledge engineering: domain expertise may be hard to find, experts may not agree, and it is very labor intensive. On the other hand, it is not data intensive. Because the expert is asked to supply the knowledge by introspection, no large corpus of observed input is required.

At the other end of the spectrum is the stochastic approach, which in its purest form concerns itself only with string relations and avoids use of any linguistic constructs. This is the empiricist approach. Its advantage is that string relations are simple and well-understood. There are a number of powerful tools that have been developed to model the relations between an observed input signal and a given output signal. These tools can produce limited but very useful descriptions of language. For example, N-gram grammars, which have been incorporated into speech recognition systems, provide the probabilities of a given N-word (or N-part-of-speech) sequence. These kinds of models lend themselves very well to automated training techniques. However, to train the system, vast amounts of data are needed. The more complex the relation between input and output, the more data are needed. And no one has succeeded to date in deriving detailed representations of meaning (e.g., suitable for natural language front-ends or database updating) from statistically observed string relations.

There is much room for experimentation between the extreme knowledge engineering approach and the purely string-based stochastic approach. Ideally we need to find ways of combining the strengths of these approaches and avoiding their weaknesses. Of course, it is hardly surprising to linguists that the purely stochastic string-based approach should have difficulty modeling meaning. The various levels of linguistic abstraction (morphemes, words, phrases, sentences, discourses) have been developed precisely to describe distributional characteristics of language that are not revealed by simple string relations. But the question for the computational linguist becomes how to combine these linguistically based units that relate structure to meaning into a trainable, stochastic paradigm. The distributional analysis approach points in the right direction, focusing on the distribution and frequency of patterns of linguistic constructs (e.g., semantic classes co-occurring in a given syntactic pattern). It lays the groundwork for automated training procedures and provides the kind of relational view that maps well into application back-ends (e.g., database retrieval or database update requests). Again, however, research is needed to demonstrate the trainability of a natural language understanding system based on co-occurrence patterns derived from distributional analysis.

3. THE OPEN-LANGUAGE PROBLEM AND MTDS

The preceding discussion has focused on issues of language openness and the development of sublanguage-specific systems to understand text. A static knowledge source, such as an MTD, clearly is at odds with the openness of language. However, the notion of an MTD is very consistent with the knowledge engineering approach to computational linguistics. Does this mean that MTDs will be of interest only to those computational linguists in the intuitionist school?

To answer this, we need to go back to the relation of a sublanguage to the language as a whole. If we believe that a sublanguage is derived from the general language in some kind of systematic way, then an MTD covering some substantial portion of the general language (or even covering the sublanguage) is an invaluable resource, so long as it is viewed as one piece of the solution, and not the entire solution. Given a good model of the general language (part-of-speech information, syntactic attributes, and ideally some information relating basic concepts to each other), this can be used to bootstrap the system into a new domain. That is, we use an MTD to parse sentences, use the parses to derive syntactic patterns, then use syntactic patterns and string relations to identify substitution classes and from there, semantic classes. These, in turn, can provide sublanguage-specific co-occurrence patterns, which will reveal the basic sublanguage relations. Also, given a good description of words and structures in the general language, it should be possible to describe patterns of specialization from the general language to the sublanguage, which can facilitate training procedures for new sublanguages or support recovery strategies for handling unknown words or constructs or concepts in a sublanguage.

4. CONCLUSION

Given that language is inherently open, what role can a static knowledge source (e.g., an MTD) play? It is clear to any practicing computational linguist that a good MTD would be an enormous asset. Static knowledge sources can be powerful tools when used to "prime" an open, adaptive language understanding system. However, we need to change our paradigm for building natural language understanding systems. We need to abandon the prevalent "closed world" model of systems and embrace an "open world" view of language. We need to develop paradigms that allow a system to bootstrap its way into new domains. This paradigm may well combine the expert-intensive knowledge engineering paradigm (especially in the early stages of learning a sublanguage) with a stochastic training paradigm that becomes increasingly effective as the system knows more and more about the sublanguage. Such a system would start from a model of the general language and use feedback to specialize this general knowledge to obtain detailed knowledge of a specific sublanguage. If we couple the notions of adaptive training, statistically based linguistic methods, and bootstrapping from the general language to specialized domains, it is clear that MTDs will play a critical role as general knowledge sources, key to building broad-coverage, robust systems. It is also clear that the same technology that enables us to build adaptive, trainable systems will make it easier to dynamically update specialized dictionaries as new words enter the sublanguage, or to (partially) automate the process of creating specialized dictionaries for new subject matter areas.

CHAPTER 4

LEXICAL KNOWLEDGE REQUIRED FOR NATURAL LANGUAGE PROCESSING

Arthur Cater
Department of Computer Science
University College Dublin

1. INTRODUCTION

There is now a substantial body of research that aims to extract information from MRDs (machine-readable versions of ordinary dictionaries), in order to provide, relatively painlessly, large lexicons for use by NLP (natural language processing) systems. This chapter sets out to provide a second perspective on such work. Rather than ask what lexical information can be extracted from MRDs, we ask what lexical knowledge NLP requires. Clearly if a gross mismatch existed between the two answers, such that MRD-derived information needed to be substantially supplemented to meet the needs of NLP, it would spell trouble for the prospects of using MRD-derived lexicons for NLP purposes.

The scope of this chapter is limited in four major ways. First, we do not consider NLP in the nonsymbolic connectionist paradigm. Second, we are not concerned with superficial kinds of processing, among which we include frequency-based processing. The third restriction in scope is that we will be mostly concerned with open-class words. There is good reason for paying less attention to closed-class words. NLP systems need a great deal of information about closed-class words, and tend to treat them in highly idiosyncratic ways. It is very doubtful that ordinary dictionaries do contain the information about these words that NLP systems require, and it is virtually certain that even if they do, it would be difficult or impossible to present that information in a way that would be amenable to the diverse idiosyncratic processing requirements of extant techniques. Yet curiously this does not matter, because by definition closed-class vocabulary is finite, and in practice is tiny by comparison to the realistic expectations of the size of open-class vocabulary that could be extracted from MRDs. So, even if developers of NLP systems were obliged to hand-code all the knowledge required for closed-class items in the worst case, they would still profit greatly from the very large open-class vocabularies extracted from MRDs.

2. TASKS IN NATURAL LANGUAGE PROCESSING

There are numerous areas of application of NLP, and there is a fair degree of agreement on what those applications are: machine translation, natural language interfaces, speech recognizers and synthesizers, and spelling and style checkers, to name a few favorites. A successful system in any area of application will require certain lexical information. However, it is not profitable to assess the lexical requirements on an application-by-application basis, because there will be a great deal of overlap. Instead we view NLP as a collection of tasks. A successful application system will need to perform some subset of these tasks, and will do so using certain techniques. We may then characterize the lexical requirements by considering the kinds of information needed to perform those tasks. We note that other approaches to the lexical requirements problem are possible: surveying individual applications, individual existing systems for NLP, or individual linguistic theories. But we have chosen a task-based approach.

Some of these tasks are simple superficial processing tasks that do not involve the resolution of ambiguity. Others are more involved, and typically are concerned with disambiguation of one kind or another. These we call knowledge-based processing tasks, and it is the lexical knowledge requirements of these tasks that concern us in this chapter:

1. Single-sentence analysis
2. Single-sentence generation
3. Discourse-level processing
4. Speech processing
5. Text analysis
6. Dialogue participation
7. Language transfer
8. Language acquisition

The knowledge-based processing tasks exhibit a nearly hierarchical pattern of dependencies. Activities at the discourse level build on sentence-level analysis and generation capabilities, and most of the

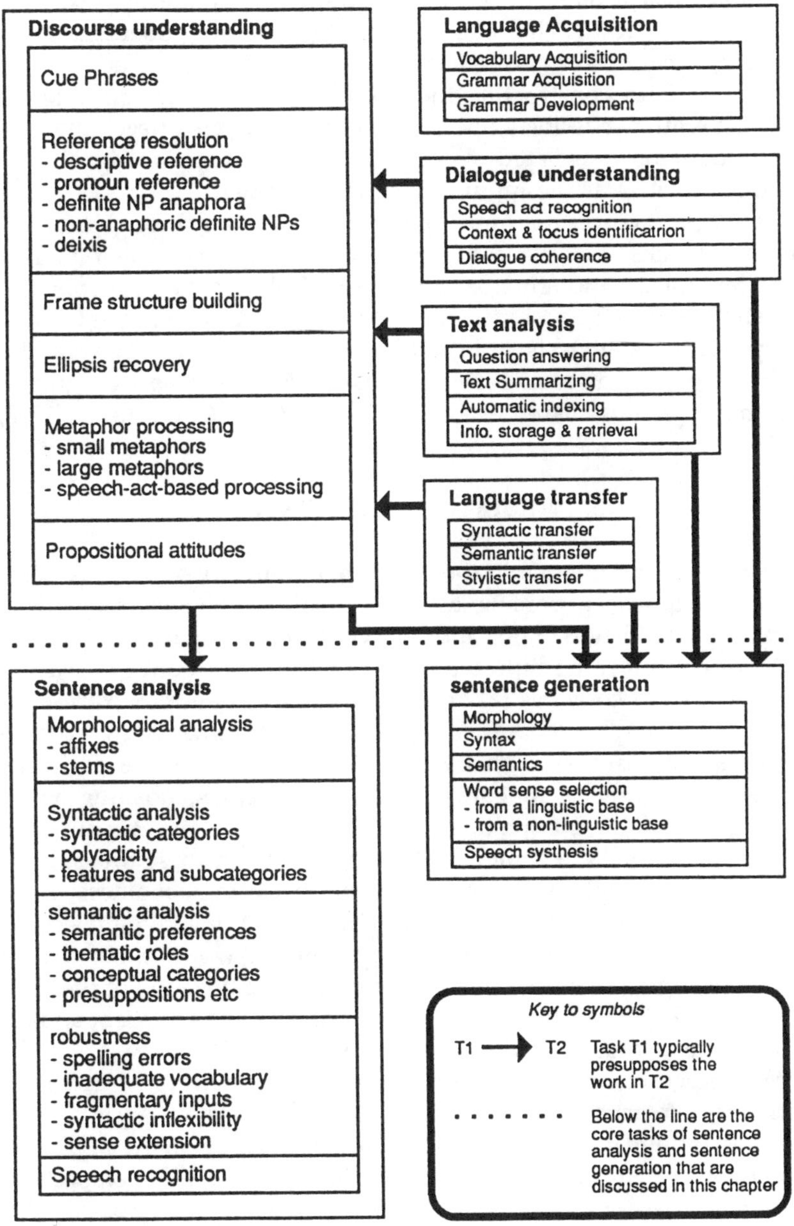

Figure 4.1. Tasks in natural language processing

remaining tasks build on sentence generation, connected-text understanding, or both. The main exceptions to this generalization are language acquisition and speech processing. Language acquisition is concerned with constructing the knowledge bases that make analysis and generation possible. Speech processing covers speech synthesis, the recognition of isolated words, and the use of speech signals rather than text strings as the input to language parsing.

Each task involves a number of subtasks, and it is through examining these subtasks that we can get a detailed understanding of lexical requirements. Although stressing that NLP embraces numerous tasks, we shall be concerned here only with the lexical requirements of two: single-sentence analysis and single-sentence generation. The additional requirements of discourse-level processing in particular are significant, and have been discussed elsewhere (Cater, Guo, & Matthews, 1990).

3. PARSING SINGLE SENTENCES

This task is fundamental in the sense that many other tasks we discuss later presuppose a parsing ability. Parsing and generation are also almost mirror images of one another. The information needed to analyze a sentence into some representation is to a large extent needed when performing the converse task of generating a sentence to express some representation. There are some special requirements in each case however. Robustness is an issue in parsing, because it is desirable to understand sentences that are faulty in some respect, violating syntactic rules or containing misspellings, for instance. However, it is not usually desirable to generate sentences that are faulty in these ways, and so lexical requirements deriving from a concern with robustness have no correlate in the generation task's requirements. Similarly, a major issue in generation is the selection of an appropriate word to express some given meaning. This has implications for the organization of the lexicon and in particular for the methods by which it can be accessed, and there is no corresponding requirement for parsing.

We structure our discussion in the following way. Morphological analysis, syntactic analysis, and semantic analysis are each discussed here as though they were exclusively subtasks of analysis. The next section gives any additional points coming from the perspective of generation. We also discuss here the analysis-specific issue of robustness. In this manner we hope to convey concisely the very similar lexical requirements of both the parsing task and the generation task.

Before proceeding with the discussion of these subtasks, two points must be made. The first concerns the role of language parsing. Some applications do not require every subtask to be performed. For example, only the most sophisticated bibliographic retrieval systems do any semantic analysis at all. Further, in some applications the result of parsing should be a complete set of valid analyses at some level. For example, parsing tools to assist grammar developers should reveal multiple parses, not conceal them. Usually, however, when parsing is subservient to discourse understanding, disambiguation is very important. In these contexts, a parser should ideally yield the one (semantic) analysis that corresponds to the speaker's intended meaning. The information required to do this includes lexical syntactic and semantic information, but in general goes beyond this to information that is held at the discourse-understanding level only.

The second point is that natural language processing draws on several qualitatively different kinds of knowledge. In particular, there are rules of grammar that express generalizations about syntactic structure. These rules need access to various kinds of information about words and phrases, and this information is (part of) what is stored in the lexicon. In some theoretical models, the rules themselves are named by, or directly associated with, particular lexical items, and so the rules are part of the lexicon. In most of our discussion however, we follow the more standard practice of assuming that a distinct grammar exists, which refers to terms and features found in the lexicon, but which is not itself part of the lexicon. Ramsay (this volume) makes the point that the structure and content of the lexicon is intimately interwoven with the linguistic theory underpinning any system that attempts to use it.

3.1. Morphological Analysis

Words are built from morphemes, typically one stem and zero or more affixes. New words can be productively formed by adding affixes to a stem, and sometimes by concatenating two stems (e.g., snowman or icebox). It is not feasible in practice, and maybe not possible in principle, for a lexicon to provide an exhaustive list of words formed from combinations of morphemes. There is therefore a need for morphological analysis, that is, a process that identifies the morphemes from which a word is built and characterizes the polymorphemic word that results. Morphological analysis requires access to several kinds of information: (a) morphemes themselves (both stems and affixes), (b) rules that determine whether a certain combination of morphemes is valid, (c) rules that specify the characteristics of the new word, and (d) whatever information is needed for these two kinds of rules.

3.1.1. Affixes. Affixes break down into prefixes, suffixes, and in some languages, infixes. Another distinction is between inflectional affixes, which provide clues to grammatical structures, and derivational affixes, which give clues to meaning. In general, these two classifications are orthogonal (English being an exception in this respect), and a lexicon must recognize this fact.

In English, derivational suffixes generally precede inflectional ones. This leads to the general observation that there exist order classes of affixes. This order class is one of the pieces of information that a lexicon should provide for affixes, because it is useful for the disambiguation of homographic affixes. In English for example we find homographic affixes *-s*, and *-ed*. The suffix *-s* is inflectional in both of its uses, forming plurals of nouns and third-person singular verb forms. The suffix *-ed* has an inflectional use, to make past-tense forms of verbs, and a derivational use, to form adjectives from verbs. In the case of a word such as *relatedness*, the order-class information is useful in selecting the derivational use of the suffix *-ed*.

For each affix, the following information is in general necessary:

1. whether derivational or inflectional (e.g., *-ly* is derivational)
2. whether prefix, infix, or suffix (e.g., *-ly* is a suffix)
3. graphic form and graphic changes (e.g.,*-ly* consists of the letters *ly*; when the sequence *yly* is formed, it is sometimes changed to *ily*, thus *happily*; but note *slyly*.
4. category change if any (e.g., *-ly* turns adjectives into adverbs)
5. pronunciation and pronunciation changes (e.g., *ly* is pronounced /li/; when /ili/ is formed, it is optionally changed to /eli/)
6. subcategorization effects (e.g., *construction* discussed later)
7. meaning changes (e.g., pre- meditate -ed; mal- practice)
8. constraints on application (category, pronunciation, semantics)

The meanings and the subcategorization properties of polymorphemic words are influenced both by the stem and by derivational affixes. The verb *construct*, for instance, takes up to three arguments: the agency constructing something, the object being constructed, and the material being used.

Bill constructed the boat from fiberglass

Construction has several senses. In one sense, it means the object constructed:

the construction }
the fiberglass construction } sank rapidly

Another sense refers to the act of constructing:

the boat's construction }
the construction of the boat } took four months

In a third sense, it refers to some aspect of the act:

the fiberglass construction of the boat }
Bill's construction of the boat } makes it dangerous

Each derived sense has specific subcategorization properties; that is, distinctive (but not necessarily distinct) mappings from surface realizations of arguments to slots in underlying semantic structure. The linking of senses to subcategorization properties must be effected, and depends in part on information about the suffix.

At the level of semantic structure, the three senses of *construction* are all straightforwardly derived from the semantics of *construct*. Numerous affixes exist that yield meanings that reflect a modification of underlying semantic structure. For example, the prefixes *un-*, *de-*, *dis-* , and *a-* all serve to negate a semantic structure. *Mis-* and *mal-* change semantic structures to indicate wrong or poor performance of an action. *Pre-* and *fore-* affect temporal components of semantic structure. The semantic properties of derivational morphology are generally not well understood. There does not seem to be any theory yet that explains why *extradite -> extradition* is possible and *expedite -> expedition* is not; or what semantic relationship there may be between *exhibit* and *inhibit*. NLP research that aims to build semantic representations therefore tends in practice to eschew derivational morphology, using instead lexicons with morphological derivatives explicitly present.

Affixes generally cannot be attached to just any base. Each affix is restricted at least in terms of the syntactic categories of bases to which it may be attached. Additional constraints may apply to the base words with which a given affix may be combined, expressible in terms of the phonetic or semantic character of the base, or even its spelling.

The importance of the phonetic character of the base is illustrated by the prefix *in-* and its variants *im-*, *il-*, and *ir-*. In practice it is convenient to have separate lexical entries for these prefixes, even though they do not have independent theoretical status. The applicability of *in-* is restricted on phonotactic grounds.

The semantic character of the base is also important, as can be illustrated by the agentive and nonagentive uses of the suffix *-er* added to verbs. The agentive use forms nouns meaning *a person who . . .*: Thus *singer* , *dancer* , and writer. Other nonagentive uses also exist. There is a use where the word formed names an instrument used in an action: *grater* and *shredder*. A slightly different use is possible with words of the "spray/load" class of verbs: *loader* and *spreader*. This class is one of several classes of verbs where members of each class are semantically related and show similar syntactic and morphological behaviors.

3.1.2. Stems. Some stems have morphological idiosyncracies that should be explicitly noted in a lexicon. That is to say, these stems do not combine with all inflectional affixes in the normal ways. We simply list here some morphological irregularities with examples. We take examples from English only, but point out that other languages certainly have morphologically idiosyncratic words of their own.

- Irregular verbs: the past of *take* is *took*. These often fall into groups which nevertheless cannot be exploited, e.g., {*brought, thought, sought* }; {*taught, caught* }.
- Multiple variant forms: go has past participles gone and been.
- *Invariable nouns: music* has no plural.
- Zero plurals: the plural of *sheep* is *sheep*.
- Pluralia tantum: *archives* and *entrails* are both syntactically plural, and have no corresponding singular forms.
- *Foreign plurals: criterion* becomes *criteria*.
- *Irregular plurals: child* becomes *children*.
- *Irregular comparative and superlative adjectives: good* yields *better* and *best* .
- Ambiguity between stem and (usually irregular) inflected form: *people* has plural *peoples,* but is also an irregular plural of *person*. *Lay* has variants *lays* and *laying,* but is also the irregular past form of one sense of *lie*.
- Morphologically complex words that must be treated as stems: *civilize* has a specific meaning, not related to *civil -ize*.

Specific lexical information is needed to allow morphological analysis procedures to treat such phenomena correctly. Morphological synthesis is the converse of morphological analysis. For purposes of generation, it is necessary to be aware that new words may be formed from old ones by derivational as well as inflectional affixation. This implies that morphological processes must be available to advise the word-sense selection component of a generator that certain words exist, even though they are not explicitly present in the lexicon. A generator must of course use all the morphological knowledge described earlier to ensure that the words it constructs are valid, and mean the right things. Thus, for instance, the knowledge that the suffix *-ize* cannot legitimately ambiguity. This is a problem that confronts earnest language learners and realistic natural language processing systems alike. The notion of a context enforcing a certain reading of a word or selecting for a particular word sense is central both to global lexicon entry design (this is the question of breaking a word into word senses) and local composition of individual sense definitions. However, current dictionaries and lexicons reflect a particular static approach to dealing with this problem. The numbers of, and distinctions between, senses within an entry are frozen into the dictionary at compile time. Furthermore, definitions hardly make *any*provisions for the notion that boundaries between word senses may (and do, as shown later) shift with context.

There are serious problems with positing a fixed number of bounded word senses, and it is not only language-processing systems that face them. In a framework that assumes a partitioning of the space of possible uses of a word into word senses—as postulated and defined by the entry for that word—the problem becomes that of selecting, on the basis of various contextual factors (typically subsumed by, but not necessarily limited to, the notion of selectional restrictions), the word sense closest to the use of the word in the given text. As far as a language user is concerned, the question is that of fuzzy matching of contexts. As far as a text analysis system is concerned, this reduces to a search within a finite space of possibilities.

Realistically, however, this approach fails on several accounts, both in terms of what information is made available (in a dictionary, or in a lexicon) to drive the disambiguation process, and how a sense selection procedure might make use of this information. Typically, external contextual factors alone are not sufficient for precise selection of a word sense. Additionally, often the lexical entry does not provide enough reliable pointers to critically discriminate between word senses. In the case of automated sense selection, the search process becomes computationally expensive, if not intractable, when it has to account for longer phrases made up of individually ambiguous words. Finally, and most importantly, the assumption that an exhaustive listing can be assigned to the different uses of a word lacks the explanatory power necessary for making generalizations or predictions about how words used in a novel way can be reconciled with their currently existing lexical definitions.

To illustrate this last point, I present some examples of a problematic nature, both for language learners and for current ambiguity resolution frameworks, as implemented in existing NLP systems.

1. CREATIVE USE OF WORDS

Consider the ambiguity and context-dependence of adjectives such as *fast* and *slow*, where the meaning of the predicate varies depending on

CHAPTER 2

POLYSEMY AND WORD MEANING

James Pustejovsky
Computer Science Department
Brandeis University

This chapter deals with systematic lexical ambiguity and the representational tools necessary to account for such phenomena in natural language. I argue that traditional approaches to representing ambiguity—and hence corresponding treatments of disambiguation—fail to account for the systematic ambiguities that exist in natural language. Current lexicons for natural language systems and linguists alike reflect, through their organization, the traditional view of word senses. In particular, they assume that the space of possible uses of a word is exhaustively carved out by an enumerated set of senses for that word. This is inadequate for several reasons. First, it cannot account for the *creative* use of words; that is, the way in which words acquire new senses from novel contexts. Second, it is unable to account for the *permeability* of word senses, namely, that many words do not have distinct senses at all, but are complex overlapping meanings. Finally, it says nothing about the predictability of syntactic forms for a word. Thus, if a word participates in distinct syntactic realizations, why should it be assigned a distinct word sense as well, as is usually the case? Finally, I briefly sketch a particular approach to lexical semantics that promotes the notion of a *generative lexicon*. I show how a lexical entry can be assigned a richer knowledge structure, and how by performing specialized inferences over the ways in which aspects of knowledge structures of words in contexts can be composed, mutually compatible and relevant lexical components of words and phrases are highlighted (for details, cf. Boguraev & Pustejovsky, 1990; Pustejovsky, in press).

One of the most pervasive phenomena in natural language is that of

> above two positions) that claims that, if the knowledge structure is adequate, then practical problems of language semantics (lexical ambiguity, etc.) do not arise. The answer to this is that, unless the domain chosen is trivial, the claim is simply false. However, I do not intend to mark cs off the knowledge realms and their formal expression. On the contrary, the position of this discussion is that knowledge of language and the world are not separable, just as they are not separable into databases called dictionaries and encyclopedias, respectively.
>
> If there is a distinctive position in this discussion, it is that this inseparability goes further than is normally thought and that particular language structures, text-structures, are in fact a paradigm for knowledge structures (Wilks, 1978) or, to put it very crudely, knowledge for certain purposes should be stored in text-like forms (as opposed to, say, predicate calculus-like ones). That fact is far deeper than the superficial claim that we, as people, normally store information as pieces of paper with writing on. (Wilks et al., 1989)

As the entire field of NLP is becoming more and more interested in processing unrestricted natural language text/speech, Wilks' *inseparability* hypothesis concerning the relationship between language and knowledge, and his *natural-text-structure* hypothesis concerning the meaning representation of natural language text as stated above, will become increasingly relevant to MTD research and development. Eventually, in the design and construction of MTDs, we have to face up to the challenge of one ultimate question: How are we going to represent natural language data in our dictionaries such that no less than *all* natural language data are represented and no less than *all* natural language processes computed? Before an adequate answer is found to this question, all approaches to MTD development remain empirical.

CHAPTER 1

PRELUDE

Cheng-ming Guo
Computer Science Department
Tsinghua University

Yorick Wilks, one of the leaders in MTD research, drafted a short passage a couple of years ago as the opening remark of a joint CRL paper on MTDs. Owing to its significance and relevance in setting up the stage for the present forum, an adapted version of the passage appears below as the prelude to the discussion on the design and construction of MTDs. It reads as follows:

> This discussion is concerned with computational semantics (cs), in a sense fairly well understood in artificial intelligence (AI) and computational linguistics (CL), but one not beyond dispute by other users of the term *semantics*. I shall just state the sense I intend, because the purpose of this discussion is not to defend the use, that has been done often enough, but to bring into focus some of the issues involved in making machine-tractable dictionaries resources for cs.
>
> As is often the case, a position can be best described by contrasting it with others, and in this case I can contrast cs usefully with three positions: syntactic analysis, logical semantics, and expert systems. There are refinements and subtleties in all those positions but, speaking broadly, cs is opposed to any claims as to the necessity or sufficiency, for computational language understanding, of logical semantics or syntactic analysis. To say that is not to deny, in certain cases, the usefulness of a limited initial syntactic analysis, nor the aesthetic pleasures of a subsequent formal axiomatization. Cs holds, however, that the real theories of language understanding, which is to say the substantive algorithms and the right level of analysis, lie elsewhere.
>
> The issue of expert systems is different. There is a position, for which it is difficult to give textual sources (in a way that it is all too easy for the

PART I

FORUM ON THE DESIGN AND CONSTRUCTION OF MTDs

be applied to the stem *civil* is particularly important for the generation of meaningful texts.

3.2. Syntactic Analysis

Abundant information is required for the syntactic analysis of a sentence. A recurrent theme in much recent NLP research has been the extent to which syntactic information can be inferred from semantic information. This issue however, is irrelevant for our purposes at this point, because we are concerned with the nature of the syntactic knowledge that is required for analysis and for generation. The issue of where this syntactic knowledge comes from, or whether it must be accorded a distinguished status within a lexicon is an important consideration in organizing the explicit information stored in the lexicon. However, for purposes of syntactic analysis, the issue of whether the syntactic knowledge is stored explicitly or is derived by inference is secondary to the issue of what that knowledge is. We will look at some general information that the syntactic analysis of natural language needs.

3.2.1. Syntactic categories. Syntactic category information is a minimum requirement in producing a syntactic analysis for sentences. For each individual language there is an agreed set of major syntactic categories. This category information is essential for all parsing tasks. Each major category is either open or closed, and is identified with sets of words that can usually be substituted for one another without affecting the syntactic acceptability of sentences. Within each major category, however, we often find numerous syntactic constructions where intersubstitutability is restricted to smaller sets of words. This is accounted for by two main techniques: identifying distinctive subsets of the major categories, or associating subcategorization frames with individual words. Either technique is sufficient for syntactic analysis, but where semantic analysis is also required, the richer structure afforded by subcategorization frames makes them the better choice.

3.2.2. Polyadicity and subcategorization. Many types of words can be seen as *pivot words*, centrally engaged in some relation with other words or arguments. This is most obviously true of verbs, but it also applies to adjectives, prepositions, deverbal nouns, adverbs, and quantifiers. We consider that words in all these classes have subcategorization frames. A subcategorization frame gives information about the cases or arguments that the pivot word accepts. It specifies for example: (a) the number of arguments, (b) which arguments are optional and which are mandatory, (c) what syntactic (and semantic/conceptual) types may realize each argument, and (d) what order(s) the arguments may appear in.

The idea that certain arguments may be optional actually betrays a presumption. Logically there are two ways in which subcategorization frames can be organized:

1. A separate word sense could be provided for each different way of using a word. For example, the English verb *open* can be used (in the active voice) in at least the following ways:
<agent> *open* <object> ; He *opened* the door
<agent> *open* <object> with <instrument>
; He *opened* the door with a key
<instrument> *open* <object> ; The key *opened* the door
<object> *open* ; The door *opened*
The lexicon could be equipped with distinct word sense entries, each with a particular pattern, but possibly the same in other respects.

2. A single entry could be provided to cover some or all of the different usage patterns. For example, the first two usage patterns above could easily be merged into one, in which the argument phrase "with <instrument>" is optional. More sophistication in pattern specification might allow the third usage also. The fourth usage however has an absolutive aspect, which conveys a different meaning. It is therefore likely that it would not be appropriate to cover this usage with the same sense definition as the others, even if the pattern-specification language is sufficiently flexible to make that possible.

There are two main objections to the first approach. If multiple lexical entries are provided giving different case frames, then there is likely to be a proliferation of entries that are in most respects identical. This will increase storage requirements, which may turn out not to be very important. It may also increase retrieval and processing times. The second objection to this approach is its failure to capture significant linguistic generalizations. Pustejovsky (this volume) argues for enriching definitions so that multiple related senses can be conflated to one, thus reducing the choices confronting a disambiguation procedure.

The second approach is therefore preferred, though it too has some drawbacks. It may prove difficult for automatic MRD analysis processes to determine a pattern just flexible enough to cover the semantically identical usages. The use of flexible patterns also increases the likelihood of errors of commission. Although both approaches are equally likely to omit usage patterns that are in fact valid, the second approach is more likely to cover usage patterns that are in fact invalid.

Whichever approach is taken to specifying the polyadicity of words, some common issues arise. Syntactic cues, such as the choice of subject or object position or the use of specific prepositional markers, have to be indicated for each of the argument cases. Syntactic restrictions sometimes also need to be stated. For example, a noun phrase may be required to be indefinite, or a subordinate clause may need to be finite. Semantic preferences often need to be stated, and semantic/conceptual defaults need to be provided for optional (missing) constituents.

Syntactic cues will play a crucial role in relating lexical entries to grammars that are used for either analysis or generation. A properly chosen set of syntactic cues, combined with a properly organized grammar, will push to extremes the difference between the two approaches to describing case frames. In the case of English, for example, it is possible to state just one case-frame pattern for a ditransitive verb like *give*, and have a grammar-for-analysis use that one pattern for all sentences derived by passivization and/or dative shift, or one could explicitly list the six permitted patterns.

3.2.3. Syntactic features and subcategories. Within each major syntactic category, subcategories exist. Each subcategory represents one particular syntactic behavior of the word. The differences in subcategories of a word result in differences in the acceptability of word sequences. There are numerous phenomena that must be accounted for, a few of which are as follows:

- Count, mass, and proper nouns
- Agreement phenomena
- Commaless apposition (e.g., *the painter Picasso*)
- Measure phrases (e.g., *three centimeters in length*)
- Nominalization (*seem* requires an NP subject)
- Predicative or attributive adjectives
- Pleonastic *it*, existential *there*
- Partitive quantifying phrases
- Postnominal adjectives, (e.g., *Attorney general*)
- Aktionsart phenomena
- Idioms, e.g., *turn turtle, give somebody a piece of one's mind*
- Passivisable or used only in the passive (e.g., be born, be rumored)

Such phenomena can be accounted for either in terms of subcategories of the major syntactic categories, or sometimes by specific subcategorization frames associated with particular words or word senses. The total number of syntactic subcategories of English vocabulary used by Sager

(1981), for instance, runs to 150. One-sixth of these belong to closed-class words. Half the remainder (around 60) belong to verb subcategories. Such a rich set of syntactic subcategories can be used to account for the same kinds of phenomena as have been mentioned previously in connection with polyadicity, and their use presupposes that a grammar-for-analysis is sensitive to those features. For example, a subcategory could be defined to cover all those ditransitive verbs such as *give* that behave as shown earlier with respect to passivization and dative shift. Other subcategories can distinguish between adjectives that are attributive only, predicative only, or either.

3.3. Semantic Analysis

There are numerous formalisms in which NLP researchers have attempted to represent meanings over the years. Most of these formalisms are intended either to allow the construction of unambiguous representations of meaning, or to allow the representations to be ambiguous in systematic ways that, it is hoped, reflect all and only the possible meanings of a sentence. Building a representation for a sentence then requires that some inference be performed, in order to determine the meaning (or range of meanings). This inference depends on knowledge about the world and about the words.

Meaning representations are not an end in themselves. They are used primarily for other processes, particularly those involved in processing discourse. A simplifying assumption is commonly made, that meanings do inhere in sentences, and that these meanings are suitable inputs to discourse-level processors. Recently there has been a trend to challenge that assumption, asserting instead that it is the attempt to integrate linguistic inputs with structures in long-term memory that is primarily responsible for disambiguation. We feel certain that there is much truth in this; but we also feel that an attempt must be made to distinguish lexical knowledge from real-world knowledge, even though the boundary between the two types is uncertain. In this section we therefore discuss some kinds of lexical knowledge that continue to be useful for semantic analysis at the sentence level. There is another problematic boundary, between sentence-level and discourse-level analysis. The single sentence is most useful as a unit at the level of syntax, and even so nonsentential fragments are quite normal. However, it is in general possible to swap a complex sentence for several simple ones, or vice versa. The characterization of a discourse as a collection of sentences is a convenient approximation. There are several phenomena, at the semantic and the syntactic levels, that we have chosen to discuss as discourse phenomena, even though in some cases they are manifest within single-sentence boundaries.

3.3.1. Semantic restrictions/preferences. Semantic preferences are an important tool for disambiguation. They can help in selecting word senses in argument phrases, they can simultaneously help in selecting word senses of ambiguous pivot words, and where arguments are optional, they can help in structural disambiguation by providing a criterion for preferring one attachment possibility over another. Finally, where an argument is present but underspecified, the semantic preferences of a pivot word can assist in comprehension. For example, the English pronoun *they* carries little semantic information. It specifies plurality, but has no inherent specification for any semantic properties such as animacy or humanness. However, when it appears as the subject of the verb *tell*, the semantic preference of *tell* (for say +human) can be exploited for purposes of anaphora resolution, to pick out if possible a referent labeled +human. These semantic preferences are also related to defaults for unspecified optional arguments. Defaults are likely to be objects in a conceptual hierarchy that have semantic properties but that are not themselves semantic objects.

Semantic preferences can be stated for all arguments of almost all classes of pivot word. Verbs, deverbal nouns, adjectives, and prepositions can all profitably state semantic preferences for their arguments. Semantic preferences are usually monadic; that is, each argument of a pivot word, in isolation from other arguments, is expected to be of a certain semantic (or conceptual) type. However, arguably there are cases where multiplace semantic preferences are involved. For example, it has been suggested that the sense-resolution of *pen* in the sentence "The baby picked up the pen," depends on a preference-like rule that states that the agent of picking up must be strong enough to pick up the object (Hayes, 1976). There also seems to be a case for regarding the interpretation of prepositions such as *of* and *with* as depending on multiplace preferences. These, however, are closed-class items, to be discussed no further here.

Aquite different kind of semantic preference is often evident, where sense disambiguation exploits general topic information. For example, Hayes (1976) cites the sentences

> The gardener picked some stock.
>
> The rancher picked some stock.

The appropriate senses of stock (a flowering plant, cattle) appear to be chosen because they are related to other entity types mentioned in the sentence. This is in contrast to, and is additional to, the normal mode of operation of semantic preferences where a pivot word seeks to restrict the ontological category of an argument. Topic-related preferences are often implemented in NLP systems by using spreading-activation models in semantic networks (e.g., Charniak, 1981a; Fass, 1988). Something of the same effect may perhaps be achievable using LDOCE's subject codes or other similar indications of topic (e.g., Slator, 1989).

Wherever semantic preferences can be stated, they bring all the aformentioned benefits. Attempting to minimize the violation of semantic preferences is a very useful technique in disambiguation, but preferences are different from semantic restrictions in that they can be violated. Furthermore, noting that preferences have been violated is one of several clues to the possible presence of metaphor.

3.3.2. Thematic role information. Semantic representations may take many superficially different forms: formulae in predicate calculus or some other logic; semantic networks, whose nodes may be words, word senses, or semantic primitives; functional structures; or theta grids, for example. What all these representations have in common is that pivot words especially (verbs and others) are associated with a template, a skeleton structure, in whatever form of representation, having variables (or gaps) where other information is to go. We will use the term *thematic role information* for whatever information is required to enable the instantiation of such variables (or filling of such gaps).

The principle of "compositionality of semantics" is that complex semantic representations are simple functions of the representations of their parts. It is the thematic role information for pivot words that is used in building the semantic representations of phrases, and it must therefore identify what simple function computes the fillers from the arguments. Often this is straightforward identity. The representation of a single argument serves as the value of a single variable. Functions other than identity must also exist, for example, to compute temporal representations from tense and aspect.

In order to construct semantic representations in this manner, it is usual (though not strictly necessary) to have an explicit syntactic parse tree, where each node has its own semantic representation. Each nonleaf node inherits its skeleton representation from one daughter node, and may flesh out that skeleton by applying specified simple functions to the representations of other daughter nodes.

Idioms present a little difficulty that is overcome by treating them as multiword lexical items. Even so, some idioms exhibit morphological complexity, agreement phenomena, and syntactic structure. In "to give *somebody* a piece of *one's* mind," *one's* is morphologically complex, and is replaced with *his* or *her* to agree with the subject; and *somebody*, the direct object, is an ordinary phrase, not a literal part of the idiom.

Another difficulty is with unbounded dependencies. This is sometimes handled by making semantic representations take the form of lambda expressions, so that the building of structures can be deferred until an argument is available at some higher node in the parse tree.

In general, therefore, thematic role information has to specify mappings (usually mere identity) from representations of syntactically realized arguments to variables in semantic structure. Thematic role information also has to somehow establish which of several phrases corresponds to a particular argument, and hence to a variable in semantic structure. The arguments may appear in varied syntactic positions because of the operation of syntactic rules.

Morphologically complex words, in which there are derivational affixes, have templates that are highly similar to those of the stem. The thematic role information however is often quite different from that of the stem. Different syntactic realizations of arguments may be permitted, and it may be either unnecessary or impossible to syntactically realize an argument that is required in the stem. In order for morphological processes to be able to modify the thematic role information, such defaulted arguments must be constructable from the lexical entry of the stem. Typically this means that the conceptual category of the argument should be explicitly stated, so that a default filler of the correct type can be supplied.

3.3.3. Conceptual category information. The semantic representation of an individual physical object is a concept, conventionally called an *instance*. Other similar objects will be represented by other instances, and all these instances will be related to another concept, termed a *class concept*. This relationship between instance and class is often termed the ISA relationship. Class concepts are often arranged in one or more subset hierarchies. This allows simple inference procedures to make available information about a concept that is only expressed explicitly at higher levels in the hierarchy. The same technique of representation is easily applied to abstract entities, such as events. When this is done, there are typically several disjoint hierarchies.

Concept networks superimpose on the basic hierarchical structure a whole set of other relationships between concepts. These may be used to encode numerous kinds of information, for example: (a) describing a prototypical member of a class, (b) expressing defining properties of class members, (c) expressing default properties of class members, and (d) expressing arbitrary associations between classes of concept.

It is important that word senses be linked to concepts for several reasons. First, concepts representing individuals, and complex concepts representing relationships among individuals and among other complex concepts, are the essence of semantic representation, and are suitable for many kinds of discourse-level inference. Second, hierarchical arrangements of class concepts allow semantic preferences to be stated in terms of a tree representing a restricted part of the ontological universe. Semantic features may be seen as a notation for one or more such trees. Finally, relationships between concepts, taxonomic and otherwise, provide an encoding of real-world knowledge. This can be used to support some kinds of inference that are needed during phrase-level parsing, and that provide clues to disambiguation processes.

With regard to the last point, a particular example is the determination of plausible meanings of noun–noun compounds. Lexicalized compounds have conventional meanings that should be recorded in the lexicon; for example, *pressure cooker*, or *starvation diet*. Novel compounds present a problem of disambiguation. Levi (1978) presents an analysis in terms of nine "recoverably deleteable predicates," and suggests that syntactic rules exist that allow phrases using these predicates to be realized as noun-noun compounds. Most of Levi's nine predicates are ambiguous though. Allowing for only those ambiguities that Levi notes, there are 28 possible interpretations of a noun-noun compound. It is not in general possible to select one reading in preference to all others, because genuinely ambiguous compounds can be found, for example, *glass tray* as "tray made of glass" or "tray for (carrying) glasses." Admittedly, two different senses of *glass* are involved. For any one compound, however, it is possible on grounds of semantic ill-formedness to rule out of consideration most of the 28 readings. The same techniques should be applicable also to some cases of morphological compounds, such as *snowman* and *icebox*. The point is that the judgement of semantic well- or ill-formedness rests on the availability of knowledge about concepts. Therefore conceptual category information is an important resource during parsing.

3.3.4. Presuppositions, entailments, implicatures. The lexical entry of a word must contain sufficient information for natural language systems to fully understand its meaning. Unfortunately, information about implied meanings is seldom made explicit. Preferably some means could be found to indicate the truth conditions associated with the content of the sentential arguments of words such as those emphasized below:

He *realized* that he was late.	; He was late.
He *pretends* he is working.	; He is not working.

It is *too* hot to eat. ; It cannot be eaten.

I believe the sun has only 9 planets. ; I do not know it.

Part of the information that must be supplied concerns whether a particular implication is a presupposition or an entailment. The distinction is that presuppositions are conveyed even when a clause is negated or interrogative. Thus, for example:

He has stopped }
He has not stopped } beating his donkey
Has he stopped }

All imply that he did beat it. The content of the clause is presupposed by *stop*. However, there is a different behavior with the complement clause of *know*:

I don't know }
I know } that he beats his donkey
Do you know }
I didn't know }

The implication here does not seem to hold in the first ("I don't know") case, but it does in the others. Clearly the behaviors of individual words with regard to when implications are and are not conveyed are nonuniform. The information about the circumstances in which these inferences may be drawn is therefore lexical in nature, and is required for inferential processing of the semantic representation of sentences.

3.4. Robustness

The past decade has seen a surge in research aiming to handle ill-formed inputs (see e.g., AJCL, 1983). Nevertheless most parsers existing today are fragile. They might work well on even a wide range of inputs, efficiently producing sophisticated analyses for intricate linguistic constructions, but fail utterly on other inputs that are only slightly different. Common causes of this fragility are (a) failure to handle spelling mistakes, (b) inadequate system vocabulary, (c) inability to handle fragmentary (nonsentence) inputs, (d) inflexible insistence on correct syntax, and (e) inability to handle sense extension and other nonliteral uses of language.

Ill-formedness is to a large extent a relative concept. For example, fragments are ill-formed inputs only from the point of view of a system that expects all inputs to be whole sentences, but natural use of language makes extensive use of nonsentential fragments. Again, although a syntax error like . . . *for my husband and I* is ill-formed in a more absolute sense, it is troublesome only for a grammar that enforces pronoun case restrictions. (It is actually less arduous for a grammar developer to ignore such restrictions than to enforce them.)

There is a strong motivation for developers to state as many restrictions as possible. For any restriction that is omitted, one can find sentences whose correct interpretation depends crucially on sensitivity to that restriction. If a parser is not sensitive to the restriction, it will find ambiguities where none exist. Unfortunately, the addition of well-motivated restrictions tends to exacerbate the problem of fragility. The challenge in designing robust parsers is making them able to exploit restrictions for purposes of disambiguation, and yet also able to tolerate restriction violations when inputs are in fact ill-formed. In particular, a parser faced with ill-formed input must decide which restriction(s) to relax.

The five listed causes of fragility in NL parsers should be treated in different ways. The first two have implications for the lexicon that we discuss. The issue of sense extension and other nonliteral use of language is also lexically significant, and is related to the topic of Pustejovsky's chapter in this volume, but space limitations preclude a serious discussion in this chapter.

3.4.1. Spelling mistakes. The situation of a word being misspelled is not easily distinguished from the situation of a legitimate but unknown word being used. Another difficulty, often overlooked, is that errors, particularly orthographical errors, may result in a word that is present in the lexicon, but is not the word intended. The words *principal* and *principle,* for example, are often used inappropriately. Lexical entries for such words might include the information that they are commonly used (mistakenly) as orthographic variants of each other. This is not strictly necessary, because more general techniques, that would in any case be required to handle typographical errors as well as nonword-forming orthographical errors, would work equally well for word-forming errors. It might nevertheless be profitable to include this type of information, because the more general techniques are typically computationally expensive. Without this information, these techniques would have to be applied to all input words, not just those missing from the lexicon, just in case an error had accidentally formed a valid word.

For general techniques, the lexical information required to handle spelling mistakes is only the orthographical and the phonemic representations of words, and both of these are required for other purposes anyway. Techniques for spelling error correction do however impose an organizational requirement on a lexicon. It must be possible to set up an index so that words may be located based on the phonemes and/or n-grams they contain.

3.4.2. Inadequate system vocabulary. The availability of a lexicon based on MRD sources can be expected to reduce greatly the incidence of valid words being unknown to NLP systems, but the problem will never go away completely, if only because language users are forever at liberty to coin new words. Novel compounds should be handled by morphological processes, which in this case will certainly need access to at least that conceptual category information that is used for syntactic compounds. For other neologisms, it is meaningless to ask what information the lexicon should contain, because the words simply are not present.

4. SINGLE-SENTENCE GENERATION

Much of the lexical knowledge needed for generation is the same as that needed for analysis. Much of the morphological, syntactic, and semantic knowledge is just as essential for generation as it is for analysis, because essentially similar processes are running in opposite directions. However, some additional information is needed for generation over and above what is needed for analysis, because generation involves making choices about how to express ideas, whereas analysis has the job of identifying the ideas. There is therefore information required by generation concerned purely with this choice-making activity, which has no correlate for analysis.

4.1. Word-Sense Selection

Natural language generators come in two major varieties: one variety, that may arise in machine translation, is required to produce text and is given a direct indication of words that can be used in the text. The other variety is given some kind of word-sense-free semantic representation, and must itself choose the words to use in the text.

In this second case, the representation will normally consist of individual complex concepts, having links to other concepts in a lattice, and being themselves structures of other concepts. In general it is not sufficient merely to annotate a concept with a word to use for it, for two reasons. First, some concepts, particularly those at a high level of generality, can be expressed using a variety of words. For example, a transfer of possession can be expressed in English using several words: the verbs *give, receive, lend, steal, give back,* and so on; and the nouns *gift, receipt, loan, theft, return,* and so on. Second, some concepts do not have names in some or in any languages, and have to be expressed by describing them in terms of their links to other concepts.

These problems necessitate selecting among possible ways of expressing a concept. Numerous factors will influence the selection, including (a) desired syntactic category, (b) satisfiability of syntactic constraints on expressions of arguments, (c) appropriateness of conceptual types of arguments, (d) discourse knowledge (*gift* vs. *return*), and (e) appropriateness of register.

The first two of these go hand in hand. Consider what goes on in choosing the words *took* and *construction* to form the sentence "The boat's construction took 4 months." The verb *take* (in this sense) requires a noun-phrase subject. In expressing the subject, therefore, the word selection procedure must be sensitive to this desired syntactic category, and must find a noun (or find a way of building a noun morphologically). It would not be syntactically acceptable to produce a verb phrase. Now suppose that the word selection procedure failed, because it could not find a noun to express the concept. This would mean that the decision to use *take* would have to be retracted, because the syntactic constraints on the expression of its arguments could not be satisfied.

Another factor is the semantic character of arguments. For example, the English verb *eat* has two translations in German, *essen* and *fressen*. The selection of which German word to use is dictated by the conceptual category of the eater: if a person is doing the eating, *essen*, if an animal, *fressen*. This ought to be a very simple inference, but other more complex inferences may be required. This may involve specific memory of the events in a narrative, in order to select between say "the gift of the book" and "the return of the book." Finally, there is the matter of appropriateness of register (formal, vulgar, etc.).

4.2. Sentence Generation as a Planning Process

The circumstances in which generation takes place in machine translation are different from those in a natural language interface. For an NL interface, the purpose of generation is to deliberately construct a fluent and grammatical text that meets the communicative needs of the underlying AI system. An MT system has no access to the goals that the author of the source text may have had, so it must either infer them from the text or go without. The generator in an MT system will have to judge whether a given piece of information is new or old, whether it can be communicated tacitly by inferencing from the choice of wording or phrasing, or whether it must be explicitly spelled out. We need effective models of the choices that the target language offers, and their consequences if used. There must be connections with inference systems and with the part of the system looking after dialogue generation. Natural language understanding involves going through the traditional stages of linguistic analysis, moving from the form of the text to the intentions behind it. In generation, on the other hand, we begin with the intentions (the goals or the list of conversation moves) and work our way down to the text, going in the opposite direction. Generation, however, is more complex than simply analysis in reverse. It is a planning process, entailing realizing specific goals in the presence of constraints and dealing with the effects of limitations on resources, (e.g., the expressive capacities of a given language, or the space available in a sentence or paragraph to express ideas) once a given prose style has been chosen. The process of text generation needs the following:

- A word-sense selection mechanism to choose appropriate target language words for the concepts to be expressed
- A knowledge of restrictions placed on the fillers of slots in a given phrase
- Knowledge about the number, grammatical gender, and so on, of noun phrases
- Knowledge about the appropriate tense, form, mood, aspect, and so on, for verb phrases in order to perform the correct morphological transformations on sentence particles
- A knowledge of permissible syntactic transformations in the target language
- Indicators as to prose style, such as whether or not to break complex sentences down into smaller phrases if that is feasible

5. CONCLUSION

In this chapter we have approached the problem of identifying the lexical requirements of the tasks of sentence-level parsing and generation. We have tried to enumerate the kinds of information required, without getting bogged down in the minutiae of snippets of information necessary for fully handling the phenomena of any particular language or linguistic theory.

We have identified many broad kinds of information, some of which are clearly lexical, but we note that there is a large gray area where the lexical or nonlexical status of pieces of information is not clear. This boundary is difficult to draw. We have taken as a guide the notion that a species of information is lexical if (a) it is required for some task in NLP, (b) it can be stated as a property of lexical items, and (c) there is no other knowledge structure in terms of which the information can be more naturally or more parsimoniously stated.

Not surprisingly, the third condition is the one that causes uncertainty about the lexical or nonlexical status of certain kinds of information, because it is not clear just what other knowledge structures exist and can be exploited in NLP. If, for example, one supposes that there is a memory composed of concepts and links between concepts, with lexical items somehow indexing some of these concepts, then certain kinds of knowledge would appear to be more naturally expressed in the memory than in the lexicon. For example, Pustejovsky's notion of qualia structure (this volume) involves recording among other things that certain objects have a telic role-books are for reading, for example. But given a concept-network memory, this would be more naturally expressed as a fact about the concept named by *book* than about the word *book* itself, even more so in a multilingual system. That is to say, this kind of information would be regarded as encyclopedic rather than lexical. Similar observations hold for many other kinds of knowledge structure, such as syntactic grammars and phonetic transduction rules. They too can provide an alternative locus for certain species of arguably lexical knowledge.

In general, those kinds of information provided by commercial human-oriented dictionaries are also needed for computer-based natural language processing. Elaboration will be needed, but little will go to waste apart from the grouping of senses into related homonyms, and the identification of etymological roots (identification of the donor language can, however, be useful information). The information available in these sources typically needs to be considerably enriched and made more explicit if it is to be tractable for NLP purposes, and some further kinds of information have been identified that do belong in the lexicon but are not to our knowledge listed in commercial dictionaries; for example the presuppositions and entailments of words like the verb *stop*.

A particular example of the need for enrichment and explicitness, one to which we wish to draw special attention, is the dictionary approach to derivational morphology. We do not believe that enough is currently known about the semantic representation of lexical items, nor about the interactions between semantic classes and syntactic properties, to allow a fully general and accurate morphological algorithm that will yield the semantic and syntactic information that NLP requires for morphologically complex words. If dictionaries are to be converted into lexical resources for NLP systems therefore, it would be advisable to provide additional information about morphological combinations, perhaps even listing explicitly new stems formed by derivational affixation that are not found explicitly in the source dictionaries. A second area where a great deal of additional information would be required is the linking of word senses to some kind of extralinguistic store of real-world knowledge. This might be organized as a concept-network memory, or in some other fashion: but it is in world knowledge, and not in the lexicon, that we will find the information that allows us to disambiguate Bar-Hillel's *pen* sentences.

Some tasks in NLP impose requirements on the organization of a lexicon that are generally quite different from those of human users of dictionaries. These fall into two classes of organizational device: links between sense entries, and computational structures for retrieval that encompass the entire lexicon. Structures of the second kind are necessary for looking up words, either by sound or by (approximate) spelling. These large-scale knowledge structures are essentially indexes, and may fortunately be constructed automatically by special-purpose programs that examine each entry in turn.

Links *between* sense entries are of many kinds, including traditional lexical-semantic relations such as synonymy, antonymy, and taxonomy, many of which one might reasonably expect to be able to derive in an almost fully automatic fashion from machine-readable forms of conventional dictionaries. However, other kinds of intersense link are also sometimes needed. For one example, there are a few verbs in English, like *hit* and *put*, whose past participles, simple past forms, and present tense forms are all the same. In processing a sentence such as "I put the book on the table," there seems to be a strong preference for the past tense interpretation, although appropriate context can override this preference. This must depend on some information in the lexicon, and we feel that the information in question is in fact a link between different senses.

In summary, conventional dictionaries provide a great deal of the information that is required for computer-based processing of natural language. But this information will need to be preprocessed in a variety of ways before it can be made fully machine tractable. It must be enriched, because certain kinds of information are usually missing, and some NLP tasks depend crucially on it. It must be made more explicit, because NLP programs do not have the robustness, selectivity, and background knowledge that humans bring to bear in using dictionary information. It also must be organized, so that lexical semantic relationships can be represented and efficiently exploited, and also so that lexical entries can be accessed by programs on the basis of approximate pronunciation or approximate spelling.

CHAPTER 5

SOURCES FOR MACHINE TRACTABLE DICTIONARIES

Nicoletta Calzolari
Istituto di Linguistica Computazionale del CNR - Pisa
Dipartimento di Linguistica - Università di Pisa

1. THE PROBLEM OF SOURCES FOR LEXICAL INFORMATION

Historically, we must notice that there has been, after a long period of indifference, a shift of interest toward the lexicon in the past decade, within both theoretical and computational linguistics. In parallel, there has been a movement toward the exploitation of MRDs for the semiautomatic extraction of different types of lexical information as an aid in the creation of MTDs. Many research groups all over the world have begun to work in this framework, and a result of this tendency can be seen, for example, in an ESPRIT Project, ACQUILEX, whose explicit purpose is the acquisition of lexical information from MRDs for NLP systems.

However, now that this tendency has finally found its most relevant acknowledgement both within academia and in funding agencies, it appears very clear that MRDs can only be one of the sources of lexical information for building a good extended lexical database or lexical knowledge base.

I try to summarize here some points concerning the relevant sources for MTDs. In a very concise and schematic way (not exhaustively, with no argumentations, and not in detail, but by means of representative types), I discuss (a) what can be found in MRDs that can be reused; (b) what are the advantages and disadvantages associated with reuse; (c) what is missing in MRDs, but is relevant for MTDs; and (d) what other sources can be taken into consideration for (c).

2. WHAT IS PRESENT IN MRDS THAT CAN BE REUSED

2.1. Types of Information

From MRDs, in general, we can obtain data such as pronunciation; etymology; grammatical information (part of speech, other traditional categories like transitive, reflexive, etc.); semantic information (synonyms, taxonomies, metonymies, other semantic relations); some idioms, collocations; and some compounds.

2.2. Advantages

One obvious advantage associated with deriving lexical information from MRDs is connected with the need for large coverage computational lexicons. The types of information that can be extracted from a MRD (see previous) can be very extensive in coverage.

Moreover, some research progress has been made, and more is expected, in the extraction of conceptual categories and of semantic knowledge in relational form from the analysis of dictionary definitions.

2.3. Disadvantages

However, on the negative side, if lexical data in MRDs is extended in breadth, we cannot claim that it is also extended in depth. For "deep" syntactic or semantic information we must resort to other sources. In addition, MRD data are not really complete, nor error-free, and extraction procedures are, in large part, not completely automatic. Some human intervention is always necessary although the amount of human involvement may vary depending on the type of information processed. Extraction processes must be guided by theoretical principles in order to be of value. Strategies must be established for the extractions.

3. WHAT IS MISSING IN MRDS THAT CAN BE EXPLOITED FROM OTHER SOURCES

3.1. Other Types of Relevant Information for NLP

Even though we recognize (and we were among the pioneers in claiming) that MRDs are very valuable sources of lexical information for NLP, we are well aware that not all that is needed is there. There is very important information that is either completely missing, very fragmentary, or rather poor, for which we have to resort to different sources.

A tentative and partial list can include the following:

- Frequency (at any level: of words, word forms, word senses, word associations, etc.)
- Subcategorization (unless you have a learner's dictionary)
- Collocations, idioms, word combinations
- Thematic roles, valency
- Semantic constraints on arguments
- Typical subject, object, modifier
- Explicit derivational and inflectional morphology
- Aspectual information
- Proper nouns

3.2. Other Sources

When we try to determine if and where we have other important sources of lexical information, we can come up with at least the following sources that are necessary to consider:

- Lexicographers' knowledge
- Theoretical linguists' knowledge
- Large textual corpora and statistical approaches to text analysis.

For each of these three sources, some problems are to be faced, alongside those specific to the area, for example, standardization, shareability, and theoretical soundness at different levels of (lexicographic, linguistic, and textual) description.

3.2.1. Lexicographers' knowledge. This refers to the (often quite large) amount of lexicographical data that is preparatory for the compilation of dictionary entries, and that is not used in the printed dictionary usually for lack of space, or due to its intrinsic nature. The data can be, on the contrary, a very rich source of information to be exploited. If lexicographers were provided with a well-designed lexicographic workstation, this valuable source of information could become immediately reusable and of great benefit for an MTD.

3.2.2. Theoretical linguists' knowledge. If we consider the different levels of linguistic description (morphology, syntax, semantics, etc.), for each of these we should ask questions like the following:

- What is the degree of accuracy and completeness of available theoretical linguistic descriptions?

- What is the present state-of-the-art?
- What has to be done?
- Do we have theories sufficiently developed to become satisfactorily implementable?

The answers will obviously differ from level to level.

3.2.3. Textual corpora. Textual corpora, in particular, can be used to obtain a large part or, at least, some information for most of the aforementioned items. Therefore, stress is placed on the importance of the use and the analysis of textual corpora exactly in the context of this discussion where we speak about LDBs or MTDs. To achieve good MTDs it is important to have access to and to use large textual corpora.

This is also a point of convergence where, for example, literary computing people can play an important role not simply because of their large collections of texts but because of their competence in dealing with texts as well.

4. CONCLUSION

It is a fact that there is, nowadays, a growing convergence of interest around computational lexicography and lexicology of areas and fields such as computational linguistics and natural language processing, literary and linguistic computing and text processing, and lexicography and publishing houses.

This convergence must be exploited. The main task is an effort toward the integration of the different types of information coming from different sources, and, in a sense, linked to the above sectors. This can be obtained only through the design of large cooperative projects where the typical data, tools, procedures, know-how, techniques, knowledge, results, methods, and so on, of all the aforementioned areas involved work in parallel, and cooperate and interact with each other. For instance, a growing number of computational linguists are now using statistics and textual corpora whereas some lexicographers are using the results of computational linguistic research and database technology. We must, therefore, be able to establish and consolidate this rather new and productive trend of cooperation between different areas of research (with different viewpoints on the lexicon), different approaches (e.g., more research oriented or application oriented), and different environments (e.g., research institutions, industries or commercial companies, public organizations).

CHAPTER 6

NEUTRAL DICTIONARIES*

Pim van der Eijk
Research Institute for Language and Speech
State University of Utrecht

1. INTRODUCTION

The past several years have seen a growing interest in lexicons. In the field of natural language processing (NLP), the move from experimental systems with toy lexicons to larger systems has generated the need for large lexicons containing rich syntactic and semantic information.

Considering the large amounts of time and money that have to be invested in the construction of large lexicons, it is essential that existing lexical resources be combined and reused, and that future lexical development work can serve a variety of purposes. Usually, the notion of reusability is restricted to a narrower sense, referring to attempts to use existing machine-readable dictionaries (MRDs) as a source for the derivation of lexical databases for NLP systems.

In a more general setting, I would like to raise the question of how the concept of a neutral dictionary, ensuring reusability in a wider sense, can be defined and implemented.

2. WHAT IS A NEUTRAL DICTIONARY?

In general, the notion of neutrality only makes sense in a context where there are several (possibly conflicting) views, and where these views

*Most of the ideas described in this paper were jointly conceived with Dirk Heylen. The research reported on in this paper has been sponsored by the European Community's Eurotra MT project and by the Lexic Project, which is sponsoredd jointly by the EEC, Phillips Research, and Van Dale Lexicograaphy.

describe partly the same or similar objects in a (linguistic, in our case) reality, and that they partly predicate the same or comparable properties of these objects (words). All views are necessarily partial, because (linguistic) reality is vast and complex, and far from well understood.

With the aim of reusing dictionaries, the design of a neutral dictionary should combine these partial *descriptions* to obtain a richer view of the data, which can then be put to wider use.[1] In order to realize this combination, it is necessary to carry out a rigorous comparison of the various sources. This comparison can be conducted on the basis of detailed descriptions of the sources and definition of the notions that are used. Appropriate description languages are discussed in Section 3.

A closer look at various dictionaries shows there can be differences at various levels, such as the *selection*of objects (which words are described) and the question of what are the relevant *properties*that are to be mentioned. Other issues include what counts as a word, for example, extensional full-form dictionaries versus intentional dictionaries that describe words abstractly by assuming closure under morphological rule application, and *structural*differences in the descriptions of objects. For instance, in a classical dictionary, a lexical entry is a word form coupled with a *tree*of word senses, where the branching of the structure may be governed by various conventions.

These descriptions constitute the basis for detailed comparison, which will result in a set of correspondences where there are overlaps in information. The correspondences can be quite complex.

In the approach discussed in Section 4, the correspondences are expressed as general constraints in a feature structure logic. Ways in which these constraints can be used-that is, to *derive* information, and to maximize *consistency* and *correctness* of data-are also discussed.

The data that are collected this way can be reused for any arbitrary new application by just adding the appropriate constraints and interpreting them as conversion rules. The interpretation of the constraints will then yield a virtual lexicon. If the application already has a small dictionary, the constraints can be used as recognizers to test whether or not the postulated correspondences indeed hold.

In the *neutral* approach advocated here, various views coexist, and similarities between these views can be exploited to achieve advantages similar to those claimed for using databases in general (e.g., Date, 1981). A difference with traditional database design exists in the fact that incompatibilities between views will *not* be resolved. In general, advocates of *standardization* choose the approach of comparing various competing views to develop a consensus to replace the existing views.

---

[1]The same objective has been pursued with UDICT as described in Byrd et al. (1987)

The motivation for *neutrality* is that, although standards may be set for relatively low-level issues (e.g., text handling, morphographemics), most of linguistics (and much of the information that will be encoded in a lexicon) is not yet ready for standardization and conflicts need not all be resolved, although they must be accounted for.

3. DESCRIBING INFORMATION

There exist several standard data models for database systems (cf. e.g., Ullman, 1988), the best of which are formal in the sense of having a solid mathematical foundation and supporting data definition using formulas in a well-understood data definition language (DDL). The Entity-Relationship (ER) model, for instance, provides a high description level of data that can be mapped to conceptual schemes in other (e.g., relational) data models, upon which real database systems are built.

To apply the ER model, it is necessary to state, for each existing dictionary, what the objects are and what is stated about them. The reverse procedure has to be followed, because the data (the dictionaries) already exist; that is, the data definition and an ER model have to be reconstructed.

The classical relational concept has several well-known drawbacks, such as the absence of ways to deal with complex structured objects, with recursion and partiality, and with sequential (ordered) data, that are relevant to the application to dictionaries. Several alternative approaches to data modeling have been pursued. I mention two of these that are relevant to the application.

The first model emphasizing *textual* data structures was proposed by Gonnet and Tompa (1987). The authors claimed commercial (relational) databases were inappropriate for text-dominated databases such as dictionaries. Instead, grammars were used as schemes and "parsed strings" as instances. Textual databases are very appropriate for classical dictionaries that have large amounts of unformalized text.

A second model has emerged in a number of recent linguistic theories, where information about linguistic objects is modeled by data structures called feature structures. Linguistic phenomena are modeled by constraints of (in)equality over feature structures and the fundamental operation of solving such systems of equations is unification (Sag et al., 1986). Recently, Carpenter (1990) has shown the relationship of an extended type of feature structures with knowledge representation systems.

One advantage of using feature structures as data type over other approaches is that it fully supports structured objects and recursion, and especially the notion of partial information (cf. Pereira, 1987) which, as argued in Section 2, is essential for the application to neutral lexicons. They may be less suited to sequentially ordered data such as text, but modern dictionaries make increasing use of these data structures.

Another advantage is that the equations that go with feature structures are more suitable to describe data on the conceptual level. That is, they allow for a higher level of abstraction, whereas the 'parse-strings' seem more closely tied to the textual representation of the primary data.

In the rest of this discussion, attention is restricted to feature structures.

4. RELATING INFORMATION

The construction of a neutral dictionary, using one or a number of preexisting sources, can proceed by *normalization*; that is, reduction of redundancies. If a piece of information in one place can be predicted deterministically from a corresponding piece in another by constraint satisfaction, it can be removed because the constraint can be used as an instruction to recover the information. As a simplified example, the constraint

$$\mathrm{dict1} \bullet \mathrm{cat} : (\mathrm{adv} \vee \mathrm{adj}) \; <-> \; \mathit{dict2} \cdot \mathit{cat} : \mathrm{a}$$

implies that the value for *cat* in *dict2* can be determined from the corresponding attribute in *dict1* but not vice versa.[2] If the constraints are not strict enough to allow for full recoverability, they can still be used as integrity constraints. As an example, the relation between being animate and being human is not derivable in any direction, as can be deduced from the following constraints. (If you are animate, you can be human but you need not be. If you're not human, you can still be animate.)

$$\mathrm{dict1} \bullet \mathrm{anim} : \mathrm{yes} \; <-> \; \mathrm{dict2}\ \mathit{human} : (\mathrm{yes} \vee \mathrm{no})$$

$$\mathit{dict1} \cdot \mathit{anim} : (\mathrm{yes} \vee \mathrm{no}) \; <-> \; \mathit{dict2} \cdot \mathit{human} : \mathrm{no}$$

As is well known, algorithms for mechanical normalization exist for the relational model. Further discussion of ways to adapt these procedures to feature structures on the basis of a set of constraints is deferred to a separate paper.

The technique of feature structure rewriting to solve constraint equations (Carpenter & Pollard, 1990; Zajac, 1990) can be applied to

---

[2] The example relates two views on Dutch, in which the difference between adjectives and adverbs is sometimes claimed not to exist.

reproduce the original data. New virtual dictionaries can be derived in the same way, combining the information found in several sources, provided the appropriate constraints are defined.

5. CONFLICTING INFORMATION

The only operation combining feature structures is strict monotonic unification. Constraints are global in the sense that they relate data schemes rather than instances. The application of the constraints on preexisting instances will help detect many errors and inconsistencies, but might also reveal local exceptions (e.g., a constraint is inapplicable to a particular lexical entry). Similarly, constraints deriving information from more than one source may reveal conflicts between the two.

In a powerful constraint language, arbitrarily complex correspondences can be defined, and because constraints can also refer to unique identifying attributes or keys, entry-specific constraints can in principle be defined. However, they may become quite inelegant, so it may be worthwhile to explore other approaches.

In knowledge representation, several approaches have been developed, such as defeasible logic (Vermeir et al., 1989), that could be incorporated, though the consequences of that move are as yet unclear.

6. COMPARISON WITH PREVIOUS APPROACHES

Early attempts at developing a reusable (in the general sense) dictionary include Daelemans' Flexible Dictionary System, Calder's Protolexicon (1987), and the Utrecht Ndict system (Bloksma et al., 1990; van der Eijk, 1990). These approaches can be considered implementations of a part of the concept of neutrality as proposed here. The more general view of neutrality outlined previously has several practical advantages over the earlier approaches.

First, there is no longer a single special "mother" dictionary from which all "daughter" dictionaries can be derived. It is possible to have several sources and to combine the information contained therein.

Second, the procedural flow of information from source to consumer dictionary is replaced by a more declarative view of combining information by constraint satisfaction. Therefore, it is possible to have dictionaries containing some information themselves and inheriting other information from sources.

Third, as a corollary of the previous point, it is now allowed that unrelatably conflicting views exist. In the current approach relatable information is shared and unrelatable information can be preserved.

7. CONCLUSION

The model of neutral dictionaries developed here has a much wider applicability than other known approaches. Principled approaches have been sketched to integration and generation of dictionaries. Work with preexisting and derived dictionaries can be combined. Benefits of database management, such as reduced redundancy, avoided inconsistency, maintained integrity, and sharing of data, can be guaranteed without imposing a notion of standard that would be naive in most contexts.

CHAPTER 7

CAN A NEUTRAL DICTIONARY BE USEFUL?

Allan Ramsay
Department of Computer Science
University College Dublin

Most of the other participants in the current discussion have sensibly approached it by looking at what is usually provided in dictionaries, in the hope that they will be able to make this information more useful for NLP systems. Given that the genesis of the discussion is the existence of several MRDs that contain information that ought to be useful for NLP systems but is not, this does seem to be an entirely sensible approach. It may be, however, that concentrating on the good and bad points about existing MRDs may unduly narrow the discussion. As an antidote to this I propose to consider briefly the information that current NLP systems require from their lexicons, and the extra information that might become essential if we are to transcend the limits of current systems.

If we are to discuss the information that current NLP systems require, we must have some view of current NLP systems. The following outline architectures capture the essence of the vast majority of current systems for analyzing and generating natural language texts. (As is only too common in discussions of NLP, all my arguments are illustrated with examples from English. I believe, but cannot prove, that similar arguments apply to systems for processing other languages.) Clearly there are minor variations, but the overall pictures are right.

Analysis systems are typical current systems for analyzing NL input that accept *typed* input. They contain words from some given vocabulary and conform to some predetermined grammar. The input text is manipulated either by some linguistically principled set of morphological rules, or more commonly by some program obtained by mangling such a principled set of rules, to yield root forms and suffixes. These roots and suffixes are used as keys into a lexical database, with the entries that are found being combined to form descriptions of linguistic items containing both syntactic and semantic information. Thus the word *hidden* might be split into a root, *hide,* and a suffix, *- en,* with the entries for these being combined to suggest that the item is either the past participle or the passive participle of a transitive verb concerned with making it hard to find something. These linguistic items are then combined into groups according to the rules of the predefined grammar, and a description of the literal meaning of each input sentence is built up using semantic rules associated with the grammatical ones. The description of the literal meaning will generally be expressed in some formal language with well-defined semantics (in older systems, formal languages *without* well-defined semantics were often used, but it is now generally recognized that this is a fairly pointless thing to do). This description may then be passed to some application program to do something with, or it may first be subjected to analysis in terms of "speech act theory" to try to elucidate the reasons for which it was produced.

It is harder to describe a "typical" generation system. This is partly because there is less agreement about the most effective algorithms for generation (and hence about the best way of organizing a generation system). There is, however, a deeper reason for the wide variation in generation systems. All analysis systems take NL text as input, no matter what the ultimate application is. Because all systems start in the same place, at least the first few stages of processing are likely to be very similar. It does not really matter what theory of semantics is chosen, or what information one thinks is important. One is almost bound to start by splitting words in text into roots and suffixes, looking them up in a lexicon, and analyzing the syntactic structure of the text using the information that this gives. Generation systems, on the other hand, all start from different places. The generation component of a translation system might be given the syntax tree of a source language sentence; a system for generating descriptions of plans might be given a sequence of STRIPS operators; a general-purpose system for carrying out arbitrary dialogues might be given arbitrary expressions in intentional logic, and so on. It is likely that each of these systems will require a different architecture, because the information that is available to them when they start their different tasks will provide different constraints on the space of possible output texts. The most that can be said about generation systems is that at some point any generation system will need to access a dictionary and a collection of suffixes in order to choose an appropriate root form and inflection, and that when it tries to access the dictionary and suffix set, the clues it has for finding the required entries will *not* be orthographic forms. The most likely clues will come as a partially specified set of syntactic and semantic features, and it is extremely improbable that the system designer will know in advance which features will be specified and which will not. Efficient dictionary access for generation, then, is likely to require rather subtle indexing mechanisms.

1. MORPHOLOGY

Most textbooks on NLP would provide similar architectures for analysis and generation systems (see Allen, 1987; Gazdar & Mellish, 1989). We see that systems for both analysis and generation generally require lexical entries to carry information about morphological classification (does *ride* have *-en* as the suffix for its past and passive participle, like *hide*, or does it have *-ed* like *decide*?); about syntactic properties (these include things like agreement and case marking, but the most important syntactic information concerns subcategorization frames); and about semantics.

Can we provide the required information in a theory-free way? We start by considering morphology. Look again at the words *hide, ride,* and*decide* and their past and passive participles. We might feel that the best way to store information about these words is simply to record all the required forms explicitly, with the inflected forms pointing to the root. This is clearly wasteful, because it fails to take advantage of numerous regularities. It ignores the fact that English past and passive participles always have the same form. It ignores the fact that all English verbs of the form *<consonant> i <t* or *d> e* that have *-en* as their passive/past participle suffix repeat the middle consonant. It ignores the fact that most English verbs of this form do have *-en* as their passive/past participle suffix. It ignores the fact that nearly all verbs that have this suffix for the passive/past participle form also have irregular past tense forms. There may well be other regularities concerning this group of verbs that could be used to save space. The problem is that the decision as to which of these facts should be used in order to condense and simplify the lexicon depends on one's approach to orthographic processing. Almost any representation of lexical items would benefit from knowing that passive and past participles are always the same-it is a universal rule, it is very easy to apply, and it saves the user from recording the same information twice over for every verb. Comparatively few systems would derive much benefit from knowing that most verbs that take *-en* as the suffix for these forms generally have irregular past tense forms. There might, however, be some generation system that took advantage of the converse rule (that most verbs that have *-ed* as their past tense suffix also have it as their passive/past participle suffix). The problem is that the decision about which of these rules should be used in the description of lexical items depends on the designer of the NLP system, not on the designer of the dictionary, so that even morphological facts cannot safely be treated in a theory-free way.

There are plenty of other similar problems. There is, for instance, a group of words whose past tense and past/passive participle forms are obtained by throwing away everything except the initial group of consonants and replacing what has been deleted by *-ought*. For example; *buy: bought, bring: brought,* or *think: thought*. A dictionary that is to be used by a generation system might well be able to take advantage of this pattern by simply labeling each of these verbs as belonging to this class. This is of no use at all for a dictionary that is to be used for analysis, though, because it is very hard indeed to imagine a rule that would enable a user to obtain *seek* as the root from which *sought* is derived. Even the best treatments of morphology, for instance Koskenniemi's (1984) two-level theory or Evans and Gazdar's (1989) default logic of morphological classes, would have great difficulty using this sort of fact in an analysis system, though it may well be useful for generation. Thus not only does the structure and content of the morphological information in a dictionary depend on how affixes are to be processed, it also depends on what the dictionary is to be used for.

Thus the specification of morphological information is not theory free or application free. If the specification uses generalizations that my affix-processing algorithm cannot cope with then it is of no use to me (if, for instance, it uses default principles such as the claim that most verbs of some kind have *-en* as their passive/past participle suffix, and my algorithm is deterministic). If, on the other hand, it ignores generalizations that my algorithm *can* cope with, then the dictionary will be unnecessarily verbose. It will remain impossible to design a dictionary whose descriptions of word morphology are universally acceptable until all agree on the best way to do affix stripping, which will not happen very soon. The only feasible approach is to use only those generalizations that absolutely everyone can be relied on to want-to go for the lowest common denominator, and hence to provide more sophisticated users with representations that they regard as redundant and wasteful.

2. SYNTAX

If there are problems in designing theory-free representations of morphology, what about syntax? Here we are in dreadful trouble. Different systems are based on different grammars, and even on different grammatical frameworks. The choice between different frameworks is not arbitrary. It reflects the beliefs of the system's designer about the best way to describe how language is organized. These beliefs can be influenced by innumerable factors, including decisions about what counts as syntactic evidence, and about what counts as significant syntactic evidence. Suppose, for instance, that you believe that the inelegance of "*John* and the cake are cooking," as a condensation of "*John was* cooking and the cake was cooking,"arises from syntactic considerations. If one thinks this is a syntactic problem, the grammar will need to include case frames and semantic markers as syntactic features. A theorist who regarded the problem as a matter to be resolved by semantic analysis, on the other hand, would not want to include these items as part of the grammar. Similarly, the choice of semantic representation can affect beliefs about how best to organize syntactic descriptions. If, for instance, one wants to use a typed logic as the representation language, then one may well be tempted to use categorial grammar as the grammatical framework, a choice that imposes some extremely specific constraints on the form of grammatical descriptions (see for instance the form of the grammar rules in Dowty et al.'s, 1981, introduction to Montague grammar). Even the direction of application of the system can influence the matter. People working on generation have a taste for systemic or functional grammar, because this framework includes places to hang information about the purpose of particular components of the text (Patten, 1985). People working on analysis do not usually know what to do with this information, and therefore tend to ignore it.

These different grammatical frameworks require radically different syntactic information to be associated with each lexical item. It is not, as was the case for morphology, just a matter of whether or not we can use some piece of information. There we could say that we would organize descriptions using just the information that we know that *every*one can understand. If we failed to take advantage of some regularity that one of our users could have dealt with, it did not matter all that much. The lexicon would be rather larger than it need be, but it would still be usable. In the case of the choice between different syntactic frameworks, however, it is not just that there is some information that we could use to simplify our lexicon, but that we chose to leave out. Somebody who wanted to use GPSG (Gazdar et al., 1985) would not be grateful if they were told that some verb belongs to the class of "raising" verbs, because this classification overlaps part of the GPSG treatment of control without actually being included in it or including it. They would be more grateful to be given this information than not to be told anything at all (as happens in for instance the entry for *want* in the Concise OED), but it is not really the information they need. Similarly someone who wanted to use case grammar (Fillmore, 1968) would not be grateful to be told that *open* can be either intransitive or transitive (Concise OED). If one wants to use case grammar it is because the user believes that case frames are useful-because, for instance, they help one understand the relation between the intransitive and transitive uses of *open,* which is entirely unlike the relation between the intransitive and transitive uses of *drink.*

We cannot transcend this problem by looking for some lowest common denominator. The lowest common denominator of any pair of syntactic frameworks is too low to provide the information that is required by an NLP system (and the lowest common denominator of any set of *N* syntactic frameworks is lower than the lowest common denominator of any *N-1* subset of them). Indeed, most dictionaries are extremely lacking in syntactic information, largely because it is impossible even to talk about such information without a theoretical framework. How can one explain the difference between "John is easy to please" and "John is eager to please," without a theory of control? How can one explain the relation between "John opened the door," and "The door opened," without a theory of semantic roles? Yet all these theories are contentious, and they are often strictly incompatible with one another.

The prospects look bleak. No NLP system can do much unless it has access to a dictionary with entries containing detailed syntactic information. Detailed syntactic information is necessarily tied to a specific theory of syntax, and different theories of syntax are generally incompatible. We are therefore led inexorably to the conclusion that we cannot have a useful theory-free lexicon. At the very least we cannot expect a theory-free lexicon to be useful until we have put a good deal of effort into imposing our chosen theory on it. This may well be less than the amount of work required to build a lexicon from scratch, but it is not going to be trivial.

3. SEMANTICS

And if there are problems in designing theory-free representations of syntactic information, the situation when we consider semantics is simply hopeless. It is almost impossible to find a single issue on which any two users agree, and yet to have any hope whatsoever of constructing useful theory-free dictionaries we must have agreement on a range of issues. These include agreement about at least the following:

1. The domain of semantic theories: Should they describe truth conditions, or constraints on utterance situations, or functions from preutterance situations to postutterance situations, or what?
2. The question of whether semantic representations should be based on a theory of thematic roles, and if so what roles should be used.
3. The nature of semantic primitives, and their connection to the general knowledge representation scheme of the application program that is to use the NLP system that uses the dictionary.

At present there is virtually no consensus on any of these matters. Consider the first issue, for instance. Someone working in classical Montague semantics would expect the meaning of a transitive verb to be a function from pairs of individuals to sets of possible worlds, and they would expect its description to be couched in terms of a combination of predicate calculus and typed l-calculus. Someone working in situation semantics (Barwise & Perry, 1983) would expect it to be a four-place relation between two individuals and two situations, and they would expect its description to be couched in some version of ill-founded set theory. Someone working in dynamic logic (Ramsay, 1990) might expect it to be a set of constraints, couched in yet another formal theory, and so on and so on. Any entry in a computational lexicon for the meaning of a transitive verb must have some such form. If we want, for instance, to specify the meaning of *seek*, we must say things about the relationship between the seeker and the thing they are seeking. We cannot do this without remarking that the thing being sought may not actually exist, and we cannot talk about things that do not exist without a theoretical framework for talking about possibilities and about alternative worlds or situations. Thus we cannot explain the relationship between *seek* (or *look for*) and *find* without choosing one of these mutually incompatible frameworks. Once we have made this choice, we will have to stick to it, because otherwise we will be unable to relate the meanings of different words. Anyone who wants to work in a different framework will have a great deal of difficulty in using our lexical entries, because there is no systematic way of translating between these frameworks.

Even if we agree on a basic framework, or if we find some underlying notation that we can systematically elaborate in different directions, we then need to decide on our attitude to the notion of thematic roles. Someone whose semantic theory assumed that there is a fixed set of thematic roles, and that descriptions of the meanings of nouns and verbs should be based on these, would require one kind of lexical entry. Someone who regarded them as some kind of *post hoc* description of a set of accidental regularities would require something different (see Dowty, 1989). As with the differences between the various underlying frameworks, people who hold one position can understand what people who hold another are saying, but there is no systematic translation between the two. As soon as one puts anything into a dictionary one is committed to some view on the nature of thematic roles, and the lexical entries will be useless to anyone with a different view.

The same problem arises when we come to consider semantic primitives. Some researchers believe that there is a set of primitive concepts that underlie the meanings of every word of a given natural language (Schank, 1972). Other people take a more holistic view of meaning, depending on a set of meaning postulates that between them provide constraints on the possible meanings of individual words (Quine, 1960). A dictionary constructed on the basis of one of these views will not provide the information required by a system based on the other.

This kind of problem is ubiquitous in semantic theory. The terms used in one theory will nearly always be incompatible with those used in another, so that there is no systematic translation between them. Sometimes the problem will be that one theory makes finer distinctions than another. In this case one could choose to use the finer theory for a dictionary, on the assumption that people who preferred the other could throw away detail that they were not interested in. In general, however, the problem is that the underlying conceptual categories of any pair of semantic theories will be so incompatible that any description in one will be unprocessable in the other. There is no naïve semantic theory in which to describe the semantics of lexical entries.

4. PROSPECTS

I have painted a fairly bleak picture. The problem is that absolutely anything said about a word will have to be said from the viewpoint of some theory. If one wants to say that *had* is an irregular form for the past tense and participle of *have*, one must have a theory of regular forms with which to contrast it. If one wants to say that *have* is a modal auxiliary, the syntactic theory must have features for specifying these properties. If one wants to say that *have* adds temporal information to the meaning of its complementary VP, one must have a theory of time and of events. At every point I might have a different theory, and if I do then I am almost certain to be unable to use the description.

This is all very unfortunate. Existing dictionaries, whether or not they are machine readable, do contain a great deal of information about words. It is obviously very tempting to try to use this information in the construction of NLP systems, because handcrafting large dictionaries is a very time-consuming job. In view of the arguments here, however, it may be that the best way to proceed is to use such dictionaries as resources that can be tailored to particular systems. For any given dictionary and any given system, some of this tailoring may be done automatically. Where this cannot be done, it will simply have to be done by hand. This can be made less tedious by ensuring that the dictionary is at least based on a consistent theory and laid out on a consistent format, but it will never be completely done away with until we all agree on every detail of our linguistic theories.

CHAPTER 8

MACHINE-TRACTABLE DICTIONARIES IN THE 21st CENTURY

Brian Slator
The Institute for the Learning Sciences
Northwestern University

Dictionaries are inert. They sit around on shelves waiting to be used, and then often, when pressed into service, they fail for one reason or another.

Sometimes dictionaries fail because they say too little. Definition by synonym can create this failure, as in the (possibly apocryphal) *furze* and *gorse* example. In this, so the story goes, a dictionary defined *furze* with its synonym, *gorse*. The puzzled reader who looked to *gorse* found that it too was defined by synonym—in this case, *furze*.

Of course, dictionary circles are a fact of lexical life. There is little else but words with which to express the meanings of other words. This never bothers anyone very much, because the definitions are usually formed of words simpler than the headword (the word being defined). Nonetheless, everyone has, at one time or another, known the frustration of following complex nestings when the words in a definition are still not simple enough, and must themselves be looked up. This never leads to infinite regress, but can be annoying all the same.

The *furze* and *gorse* problem is worse. A persevering reader can learn about the spiny, thickset shrubs with fragrant yellow leaves, but they must go out and get another dictionary to learn that.

Sometimes dictionaries fail because they say too much. One example of this appears when dictionary makers, in their zeal to outdo the competition, seemingly create new word-sense distinctions for the sake of it. Lexicographers are judged, in part, according to the new words they discover and to the refinements they can make to existing words. This is undoubtedly good for the science of lexicography, but is does not guarantee that dictionaries will be better, and certainly does not make them easier to use. If the problem at hand is to choose the correct sense for a polysemous word (a major component of the natural language understanding problem), it only follows that this choice is easier if there are fewer senses to choose from.

Dictionaries also say too much about closed-class words. One illustration of this is the dozens of definitions of the "be" verbs in the average dictionary. The Longman Dictionary of Contemporary English (LDOCE), for example, has at least 21, or more, depending on how you count. This is particularly odd when the general consensus in AI is that there are really only two useful sense distinctions for *be*: "is of identity" and "is of predication" (Charniak, 1981b). These are contrasted by, in the first case, "Mark Twain is Samuel Clemens," and in the second case, "Mark Twain is a man."

Compounding the too much/too little failures of dictionaries is the allied problem of representational ergonomics. The sublanguage of dictionary definitions is inconsistent, and the vocabulary of that sublanguage is ill defined. This is of little consequence when dictionaries are used as they are intended-as a resource for individuals who already understand the sublanguage of dictionary definitions. However, when a dictionary is the foundation of an MTD, a well-defined system of semantics is crucial.

This is not to say, as some do, that the semantical system needs to be prescribed by someone's particular linguistic theory. Rather, an MTD must be composed of both representational and procedural components.

The representational difficulties of the "neutral" lexicon are well documented in this discussion and elsewhere. Differing theories of linguistic semantics hold different schemas in high regard. The representation designed for one theory will likely not satisfy the needs of another, and the lexicon designed to service all theories will likely be intractably immense.

The "super neutral" lexicon that attempts to be all to everyone is probably a bad idea for a couple of reasons. Theories are prone to revision, and the lexicon is prone to change, independent of linguistic theory. At the First International Lexical Acquisition Workshop, held at IJCAI-90 in Detroit, Donald Walker related a story about how the newswire was monitored for new words, how it produced new words every day, and how every day these were added to the set of known words. On each successive day the newswire produced another set of new words, these were dutifully added, and it turned out that the growth curve of the set of known words never flattened out. Every new day brings more new words: new companies, new newsmakers, new devices, new technical terms. The "super neutral" lexicon, if it were ever constructed, would be out of date within 24 hours.

This returns us to the procedural component of MTD. The MTD of the 21st century will not merely be a thing. The evolution of theories and the growth of language make that fruitless. Dictionaries can afford to be inert, an MTD cannot. Rather, the MTD of the 21st century will be an agent that brokers between the needs of NLP systems and the world of words.

Part of this will be translation procedures that act as the interface between NLP systems and their lexicon. Differing theories will require different procedures to retrieve and reformulate according to theoretical and notational necessities. These will not be trivial procedures, because they will require theory-specific knowledge, much like that required of a computational linguist who wishes to build a test lexicon for, say, a GPSG parser (Gazdar et al., 1985). The data are in the dictionary, as well as other places, and the trick is to craft that into the proper form. Of course, every theory, and every revision to every theory, will require a new procedure, but this will surprise no one.

The other procedural component of MTD will be the agent that constitutes the interface between the lexicon and the world. This will be a program for lexical acquisition that, at the very least, monitors the newswire looking for new lexemes. Upon finding one, the acquisition agent will process the surrounding text to discover the meaning of the unknown lexeme, and then it will add that lexeme to the lexicon.

This is also, pretty obviously, a nontrivial procedure. In fact, it is so nontrivial that it approximates a solution to (a nontrivial subpart of) the natural language understanding problem.

As anyone reading this might guess, solving the MTD problem will mean solving a very hard problem indeed. So be it. The MTD of the 21st century will not be a static representational artifact. It will be an intelligent agent out in the world that explores and learns and knows the language. The MTD of the 21st century will know the language as well as any of us, and perhaps better.

CHAPTER 9

IDEAL MRDs: THE PERSPECTIVE FROM OUR EXPERIENCE*

J. Terry Nutter
Department of Computer Science
Virginia Polytechnic Institute and State University

1. INTRODUCTION

For several years now, a joint research team led by Fox and Nutter at Virginia Polytechnic Institute and State University and Evens at Illinois Institute of Technology has been engaged in trying to construct a very large scale relational lexicon from machine-readable dictionaries (MRDs). So far, work has centered primarily on *Webster's Seventh Collegiate Dictionary (W7)* (Olney, 1968) and the *Collins English Dictionary* (*CED*; Carver, 1974).

Experience with tapes of these dictionaries has led to an ever-growing list of desiderata, features we would dearly love to find in any MRD. Some of these grow out of our particular approach to lexicon formation; others are more general, and involve the differences between machine readability and computer tractability. All of them are in some sense new to the evaluation of dictionaries, in that they are geared toward *usability by computers and algorithms* as opposed to accessibility to a human audience. It will be some time before the computational industry is even a major audience, let alone one that overwhelms the more traditional dictionary audiences. But our desiderata do not necessarily contradict what one would like in a dictionary for people. They are additional, and

*This research was supported in part by the National Science Foundation under gtrant IRI-87-03580 to Virginia Polytechnic Institute and State University. Permission to use dictionary tapes was kindly granted to Illinois Insitute of Technology by the G&C Merriam Company and to both universities by Collins.

(we hope) compatible criteria, not competing ones, and so there may be some hope of achieving them. In this discussion, we look at some of the more pressing of these wish list items.

2. SYNTACTIC ISSUES

At the very least, a lexicon constructor should be able to get straightforward syntactic information out of dictionaries easily. At present, we can in fact break out the top-level part-of-speech information for most entries fairly easily. When we cannot, there are usually fairly decent reasons for that (some phrasal entries are particularly touchy), but a few cases are irritating. The most obvious concerns run-ons, which may not have any specific information at all.

But there is more to syntax than noun/verb/adjective classification, and getting more out of dictionaries is often awkward at best, even when the information is present.

2.1. Principled Classifications

Most dictionaries at least indicate whether verbs are transitive or intransitive. Some, such as the Oxford learners' dictionaries, give quite sensitive subcategorization information. This kind of information can be highly useful for lexicons, and not only for verbs. The mass/count distinction for nouns, for instance, has strong effects on sentential syntax. For numerous reasons, lexicons may want to capture this distinction.

There are two difficulties here. First, many dictionaries do not record information at this level at all. Second, when they do, they do not always have a particularly solid linguistic rationale behind the distinctions they reflect.

Information that is not present obviously cannot be extracted, but information that is present and not consistently motivated may be of little more use, in the long run, than information that is entirely absent. We cannot expect that all dictionaries will adopt the same set of categories. For one thing, not all dictionaries are written for the same purpose or the same audiences. Dictionaries intended for native speakers can be expected to include different kinds of information from what is provided in learners' dictionaries, for instance. For another, as theories change, dictionaries change with them. We would not necessarily want to freeze a single set of distinctions into place. In addition, dictionaries deliberately distinguish themselves from one another to provide reasons to buy one rather than another. So we must expect that information content will vary. However, a well-motivated, internally consistent set of subcategories will surely be easier to deal with, and more likely to prove useful, than none at all or an ad hoc set.

2.2. Clear Indications of Information

Location of information also matters. Syntactic information like subcategorization may be included as part of the part-of-speech field, or as a field of its own, or as implicit information buried in usage examples. Fields are easy to break out. Definitions are relatively harder to deal with, but can be made reasonably tractable (for information on our work in this regard, see Ahlswede & Evens, 1988a, 1988b; Fox, Nutter, Ahlswede, Evens, & Markowitz, 1988; and Nutter, Fox, & Evens, 1990). Usage examples are, by their very nature, arbitrary chunks of English, and so by far the least tractable. Up to now, dictionaries have been designed for human audiences (not surprisingly!), and so most of their designers have based their decisions of where and how to express information on what people find easy or hard. From the standpoint also of machine tractability, syntactic information is easy to present in simple, tractable ways. Users of MRDs will strongly prefer information that is coded in separate, well-defined and easily identified fields over anything they have to go electronically looking for.

3. SEMANTIC ISSUES

Syntax is simple, compared to semantics. The largest single difficulty here is that there is no single, dominant linguistic theory of lexical semantics. Although there are many competing syntactic theories, it is relatively easy to get agreement at least on categories like *noun* and *verb*. No such agreement can be reached about a minimal analysis of semantic content. It is even less reasonable, therefore, to hope for standardized presentation of definition content than it is to hope for standardized subcategorization information. Still, as with syntactic information, the semantic information within any single dictionary should be guided by a uniform view, and both the view itself and its manner of expression can contribute to or hinder the tractability of the resulting text.

3.1. Theoretical Influence on Definition Structure

Our approach is based on the theory of lexical relations (see Nutter et al., 1990, for a theoretical discussion, and Nutter, 1989, for a discussion of the particular relational hierarchy we are developing). Obviously, any dictionary consciously based on that theory will be particularly attractive to us. But short of so strong a requirement, there are a number of desirable features of the semantic portion of definitions that would simplify tractability greatly.

If definitions are structured randomly, we have no hope. If they are not, then there is some theory (linguistically accepted or otherwise, highly developed or otherwise, shared with other communities or otherwise) underlying their formation. That theory should shape the definitions. The better the theory is (in terms of linguistic soundness, clear articulation, etc.), the better the definition shape will be. Ideally, it should be possible to find out in the front matter what information each definition contains, and within limits, the form in which it contains it.

3.2. Limited Defining Vocabulary

Some dictionaries, notably learners' dictionaries, have gone to restricted defining vocabularies. Whether this helps the computational lexicographer's task depends on the details of the individual approach. Certainly in the early phases of dealing with*W7*, the choice of parser at IIT led to difficulties in part because the parser required detailed lexical entries for the parsing vocabulary, which could not necessarily be bootstrapped in any reasonable way (Ahlswede & Evens, 1988a). In this case, even though our theory of the lexicon in no way presupposed a primitive vocabulary, a limited defining vocabulary would have helped a lot.

3.3. Consistent Defining Structures

More important than limited vocabulary is consistent defining structure. Our approach depends heavily on identifying what we call defining formulae. For example, the phrase "of or pertaining to" (as in "solar: of or pertaining to the sun") usually indicates that the lexeme being defined is a nominal adjective related to the noun that follows. Most dictionaries contain many such formulae. This, indeed, is what makes their definitions tractable to current natural language techniques at all.

Containing such formulae is one thing, and using them consistently is another. It is frustrating to miss definitions because a rare variant of a formula that we had not identified has been used. Ideally, it should be possible to look up a list of such formulae and their significance, and use this as the core of the processing system. Failing that, the community should at least be able to hope that the actual formulae will be used consistently (with both the same wording for all instances of a given meaning structure and the same meaning for all instances of a given formula), so that text analysis techniques that reveal common phrases can be used to identify reliable bases for semantic analysis.

4. PRESENTATION ISSUES

Compared to the issues in the previous sections, these are relatively trivial, but they can nonetheless provide either major help or real barriers to dealing with MRDs. Typesetters' tapes were never really meant to be manipulated by computer programs under standard operating systems using high-level languages. A tremendous amount of effort can go into simply preparing the tapes for manipulation by the programs. This process tends to be very error prone. Format and font change codes carry content with them when they go, words with such codes in the middle get broken apart, and so on. Information gets lost. All this before the real work ever begins.

4.1. Standardized Field Indications (SGML)

Any standard for identifying fields is better than none. General use of something like SGML would simplify the transition from typesetters' format to program-accessible form immensely. Indeed, at present, the obvious choice is SGML itself. Although we cannot expect that choice to remain engraved in stone, we should be able to hope that this or some similar standard will in fact be adopted generally, and that it will not be abandoned without adopting a new one that is at least as good.

4.2. ASCII, Please

Non-ASCII characters cause natural language and text-processing software grief to no end. Once we have allowed for section indicators, the best case leaves no non-ASCII characters at all. The next best case involves a clear protocol, circulated with the tape by the publishers, for stripping all the non-ASCII characters without losing textual information. In any case, a tape that needs heavy human editing before it can be reduced to ASCII form is not machine tractable.

5. CONCLUSION

There are many issues this discussion has not touched. For instance, dictionaries usually contain pictures, which are included because they contain important information. At present, this information is generally a dead loss. Usage examples often contain very helpful information about such issues as selection restrictions, which can be so difficult to extract that it, too, is usually a dead loss. These are deep problems, which at present are hard to address.

However, much of what we would like in a machine-tractable dictionary would not be particularly difficult to include in a new dictionary, if the dictionary-designing community knew what we wanted. Until we know what we want ourselves, no one can tell them.

CHAPTER 10

SOME MATTERS EXAMINED IN DRIVING MTD DEVELOPMENT

Toshio Yokoi
Japan Electronic Dictionary Research Institute, Ltd. (EDR)

The EDR Electronic Dictionary project started in 1986, and has now yielded concrete results. For propelling similar projects, active discussions have been conducted all over the world. EDR would like to keep wide associations with these activities. Because electronic dictionaries have an effect, naturally, on natural language processing technology and knowledge processing technology, and also have a large effect on overall information processing technology, it is most important to create worldwide cooperative relationships.

This discussion gives an overview of the basic matters that we should consider when we drive the development of the electronic dictionaries, from EDR's experiences. According to our definition, electronic dictionary (ED) and machine-tractable dictionary (MTD) are almost synonymous. Hereafter, I use MTD, according to the main point of this book.

1. MTD SHOULD BE LARGE-SCALE

It is not too difficult to make a small-scale, precise and elaborate dictionary. However, users want large-scale ones. Currently, research and development of methodologies, techniques, and systems to develop, maintain, and enlarge large-scale MTDs are strongly needed. Therefore, EDR is not particular in dictionary specifications (especially that of the word dictionaries), but attaches greater importance to the methods of development and computer support system in our research and development.

2. CLOSE ASSOCIATION WITH USERS

MTD should be utilized. The purpose of MTD is not to be made but to be used. MTD should be made with sufficient reflection of the opinions of researchers of natural language processing systems and knowledge processing systems. The more often an MTD is used, the more valuable it becomes and the more feedback for effective improvement and enlargement we can get. Many of the EDR staff have been engaged in research and development of machine translation before. Therefore, requests made in development of large-scale natural language processing systems are reflected directly in the development of our MTD. Further, although the EDR dictionaries can be treated in many different ways as master dictionaries when they are used for various applications, they are originally designed to be able to function for themselves and to be put in systems.

3. APPROPRIATE ASSOCIATION WITH COMPUTATIONAL SCIENTISTS AND LINGUISTS

The development of MTDs must be propelled in appropriate association with the field of computers (natural language processing) and that of linguistics and lexicology. A large-scale MTD is a large-scale system in itself. The system for the development of large-scale MTDs is also large scale. As for design, development, debugging, maintenance, and administration of a large-scale system, persons in the computer field have abundant experience. Computational scientists with sufficient knowledge of linguistics and linguists with sufficient familiarity with computers and systems are necessary. However, there are only a limited number of such people in Japan, and EDR has only a few of them. So, EDR gives priority to the completion of the dictionaries with some degree of quality, led by the persons from the computer field.

4. ADEQUATE UTILIZATION OF EXISTING DATA

The largest information resources in MTD development are the existing dictionaries for humans. However, dictionaries for humans are basically different from those for computers. Accordingly, MTDs must be newly designed and produced just for computers. Moreover, the development of MTDs will generate insight into the development of dictionaries for humans. The EDR entrusted the production of the materials of dictionary data to publishers. They have been implementing this productive work, basing their work on the data from dictionaries for human use and the expertise they possess.

5. MTD MUST KEEP GROWING

Usually, an MTD that has just been developed is not highly refined. Therefore, efforts must be continuously made in order to ensure its refinement. Also, an MTD itself needs to be improved and expanded perpetually so that it can deal with an even wider range of languages and can cope with changes that constantly occur in languages. Moreover, once a widely usable MTD is realized, various MTDs based on new theories will be developed easily by using it. The design and development of MTDs must be carried out with full consideration of these matters from the very beginning. The dictionary development support system that EDR is going to develop is designed to be usable for future improvement and expansion, and also for future management and maintenance of the dictionaries.

The structure of the EDR Electronic Dictionaries is described in the following EDR reports:

TR-024: An Overview of the EDR Electronic Dictionaries EDR, 1990
TR-025: Japanese Word Dictionary EDR, 1990
TR-026: English Word Dictionary EDR, 1990
TR-027: Concept Dictionary EDR, 1990
TR-029: Bilingual Dictionary EDR, 1990

CHAPTER 11

A LEXICON SERVER USING LEXICAL RELATIONS FOR INFORMATION RETRIEVAL*

Edward A. Fox and J. Terry Nutter
Department of Computer Science
Virginia Polytechnic Institute and State University

Martha W. Evens
Computer Science Department
Illinois Institute of Technology

1. INTRODUCTION

Desirable structures for machine-tractable dictionaries (MTDs) cannot be determined without looking at their desired uses. Our work has centered on designing online thesauri to enhance information retrieval efforts. The principles underlying the thesaurus design have a major impact on what features we believe MTDs should have to promote this and similar efforts.

Most retrieval systems provide two simple mechanisms for extending a user query to capture more relevant documents. The first is truncation, where users enter expressions like "govern*" to indicate matches to words like *govern, government, governing,* and so on. The second is thesaurus lookup, where a domain-specific thesaurus has been constructed, usually through the efforts of a committee of experts, and users or search intermediaries search for broader, related, or in some cases narrower terms. Our work deals with the need for a lexicon server to act as a general thesaurus for English, so that retrieval systems can

*This research was supported in part by the National Science Foundation under grant IRI-87-03580 to Virginia Polytechnic Institute and State University and under grant IRI-87-04619 to Illinois Institute of Technology. We also want to thank the G&C Merriam Company and Collins Publishers for permission to use machine readable versions of their dictionaries.

use such a server to find more relevant documents for users. The key to this approach is to extend lexicon servers to have knowledge of lexical relations.

2. LEXICAL RELATIONS

Lexical relations are central to a lexical-level linguistic theory. Lexical relations were originally developed to express semantic (and some syntactic) information, most notably in the context of the *Explanatory Combinatory Dictionary (ECD)* for Russian (Apresyan, Mel'cuk, & Zolkovsky, 1969). In our work (Evens, Markowitz, Ahlswede, & Rossi, 1987; Fox et al., 1988; Nutter, 1989; Nutter, Fox, & Evens, 1990), we have extended them to also cover syntactic and morphological information, to provide a more complete linguistic theory of lexical information.

Lexical relations link words that are semantically or morphologically akin in a number of different ways. The most familiar relations are the synonymy and antonymy relations explicitly marked in commercial dictionaries. Many artificial intelligence applications have used the ISA (or taxonomy or hyponymy) relation, exemplified by "a lion is a kind of animal." But there are many other lexical relations. These relations encode much of the information needed for using natural language and for common sense reasoning:

lamb	**CHILD**	sheep
ram	**MALE**	sheep
ewe	**FEMALE**	sheep
wool	**PART**	sheep
solar	**ADJNOM**	sun
ice	**SOLID**	water
to send	**CAUSE**	to go
to blush	**BECOME**	red

Lexical relations specify associations, such as *sun–solar* and *die–death–decease,* that common retrieval system techniques like truncation or affix stripping do not identify, and can also prevent invalid associations like *convene-convenience* that most affix-stripping algorithms will conflate.

3. THE CODER LEXICON SERVER

The CODER (COmposite Document Expert/extended/effective Retrieval) system (under development at VPI & SU since 1985) has been designed as a testbed to explore the use of AI methods (including use of lexicons) for information retrieval.

CODER uses a large external network database (LEND) to store lexical data. This is an object-oriented database specially designed for semantic network, hypertext, and other modes of processing. The lowest level supports nodes, which can be numbers, character strings, media objects, or concepts of various types. Arcs connect nodes, and allow path based inference as well as other graph-style manipulations.

One requirement for the lexicon server is to return related words and phrases for each term in a query, a process known as *query expansion*. Query expansion involves identifying and retrieving the node representing the appropriate word sense, and then expanding along paths through useful lexical relations to retrieve related terms that may enhance retrieval. Previous studies have involved hand expansion from very modest lexicons. LEND provides a facility for semiautomated expansion (using feedback from the user) over realistically large lexicons.

Fox (1980) showed that bibliographic information retrieval could be enhanced by the use of relational thesauri (in which words are linked by lexical relations). Wang, Vandendorpe, & Evens (1985) ran another series of experiments showing similar results. Both series of experiments used thesauri to enrich the query by adding related index terms. Results showed that all relations tested, except antonymy and other "opposite" relations, caused improvements in precision at each fixed recall level.

4. CONSTRUCTING THESAURI FROM COMPUTER-READABLE DICTIONARIES

Once it has been demonstrated that relational thesauri can make a valuable contribution to information retrieval, we need to figure out a cheap and effective way to develop such thesauri. MRDs are an ideal source for such information. Ahlswede and Evens (1988b) built a thesaurus used in the research described here from a machine readable version of *Webster's Seventh Collegiate Dictionary* (Olney, 1968).

Building lexicons from MRDs could theoretically have required solving the full natural language understanding problem. It does not, because dictionary definitions have always exhibited certain regularities, based on theoretical views of the nature of definition. Ever since Aristotle decreed that the ideal definition consists of a genus term (hyponym) plus differentia (information that separates the term being defined from others in the same taxonomy), formal dictionary definitions have tried to follow this pattern. As a result most dictionaries contain a great deal of taxonomic information that can be extracted fairly easily (Amsler, 1981).

But many real lexical relations lie outside the Aristotelian model. Defining formulae such as "of or related to" are often used in commercial dictionaries to identify significant relationships and can often be used as clues in detecting the presence of other lexical information. "Run-on words" that appear in lexical entries for other words are usually related morphologically to the headword. It is thus possible to figure out consistent patterns for such morphological relationships. To the extent that dictionaries reflect these relationships systematically and consistently, their tractability increases.

5. CONCLUSION

It is quite likely that the effectiveness of information retrieval systems can be significantly improved through the use of a lexicon server. There is the obvious application of looking up words, during automatic indexing or query entry, to find root forms, with the assistance of a morphological analyzer (which must apply different rules for loan words and other specialized terms). This should replace the traditional "stemming" or truncation process, which typically introduces at least a 5% error rate.

Probably more important, however, is the application of providing related terms to those supplied in a user query. This requires that the lexicon server be able to look up words rapidly, and find those with the proper associations. This process may involve automatic tracing of association chains, following constraints on types of lexical relations, and other manipulations.

Our project has investigated the design of such a lexicon, and the loading of it with data from a variety of MRDs. We hope that our findings will help influence the development of other lexicon servers, and that our system, CODER/LEND, may validate our hypotheses regarding the use of lexical knowledge in information retrieval. Another long-term influence that this and similar research may hope to have is on the design of dictionaries themselves, to make the transition from dictionary to usable lexicon easier and more feasible.

CHAPTER 12

SOME DICTIONARY INFORMATION FOR MACHINE TRANSLATION*

Makoto Nagao
Department of Electrical Engineering
Kyoto University

1. THE AGE OF DICTIONARIES

Dictionaries are drawing more and more attention from more and more types of people. This is true not only of language dictionaries, but also of terminological dictionaries of every specific field and encyclopedias. People are interested in knowing the meaning of terms that appear in newspapers, books, TV programs, and so on. Particularly, they want to know not only the meaning of a term itself but also its related terms. People want to know the specific details of a problem on the one hand, and to grasp the total figure or to get the general understanding on the other hand. This is one of the main reasons for consulting dictionaries of every kind. In the language area, a few new good language dictionaries appeared, such as the Longman Dictionary of Contemporary English and COBUILD English Language Dictionary. These dictionaries provoked discussion of what a good dictionary is.

Dictionaries are becoming more and more important in computer processing of natural language. Not only machine translation but also man-machine dialogue systems, information retrieval systems, and so on, require good dictionaries for their own purposes. Here we have to clarify what kind of information must be included in a dictionary.

---

*This article, after its submission for publication in this book, was delivered as the keynote speech at the International Workshop on Electronic Dictionaries held at Oiso, Japan on November 8-9, 1990. It appeared subsequently in the workshop proceedings on pp. 1-9.

Dictionary construction requires much time and expense. It is quite difficult to change and reconstruct a dictionary. Therefore there must be a careful design at the starting point of the construction. In the past, dictionary contents were severely limited by the page size of a dictionary. This condition is no longer true of the electronic dictionaries, which can memorize large amounts of information. A problem in an electronic dictionary, particularly for use by computer programs, involves the representation structure, as well as the kinds of information to be memorized. Humans can interpret dictionary contents in a flexible and adaptive way, but the computer does not have such flexibility. Therefore we have to provide all the detailed information explicitly for the computer.

There are varieties of dictionaries. We can classify dictionaries from different points of view as follows:

- Ordinary language dictionary
- Terminological dictionary
- Encyclopedia
- Knowledge representation of encyclopedia in a computer
- Ordinary word dictionary
- Phrasal dictionary
- Thesaurus, and synonym dictionary
- Monolingual dictionary
- Bilingual and multilingual dictionary

What interests us most is the distinction between linguistic knowledge and extralinguistic knowledge in the dictionaries, and to what extent the latter information can be put in a dictionary.

2. LINGUISTIC KNOWLEDGE

There is a general agreement or common sense about the linguistic information that must be included in a language dictionary. This includes the headword, abbreviations, conjugations, the pronunciation, the part of speech, subcategorizations of a part of speech, derivatives, collocational phrases, and so on. Besides these, the following information is very useful in Japanese: indications of standard words, formal words, or colloquial words, and words solely used by the male or the female. The language has many honorifics, which must also be listed in a dictionary.

A verb has the most important information for parsing a sentence automatically. It must have such information as case structures with pre/post-positional information. The distinction between the volition verb and the nonvolition verb is important in Japanese. The same must be true in English because there is a phrase: One may listen, but not hear.

Another important distinctive information found in Japanese verbs is the temporal properties, including instantaneous, durative, repetitive and stative. The following are some examples:

ONGAKU-O KIKU. (I) listen (to) music.
ONGAKU-O KIITEIRU. (I) am listening (to) music.
(music) (listen)
where TEIRU indicates the durative property of the verb.
KURUMA-GA TOMARU. A car stops.
KURUMA-GA TOMATTEIRU. (?) A car is stopping.
(car) (stop) A car is parking.
where TEIRU indicates the stative property of the verb.
KARE-GA TOOCHAKU-SURU He arrives.
KARE-WA TOOCHAKU-SHITEIRU. He has (already) arrived.
(he) (arrive)
where TEIRU indicates the stative property of the verb.
HITOBITO-GA TSUGI-TSUGI-NI TOOCHAKU-SHITEIRU.
(people) (one by one) People are arriving one by one.
where TEIRU indicates the repetitive property of the verb.

An important piece of information from the standpoint of language generation is the derivational relation among words. We can construct varieties of sentences that express the same meaning such as:

It is a matter of politics.
It is a political matter.
You'd better do ...
I recommend you to do ...
I advise you to do ...
Try to do ...

More and more associative links must be provided between synonymous words. For example, a sentence generation program must be able to generate the following sentences from the same internal representation:

The house collapsed in the tornado.
The tornado destroyed the house.
The tornado broke down the house.
He is not a careful person.

He is a careless person.
It is not dark yet.
It is still bright.

In this way the synonym dictionary plays an important role in the sentence generation process. Particularly important in a synonym dictionary for machine use is the need to provide the condition or the distinction in usage of synonymous words explicitly. It is not sufficient to describe word meanings independently for each word without any consideration of other related words. Comparative description of similar words is quite important. It must clarify both common and distinctive meanings of two similar words. It is also important to show what expressions are acceptable and what are not in terms of correct usage. These examples suggest the limitation and the boundary of the word usage variations. In some contexts *need* and *require* are replaceable, but in certain other contexts they are not. If there is not explicit information about the replaceability or nonreplaceability of synonymous words, the machine cannot do anything.

3. EXTRALINGUISTIC INFORMATION

It is difficult to draw a boundary line between linguistic information and extralinguistic information. The expression

(A) I read Shakespeare.

is a good understandable sentence. Let's replace *Shakespeare* by *a man* in (A) because Shakespeare is a man. Then we have

I read a man.

but this is a strange sentence, if not ungrammatical. Therefore, there must be some reasonable explanations about sentence (A). We normally interpret it as:

(A′) I read plays or sonnets by Shakespeare.

because read plays and plays by Shakespeare are both reasonable in our ordinary sense. If we had a sentence:

(B) I read Mr. Shakespeare.

then the interpretation would be totally different. *Mr. Shakespeare* represents only the person himself, and does not represent his works. Therefore sentence (B), if it is actually uttered, must be interpreted as:

(B′) I read the mentality or personality of Mr. Shakespeare.

In these interpretations, *read plays* will be interpretable in the scope of linguistic dictionary information. But the inferences

Shakespeare -> playwright, poet -> plays, poems

and

Mr. Shakespeare -> a man

read a man -> guess a man's mind or personality

are rather difficult to handle in a linguistic dictionary. They must be regarded as extralinguistic information, and should be treated in a knowledge base.

Sentence (B) is interpretable in another way. Imagine the situation where there is an old plate where something is written, but that is hard to read. Then the interpretation of (B) may be:

(B″) I read a word "Mr. Shakespeare" on the plate.

This is an interpretation that is strongly dependent on a particular situation of the utterance.

The difference in interpretation comes from the difference of information available for the interpretations, which can be classified as follows:

1. linguistic knowledge (grammar, ordinary word dictionary)
2. extralinguistic knowledge (associative relations of words, metaphorical inference, all of which are based on the knowledge of a culture)
3. factual knowledge (facts about the scenes of the utterance)

The first is the most stable information. The second is also essential for smooth conversation in our ordinary life. People have this kind of information as common knowledge. Otherwise, communication would be very difficult, much like conversing with foreigners. The last category of information can be obtained from the actual scene or through the knowledge representations of the previous sentential information. We have to provide a mechanism to analyze, store, and utilize discourse information because we cannot prepare the information beforehand.

Extralinguistic information must include words that are derivable by (a) functional relation, (b) componential decomposition relation (part-whole relation), (c) the attribute-property relation, (d) the object-target relation, (e) the cause-effect relation, (f) the historical relation, and (g) other associative relations, including metaphorical relations.

For example, the word *car* can have the following words in association with it:

car-automobile, vehicle
parking lot, road, highway, trip, ...
drive, speed, ...
gasoline, ...

Metaphorical relation is very important for the interpretation of a sentence. It is culture-dependent. Cherry blossoms often mean spring in Japan. A full moon implies perfectness, a completely satisfied mental state, and so on. The White House means the U.S. President's office and its function. All the words have many such metaphorical meanings. Without such information and interpretation it is almost impossible to get a deep understanding of a sentential meaning.

If we enrich the extralinguistic dictionary information in this direction, we encounter the interpretation problem of such questions as:

1. What do you call the Japanese counterpart of the President of the United States of America?
2. What do you call the U.S. (Japanese) parliament that has the same function as the British House of Commons?
3. What do you call the Buddhist priest who corresponds to a bishop in Christianity?

To answer these questions, we have to find out some analogical information in different social and cultural structures such as the following:

Japan	National Diet
	House of Councilors
	House of Representatives
United States	Congress
	Senate
	House of Representatives
Great Britain	Parliament
	House of Lords
	House of Commons

The framework of natural language understanding forces us to store such contrastive information in different cultural systems, but such information is almost infinite, and it is impossible to store all the information in a computer. We have to develop an algorithm to find such analogical structures from two independent knowledge sets.

4. BILINGUAL DICTIONARIES

It is difficult to construct a bilingual dictionary because a word of a source language has varieties of meanings or concepts, and for each such meaning there exist many corresponding words and expressions in a target language. There is, very often, a case where a concept in one language corresponds to several concepts in another language, and it is not easy to fix a minimum grain of concepts that has a one-to-one correspondence to linguistic expressions in both languages.

For example the word *play* in "play piano" and "play flute" can be classified into the same concept in English, but in Japanese there are different expressions for them, and they belong to different concepts. This is illustrated in the following:

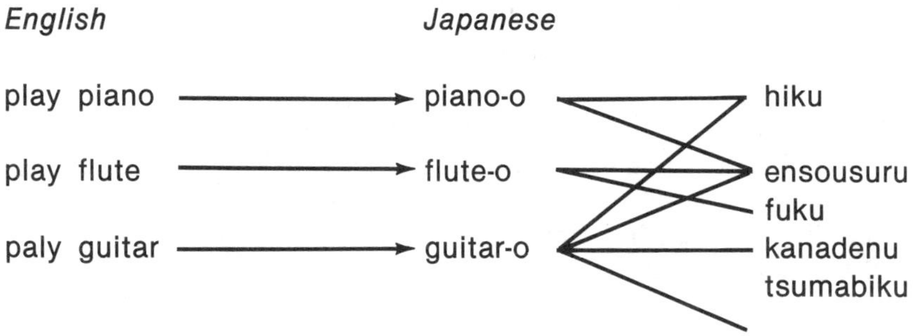

We do not know what kind of musical instruments can be kanader-ar*eru* or *tsumabik-areru* (-areru means passive form). Some Japanese dictionaries suggest that *kanaderu* can be used for string instruments, but others give an example, *flute-o kanaderu*. We certainly do not say *piano-o kanaderu*, but we do say *harpsichord-o kanaderu*, although a harpsichord looks just like a piano. Nobody has confidence in the kind of instruments with which these words are associated.

It is difficult to find key information that is effective for the determination of words that can or cannot be used with a particular verb.

The word *play* has 38 distinctive meanings according to the COBUILD English Language Dictionary. Kenkyusha's English-Japanese Dictionary has 44 major distinctions, and more than 80 subclassifications for the English-Japanese correspondence of *play*. It is almost impossible to give reasonable distinctive explanations for the choice of a proper translation to a given phrase by the semantic primitive approach for these 80 cases.

To cope with this difficulty in constructing a bilingual dictionary, The "translation by analogy principle" was proposed a few years ago (Nagao, 1984). This is now actively studied under the name of "example based translation" (Sato and Nagao, 1990; Sumita, Iido, & Kohyama, 1990). The basic idea is explained here. It is very difficult to represent a word meaning by the combination of semantic primitives, particularly when the meaning is very delicate and sophisticated. In such a case, a translation pair of a word in a language and another is very helpful. For example, the meanings of *play* in the usage of *play piano* and *play flute* may not be distinguishable in English, but in Japanese there are different translations for these, such as *piano-o hiku* (play piano), but not *flute-o hiku,* and *flute-o huku* (play flute), but not *piano-o huku.* In this method we accumulate typical different translation pairs for a word in a phrasal form. When a new phrase, for example *play tennis,* is given for translation, this phrase is compared with the stored translation pairs, and the most similar translation pair is selected for the translation candidate. In the case of *play tennis,* the translation pair, play game: game-o suru is selected, and *game* is replaced by *tennis,* and the translation, *tennis-o suru* is constructed as the translation. The selection of similar phrases is done with the help of thesaurus information.

The method is simple and the translation quality can be improved easily by increasing example translation pairs. These translation pairs do not depend on any linguistic theories or any set of semantic primitives. They remain as useful knowledge for a long time. Therefore, examples of citations are important not only in dictionaries for human use, but also in dictionaries for machine use.

5. CONCLUSION

When we consider a multilingual dictionary, we have to first find out the minimum grains of concepts in each language and culture, and then determine the minimum grains that are common to the concept sets of all languages concerned. In this way, a neutral multilingual dictionary depends on the language set. Bilingual dictionaries are difficult to construct, and so multilingual dictionaries of several languages are quite difficult to construct, particularly when the languages have very different cultural backgrounds. It is difficult to find pivot concepts through which words and phrases can be exchanged between every language pair. It would be possible to establish pivot concepts for major conceptual words, but it would be very difficult for many other concepts in ordinary life. These concepts, particularly those heavily related to human life, must be explained in terms of the cultural background of the language. Therefore if we want to have very detailed machine translation dictionaries of ordinary words, it would be inevitable to construct bilingual dictionaries. It is very difficult to construct multilingual dictionaries for several languages of completely different cultural backgrounds.

Multilingual dictionaries will be possible, however, for the concepts in natural science and technology, which are common all over the world. Or, if we do not need high-quality translation, we may be able to construct multilingual dictionaries among certain sets of languages.

Another question that we have to discuss is how to utilize the dictionary information. Dictionaries are useful not only in machine translation but also in any natural language processing systems, such as dialogue systems and information retrieval systems. Internal organization of a large dictionary is important from the standpoint of speed and flexible reference to the related information. Hypertext structure will be useful for people to use complex electronic dictionaries. We must develop more powerful uses for electronic dictionaries.

CHAPTER 13

ASPECTS OF A MACHINE TRACTABLE DICTIONARY FOR KNOWLEDGE-BASED MACHINE TRANSLATION*

Sergei Nirenburg
Center for Machine Translation
Carnegie Mellon University

In knowledge-based machine translation (KBMT) systems, lexicons play as central a role as in any other approach to machine translation. However, the amount of information included in KBMT lexicon entries is typically much larger than that in other systems. This is because lexicons in this kind of application must support more types of processing. KBMT lexicons rely on the existence of an independently motivated ontology and a sufficient number of domain models to provide the vocabulary for describing the meaning of various lexical units. The content of the entries is also influenced by a particular representation language (in the machine translation this language is called interlingua) selected for representing text meaning. In fact, several kinds of entries make use not only of instances of ontological concepts but also of specific constructs in the text meaning representation language to record the meaning of a lexical unit.

In some KBMT systems there can be two lexicons, one for analysis and one for generation. This approach was advocated by Nirenburg and Raskin (1987). In some other systems, the information needed for both types of processing can be incorporated into a single lexicon.

Lexicons for KBMT can take a large number of shapes and forms. However, all of them must support all of the morphological, syntactic,

*This is an abridged version of an article by the same author that previously appeared in the Proceedings of the International Workshop on Electronic Dictionaries (pp 107-117) held at Oiso, Japan on November 8-9, 1990.

semantic, and pragmatic analysis, as well as text planning, including lexical selection, and realization in generation.

In this chapter I illustrate the lexicon structure appropriate for KBMT using the lexicon of the DIONYSUS project at Carnegie-Mellon University. First, I give an informal overview of the lexicon structure. Next, I go through two annotated examples. Finally, I describe the motivation behind certain lexicographic decisions, specifically those referring to lexical semantics.[1]

1. THE LEXICON STRUCTURE

The lexicon is an alphabetical list of superentries. Superentries are lists of entries. The entry corresponds to a word sense and is a FrameKit (Nyberg, 1988) frame identified by a lexical unit, which is the headword symbol with the symbol "+" prepended for easy detection. An indicator of grammatical category and a numerical index of this wordsense are added after a dash (-), for example, +smell-v1, +smell-v2, +smell-n1, +smell-n2, and so on. The structure of the lexicon can be summarized as follows:

```
(LEXICON
    (SUPERENTRY 1 ; headword 1
        (make-frame +ENTRY-x1 ...) ; (cat x, sense 1)
        (make-frame +ENTRY-x2 ...) ; (cat x, sense 2)
        (make-frame +ENTRY-y1 ...) ; (cat y, sense 1)
        (make-frame +ENTRY-y2 ...) ; (cat y, sense 2)
            ....
            ....etc...)
            ....
    (SUPERENTRY 2 ; headword 2
            ....
            ....etc...))
```

Each entry can have up to ten zones, each zone realized as a slot in the entry frame:

1. Grammatical category (CAT slot)
2. User information (STUFF slot)
3. Orthography (ORTH slot)
4. Phonology (PHON slot)

---

[1]A comprehensive description of the lexicon in the DIONYSUS project is given in Meyer et al. (1990).

5. Morphology (MORPH slot)
6. Syntactic features (SYN slot)
7. Syntactic structure (SYNSTRUC slot)
8. Semantics (SEM slot)
9. Lexical relations (LEXICAL-RELATIONS slot)
10. Pragmatics (PRAGM slot)

Two illustrative examples are as follows:

```
(doughnut
    (make-frame
        +doughnut-n1
        (CAT (value n))
        (STUFF
            (DEFN "pastry cooked in fat, usually in the shape
            of a ring or ball")
            (EXAMPLES "Dunkin' Donuts produces more doughnuts
            than all other fast food outlets put together"))
        (ORTH (VARIANTS donut))
        (SYN
            (count +) (proper -))
        (SEM
            (LEX-MAP
                (%doughnut)))))
```

This is the lexical entry for one nominal sense of the English word doughnut. The STUFF zone in the definition contains human-oriented information and is not used by the system itself. The ORTH zone lists spelling variants. The SYN lists paradigmatic syntactic features, in this case, the fact that the English noun *doughnut* is uncountable and common. The SEM zone in this example is a simple lexical mapping of the meaning of this sense of doughnut into a corresponding ontological concept, which happens to have the same name due to the decision of the domain model builder.

```
(find
    (make-frame
        +find-v1
        (CAT (value v))
    (STUFF
        (DEFN "to discover by chance, to come across")
        (EXAMPLES   "drop by your old favorite Dunkin Donuts
                    shop and you'll not only find fresh donuts
                    made by hand" "when I arrived home last
```

```
                  night, I found a drunk sleeping on the porch/
                  that a drunk was sleeping on the porch"))
  (MORPH
     (IRREG (*v+past* found) (*v+past-part* found)))
  (SYN-STRUC
        (*OR*       ((root $var0)
            (subj (root $var1) (cat N))
            (obj (root $var2) (cat N)))
            ((root $var0)
            (subj (root $var1) (cat N ))
            (xcomp (root $var2) (cat V ))(form pres-part)))
            ((root $var0)
            (subj (root $var1) (cat N ))
            (comp (root $var2) (cat V )) (form fin))))))
  (SEM
     (LEX-MAP
        (%involuntary-perceptual-event
        (experiencer (value ^$var1))
        (theme (value ^$var2))))))
```

This entry demonstrates our way of recording inflectional irregularities. The SYN-STRUC zone describes the subcategorization classes of the entry head. In this entry there are three subcategorization variants, all with different types of direct objects that find may take. The variables in the specifications are used for binding the values of arguments. In the LEX-MAP slot of the SEM zone, these bindings help determine to which syntactic entitles the intentions (semantic interpretations) of the arguments correspond (the "^" prefix marks the intentions). Intuitively, the lexical mapping says that the given sense of *find* is mapped into the interlingua as an instance of the %involuntary-perceptual-event ontological concept. Moreover, the semantic interpretation of whatever occupied the subj position in the f-structure should be assigned as the value of the 'experiencer' thematic role in this concept instance, whereas the meaning of whatever occupied the obj, xcomp, or comp position in the f-structure should be assigned as the value of the theme (thematic role) in the concept instance. See Section 2 for a more detailed discussion of the treatment of lexical semantics in this lexicon.

2. TREATMENT OF LEXICAL SEMANTICS

In this section I discuss the types of semantic mappings used in the SEM zone of the entry in our lexicon in greater detail.

The general format of this slot is:

```
(SEM
        (LEX-MAP <meaning-pattern>)
        (MEAN-PROC {* <lambda-expression>)))
```

LEX-MAP provides a declarative (static) specification of meaning through (a) a mapping to the ontology, (b) a mapping directly into interlingua structures (attitudes/relations), or (c) a combination of both. It establishes a semantic dependency structure using the meanings associated with the lexemes to which the variables are bound from the syntactic functional structure pattern.

MEAN-PROC invokes procedural semantic functions. In the current version of the lexicon, only one such function has been implemented, namely, intensify-range, used to realize the meaning of intensifiers, for example, *very.* This function operates on scalar attribute ranges, returning modified input ranges. For example, the meaning of the English word *old* may refer to the range (> 0.8) of the AGE attribute (which is defined for the {0,1} continuum. Intensify-range would be invoked for the phrase *very old,* for example, returning (> 0.9). Similarly, for *very young* this function would return (< 0.1), when given (< 0.2). For *very* average (if the semantics of average is defined as (< >0.4 0.6) on any scale to which it applies), this function would return (< >0.45 0.55).

In what follows we concentrate on the mapping part of the SEM zone. We distinguish four kinds of mappings

1. Mapping between lexeme and ontological concept
2. Mapping between lexeme and interlingua structure
3. Identification of a relation between ontological concepts
4. Ontological and interlingua mappings

The lexicon-building strategy involves a mapping between one sense of a word in a given language and a concept in a language-independent ontology. This mapping is further complicated by the instantiation relations that exist between a particular instance of the ontological concept and the entire class. So when we say, "My cat ate yesterday," we identify a specific instance of a cat, as well as a specific instance of the eating event.

The fundamental philosophical and methodological issue that comes up with regard to lexeme-ontology mapping is how to decide when it is appropriate to create a new ontological concept for a particular lexeme in a given language. There are two extreme positions that can be taken:

1. Maximal number of ontological concepts (minimal burden on lexicon). According to this position, a new ontological concept would be created every time one encounters (in a given language) a new lexeme for which a univocal correspondence in the ontology does not already exist. This would result in a one-to-one mapping between lexeme and ontological concept for all languages, and thus the least possible burden on the lexicon. This extreme is undesirable for two reasons. First, on the most fundamental level, it is in contradiction with the principal characteristic of an interlingual ontology, namely that the ontology be language independent. Second, on the practical level, it would lead to an uncontrolled proliferation of ontological concepts as new languages are described.

2. Minimal number of ontological concepts (maximal burden on lexicon). Following this position, an ontology consisting of a minimal number of primitives could be created, with all additional information needed to distinguish individual lexemes carried in the lexicon. This extreme has two disadvantages as well. First of all, there exists no consensus on a set of primitives, both in terms of their number and content, nor does there exist any consensus on a methodology that would lead to the discovery of such a set. Our position, described further in what follows, has been that such a set of concepts cannot be established a priori, but rather will evolve as more and more languages are added to the MT system's capabilities. Secondly, even if a minimal set of primitives could be established a priori, it would place an extremely large burden on the lexicon. A very general concept like MOVE (assuming that this were a primitive) would have to suffice for hundreds or even thousands of lexemes in a given language. We do not believe that, given the current state of our knowledge, adequate mechanisms for handling such a large burden could be developed in the short term.

Our methodology strikes a balance between these two extremes. We adopt the practical approach outlined in Nirenburg and Goodman (1990), according to which the interlingua-and consequently, the ontology-should be regarded as both an object and a process:

> Viewed as an object, developed in a concrete project, an interlingua should be judged by the quality of the translations that it supports between all the languages for which the corresponding SL-interlingua and interlingua-TL dictionaries have been built. As a process, its success should be judged in terms of the ease with which new concepts can be added to it and existing concepts modified in view of new textual evidence (either from new languages or from those already treated in the system. (p. 9)

That is, the idea of requiring "completeness as proof of feasibility for interlinguae" (Nirenburg & Goodman, 1990, p.10) is rejected. Our interlingua—and consequently, our ontology—is not determined a priori, but rather, is revised and refined in the light of new linguistic evidence, and new requirements for specific domain knowledge.

In the following, we suggest a number of general heuristics for making decisions on the lexicon-ontology interface, and describe the two basic strategies used to achieve the lexicon-ontology mapping: univocal mapping and constrained mapping.

The univocal mapping is the simplest (though relatively uncommon) kind of mapping, used when there is a one-to-one correspondence between a lexeme and an ontological concept. This kind of mapping should be used sparingly, because of the potential for uncontrolled proliferation, as mentioned previously.

As a general rule of thumb, we employ this strategy only when we strongly suspect that the concept denoted by the lexeme is rather "universal." (For practical reasons, as explained earlier, we redefine universal to mean common to the languages we, or our informants, know.) Examples might be the lexeme die–v1 (in the most literal sense of *cease to live*); lexemes denoting natural kinds such as *tree, dog*; lexemes denoting artifacts in technical sublanguages; and so on. When in doubt, we have relied on our own linguistic intuition for the languages we know, and/or consulted informants who know a number of other languages, in order to see how universal the concept denoted by a lexeme actually is. For example, when we were faced with the problem of creating an entry for shop, we learned that neither German nor French possessed words corresponding exactly to *shop* in its sense of a small store. Therefore, it was clear we should not create an ontological concept for *shop*, rather map onto the concept STORE (which we might eventually rename BUYING-PLACE), which appears much more generally lexicalized in the languages we know.

In a terminological lexicon (i.e., a lexicon for the nomenclature of an expert domain, e.g., the sublanguage of a particular scientific or technical field), the proportion of univocal mappings will increase, reflecting the higher tendency for terminological nomenclature to correspond to conceptual objects precisely (e.g., chemical compounds, machinery, electronic components, etc.).

The notation for a univocal mapping is as follows (% indicates the ontological concept that is to be instantiated in the interlingua):

```
(make-frame dog-n1
...
(SEM
        (LEX-MAP (%dog)))
...)
```

Note that the name of the ontological concept need not be the same as that of the lexeme in question. Ontological concepts being language independent, their names should be seen only as labels (which happen to be expressed in English for mnemonic purposes, although random symbols would serve just as well). In naming our ontological concepts, we use the following conventions:

1. Whenever possible, we use scientific, rather than lay terms. For example, to represent the notion of reflected light, we use LUMINANCE for the ontological concept, rather than BRIGHTNESS, because LUMINANCE has a scientific definition, in terms of which specific criteria for measuring reflected light can be stated.
2. We try to be consistent in the names of ontological concepts going down a subtree: EVENT has subclasses MENTAL-EVENT, PHYSICAL-EVENT, and SOCIAL-EVENT.
3. Whenever possible, we attempt to include in the name an indication of some distinguishing characteristic of the ontological concept (i.e., a characteristic distinguishing the concept from its sister concepts). For example, VOLUNTARY-VISUAL-EVENT and INVOLUNTARY-VISUAL-EVENT indicate events that involve vision, with voluntary or involuntary participation, corresponding to the English words look and see, respectively. One problem caused by this approach is that, as the subtree gets deeper, the names can become unwieldy, so some telescoping of distinguishing characteristics is also necessary (mechanisms for such telescoping remain to be developed).
4. Consistently throughout the ontology, we use English words in one sense only as names of ontological concepts. We therefore provide definitions for all concepts, so that when the name of a concept (e.g., STORE) corresponds to a polysemous word, the intended meaning will be clear. The ontological concept STORE is defined as "an establishment where merchandise is sold," and will therefore not be confused with the other nominal sense of a "supply of something" or with the verbal sense of "take in or hold goods."

Aunivocal mapping between lexeme and ontological concept implies that all constraints on an ontological concept (i.e., all information provided within the frame for that concept in the ontology) are consistent with the meaning of the lexeme. Below, we illustrate the constraints that apply to the ontological concepts VOLUNTARY-OLFACTORY-EVENT and INVOLUNTARY-OLFACTORY-EVENT, which correspond univocally to the lexemes smell–v1 and smell–v2.

smell-v1 = = > VOLUNTARY-OLFACTORY-EVENT

where VOLUNTARY-OLFACTORY-EVENT is identified in the ontology as having the following case roles:

(AGENT	(SEM MAMMAL BIRD REPTILE AMPHIBIAN))
(THEME	(SEM PHYSICAL-OBJECT))
(INSTRUMENT	(SEM OLFACTORY-ORGAN))

smell-v2 = = > INVOLUNTARY-OLFACTORY-EVENT

where INVOLUNTARY-OLFACTORY-EVENT is identified in the ontology as having these case roles:

(EXPERIENCER	(SEM MAMMAL BIRD REPTILE AMPHIBIAN))
(THEME	(SEM PHYSICAL-OBJECT))
(INSTRUMENT	(SEM OLFACTORY-ORGAN))

In the majority of cases, the simple strategy of establishing a univocal correspondence between lexeme and ontological concept is not possible. Rather, the mapping is the concept that is the "closest" in meaning. By this, I mean the most specific concept that is still more general than the meaning of the lexeme in question. Once the most directly corresponding concept is determined, constraints/information are specified in appropriate slots in the lexicon. These slots may have a number of specialization facets indicating the nature of the additional information or constraints. The list of specialization facets includes:

1. VALUE–a specific value (e.g., number of sides for triangle = 3, sex of a man = male). This is the facet where actual information is represented. The other facets are constraints on what goes into the VALUE, or information about the information in the VALUE facet. Typically, in the ontology, this facet is not specified–information is added to this facet by (a) lexicon entries (examples above), or (b) semantic processing and dependency structure building (e.g., for VISIT132, the AGENT case role slot may have a VALUE of HUMAN134). In many cases, the VALUE facet in the meaning pattern of a lexical entry will contain a caret (^) prepended to a variable, for example:

(%visit (AGENT (VALUE ^$var1))...)

The caret is an operator (akin to an intention operator) that dereferences the variable (retrieves the lexeme to which the variable is bound) and then retrieves the concepts that are instantiated by that lexeme's meaning pattern (SEM zone). So any place in a meaning pattern (typically in VALUE facets or in head position) where a ^$var appears is an indication to the semantic dependency-building portion of the analyzer (or the converse process in the generator) as to how to attempt to combine the indicated concepts into a meaning representation.

2. DEFAULT–usual (i.e., typical, expected) value (e.g., color of diapers = white). If a VALUE is needed by some inference process (such as NL generation) operating on a TAMERLAN representation, and the VALUE is unspecified, the DEFAULT is used. This usage is consistent with standard artificial intelligence and logic default mechanisms.

3. SEM–akin to a traditional selectional restriction (e.g., color of diapers has to be a COLOR). This is essentially a constraint on what the VALUE may be. Instead of using some small set of binary features, we allow any concept (or Boolean combination of concepts) from the ontology to be a semantic constraint. A VALUE then needs to be a descendant node of (or equal to) the SEM concept in the ontology. All slots have SEM nodes in the ontology, but often these need to be modified (typically, constrained further) for a specific lexeme. This semantic restriction is not absolute-it may be relaxed or violated in controlled ways in cases of metonymy or metaphor.

4. RELAXABLE–TO–maximum relaxability of SEM restrictions (e.g. normally, the THEME of eat is INGESTIBLE (i.e., food or liquid), but this could be relaxed to PHYSICAL-OBJECT.

5. SALIENCE–a scalar value in the range {0.0, 1.0} designating the significance of a specific attribute slot or role (partly reflecting the notion of defining vs. incidental properties). This is primarily used in generation as an identification of the slots (attributes) that are more or less crucial to the meaning of a particular lexical item. For example, the AGE and GENDER slots of the meaning pattern of the English word boy are more significant (salient) than the HAIR-COLOR or LOCATION slots.

3. CONCLUSION

This chapter has described a small subset of concerns that face lexicon builders for realistic knowledge-based computational applications, such as machine translation. There are many more lexical phenomena to be covered and problems to be solved than those mentioned here. Hopefully, this discussion has given the reader an appreciation of the complexity of our problems in building a MTD for advanced natural language processing applications.

CHAPTER 14

A CONNECTIONIST MACHINE-TRACTABLE DICTIONARY: THE VERY IDEA*

Noel E. Sharkey, Paul A. Day, and Amanda J.C. Sharkey
Department of Computer Science
University of Exeter

Now that we are moving into the age of high-speed parallel computing, it is time to begin thinking about how the new technology can be exploited in the construction of MTDs. Already there has been an explosion of connectionist natural language processing research (see Sharkey & Reilly, 1990, for a review), that meshes with the latest parallel hardware developments. Moreover, the new connectionist research offers a number of features that could prove invaluable in the construction of lexical components for natural language processing systems. The aim of this chapter is to outline some of the main characteristics of uniquely connectionist representations, and to consider the advantages that such representations could offer for the design and construction of MTDs.

Although connectionism per se has attracted a great deal of scientific interest, there has been an extensive debate in the late 1980s about the feasibility of connectionist natural language processing. In essence, it has been argued (e.g., Fodor & Pylyshyn, 1988) that connectionist natural language processing systems will only have the necessary properties for natural language processing if they implement classical (traditional linguistic) representations. However, this debate has inspired an intensive research effort into the nature of uniquely connectionist representations; that is, representational types that have come into existence only as a result of connectionist research, and that are not

*We would like to thank the Leverhulme Trust (A/87/153; S/87/2693; F.213H) for supporting this research.

mere implementations of classical representations. As a result, it now seems clear that the new approach embodied in connectionist natural language processing promises to change the way we think about language research (and human language use). The new style of representation also has important implications for the construction of MTDs, or even connectionist MTDs.

We begin with an examination of some of the terminology and relevant issues in connectionist semantics. This provides a background for the remainder of the chapter that focuses on compact distributed representations (CDRs). CDRs are a type of representation that is unique to connectionist research. A report of a small-scale simulation is provided at the end of the chapter, as a more tangible illustration of a connectionist approach to MTD, although this simulation is of too limited a nature to exemplify all the advantages of CDRs. As we shall see, the main advantages of CDRs lie in the content-addressable memory storage they provide, and their ability to learn by encoding statistical regularities in their input. The content-addressable memory embodied in CDRs uses pattern completion to enable fast parallel access of information. It also allows property inheritance and generalization. Property inheritance reduces the amount of duplicated information required (e.g., Clyde is known to be grey, by virtue of his being an elephant). Generalization of lexical entries could enable the calculation of a meaning for previously unencountered lexical items, or for words used in a new sense in a novel context. The learning exemplified in the system means that, as a result of exposure to language samples, CDRs could be evolved that reflect meanings of words in a manner that takes into account the context in which that word occurred.

1. CONNECTIONIST SEMANTICS

There are two major ways to represent semantic information in a connectionist system: localist and distributed. Localism is similar to the type of representation used in semantic nets (e.g., Quillian, 1968). In this style of connectionist semantics, each concept or proposition in a net is represented as a single node or processing unit. Figure 14.1 illustrates a partial example of a localist connectionist net for representing the concepts KNIFE, FORK, BREAD, and BUTTER. The main difference between a semantic net and a localist connectionist net is that the latter relies only on local computations that are made by each processing unit without regard for any global consequences or symbolic evaluation functions. The sample net shown in Figure 14.1 would retrieve appropriate concepts only by local computation of the amount

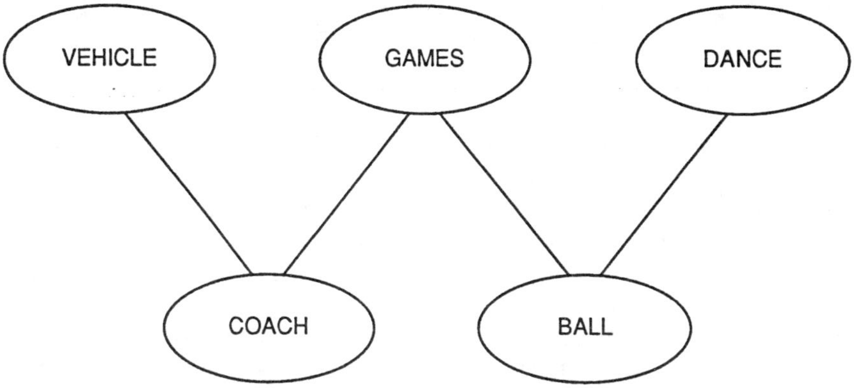

Figure 14.1. Fragment of a net employing localist representations

of activation received by a processing unit. Processing units may interact, but only by propagating activation states. One advantage of localist representations is that they are, by nature, transparent to the user and could be useful for coding dictionary queries into a net. Localist nets have already been exploited in MTD research (e.g., McDonald, Plate, & Schvaneveldt, 1989; Wilks et al., 1989). Such an approach is a useful first step to blueprint the requirements of connectionism for MTD, but our interest here is with the novel forms of connectionist representations that are exemplified in distributed systems.

In contrast to localism, distributed systems represent each concept by a number of units such that (a) an entity that is described by a single term in some descriptive language is represented by more than one element in the connectionist implementation, and (b) each of the elements in the connectionist implementation must be involved in representing more than one entity described by a single term in the descriptive language (Hinton, 1989). For example, if the letter *F* is a term in the descriptive language, then the distributed elements in the descriptive language might be the three features ' ,' ' ,' and '_' and each of these features could also be used as part of the representation of the letter *E*.

In connectionist semantics the atomic features of a distributed representation are known as microfeatures (Hinton, 1981). Sharkey (in press) classifies microfeatural representations into symbolic and nonsymbolic types.[1] Symbolic microfeatures are like the older idea of semantic features (e.g., animate, human, female, etc.) and are employed widely

---

[1]In Smolensky's (1988) terminology, both of these would be described as 'subsymbolic' microfeatures.

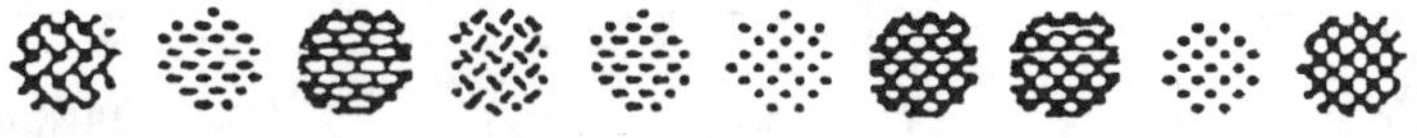

Figure 14.2. Activation pattern across ten hidden units representing a proposition

in connectionist natural language processing as output representations. Indeed, this type of output representation could mesh very well with more traditional computational semantics approaches to dictionary research (e.g., Wilks, this volume). For example, the input to a connectionist MTD could be the word *ball* and the output could be ROUND, INANIMATE, INFLATABLE, and so on. Of course the problem for a connectionist MTD net is to recognize what type of ball is being queried. This will determine the output features. For example, a cricket ball is not inflatable, or in the extreme case *ball* can refer to a formal dance. Thus, the features of a word may be determined by its linguistic context, and, as we shall see later, context sensitivity is one of the natural properties of some kinds of connectionist nets. The second type of connectionist-distributed representation is the nonsymbolic. Nonsymbolic microfeatures do not individually refer to properties in the world. They are semantically interpretable only as a pattern of activation across a collection of units. Figure 14.2 shows the use of ten units to represent an input proposition for a given output task. The shading from light to dark across the units shows the levels of activation in Figure 14.2. A common practice in connectionist research using nonsymbolic distributed representations is to map these representations onto a space of lower dimensionality. It is these lower dimensional representations that we are particularly interested in here.

Some of the important properties of CDRs for connectionist MTDs can be illustrated by examining an early connectionist implementation of semantic networks that used two types of distributed representations (Hinton, 1981). First, Hinton arbitrarily assigned to each word a set of binary microfeatures.[2] Some of these features represented type information. For example, CLYDE and ERNIE were tokens of ELEPHANT, and thus they had both individual microfeatures and shared type microfeatures as shown in the following example:

111000 000000 ELEPHANT

1101000 111000 CLYDE

111000 000111 ERNIE

000111 000000 PERSON

[2]It is not possible to say whether these microfeatures are intended to be nonsymbolic or simply symbolic without labels.

Distributed microfeatural representations from Hinton (1981). The first six bits represent type information. Three bits represent the type ELEPHANT and three bits represent the type PERSON. The last six bits are used to represent information about individual tokens such as CLYDE and ERNIE.

The Hinton net was trained by presenting it with the microfeatural representation of propositional triples such as ELEPHANT COLOR GRAY. The task of the net, during learning, was simply to reproduce the inputs as outputs (autoassociation). The network architecture is illustrated in Figure 14.3.

The input microfeatures are mapped onto CDRs (Hinton's PROP assembly) by coarse coding with fixed random weights between the inputs and the CDRs (c.f. Hinton, McClelland, & Rumelhart, 1986). The net was then trained (using a perceptron convergence procedure) to reconstruct the input by mapping compact distributed representation states back onto the higher dimensional triple space. The trained system could then be used to demonstrate some of the properties of CDRs that are important for connectionist MTDs. First, when given an agent and a relation (e.g., ELEPHANT, COLOR), the trained system filled in the missing property (e.g., GRAY), by completing the partial description of the input. This was made possible because the activation patterns on the CDRs, created by the partial inputs, contained information about the 'whole' triples. It is readily apparent that such pattern completion would be employed in fast content addressing and automatic cross-referencing.

Moreover, the CDRs exhibited a capacity for correct generalization using the type information (i.e., property inheritance). That is, when the Hinton (1981) system was presented with a novel agent/relation pair

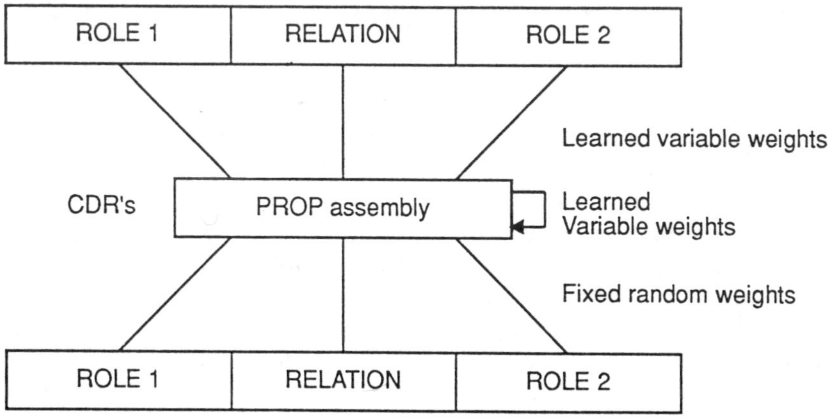

Figure 14.3. The architecture employed by Hinton (1981)

(e.g., ERNIE COLOR) it completed the triple with the correct information (e.g., ERNIE COLOR GRAY). This generalization works providing that the agent shares properties with another agent that had been paired with the relation during training. Such generalization properties, it turns out, are built into CDRs. They are difficult to capture in pure localist representations because all of the vectors representing items are, by definition, perpendicular to one another and equidistant in Euclidean space. It is, therefore, difficult to capture similarities and differences between items in localist representation space (although it can be done by explicit marking). CDRs, on the other hand, can form a denser representation such that similar items cluster on the surface of the pattern space. Thus, items that share features are more likely to produce similar results.

For simplicity of exposition, imagine that a set of distributed representation vectors are unit normalized (i.e., are all set to length 1). These vectors may then be described geometrically as points on a unit hypersphere as illustrated in the sphere in Figure 14.4. The point here is that similar items will cluster on the surface of the hypersphere (two clusters are shown at a and b in Figure 14.4). It is then relatively easy to develop a process model in which similar items produce similar or identical results. For example, if a net was trained to take microfeatural representations of HORSE, CAT, and COW as input and map them onto ANIMAL in the output, then we would expect a microfeatural representation for DOG, which was not in the training set, to also produce the response output ANIMAL. That is, we would expect the vector representation for DOG to be sufficiently close to the vector representation for the other animals to have a similar effect. We shall see later how this property of generalization can be combined with a context-sensitive mapping function for extensibility of the representations.

In sum, the CDRs in the Hinton semantic network illustrate three of the advantages referred to in the introduction to this chapter. That is, they show (a) compact content-addressable memory storage affording parallel access as a result of the systems pattern completion facilities; (b) property inheritance, exploited by the system to attribute the general properties of the type to each of its tokens, and (c) automatic generalization, exhibited by the system's ability to complete triples that had not been part of the original training set.

A further advantage of CDRs lies in their memory capacity; whereas localist networks can encode up to n items, where n is the dimension of the representation space, distributed networks have the capacity to encode $2n\text{-}(n+1)$ items. For example, in R10 the maximum number of

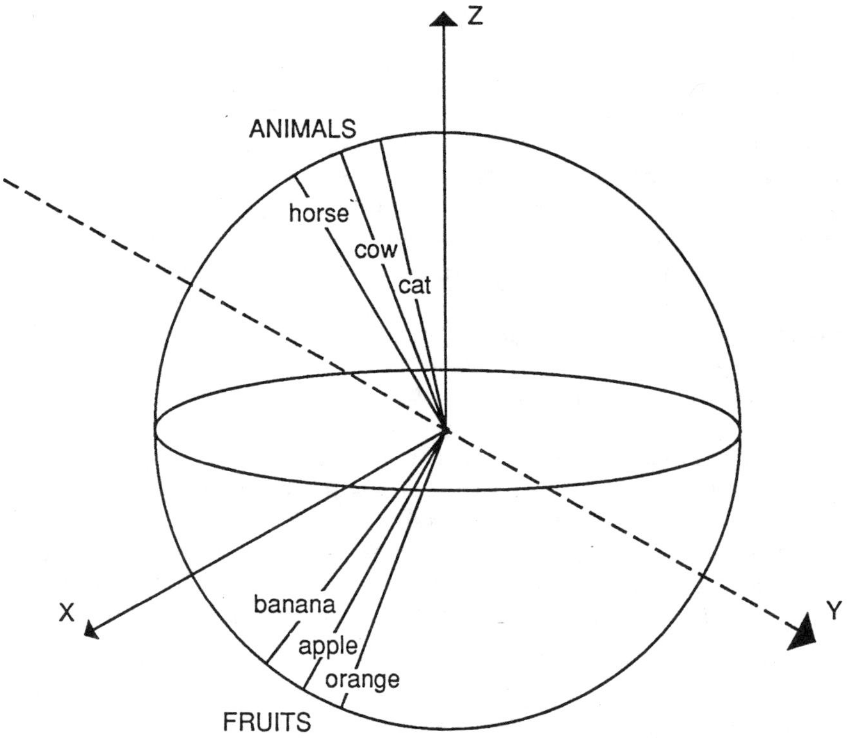

Figure 14.4. Two clusters of patterns on the surface of a unit sphere

localist representations would be 10, whereas for distributed binary representations it would be 1013 – a hundredfold difference. With superimpositional representations (e.g., Van Gelder, 1990) in which the activation values are continuous, the number of discriminable representations could be of a much higher order of magnitude. Such representations are generally learned using some variant of the backpropagation algorithm to which we now turn.

2. LEARNING

One of the major advantages of connectionist nets is that they are extensional. That is they can learn to develop their representations from exposure to some world (Jackson & Sharkey, 1991). We briefly mentioned earlier how Hinton (1981) used a learning algorithm for one layer of his net. Since then, many more powerful learning algorithms have been explored for natural language research. Probably the most commonly employed learning rule is the Generalized Delta Rule (or backpropagation; Rumelhart, Hinton, & Williams, 1986).

In the simplest backpropagation net, there are three layers of units: input units -> hidden units -> output units, with weighted connections between the layers. (The weight between two units can be thought of as representing the strength of connection). An example of a backpropagation net is shown in Figure 14.5. For the purposes of illustration, imagine that you wish to train the net to output semantic information (say a featural representation) for a particular word appearing in different contexts. The procedure is as follows:

1. Code the language strings (word + context) onto the input units. In other words, the input vector v is set to the activation states (usually binary) of the first input pattern.
2. Map the input states onto the lower dimensional hidden unit space (creating the CDRs). This mapping is carried out by post multiplying the first weight matrix $W1$ by the input vector v (i.e., $W1v$) and then applying an output function for the hidden units $f{:}W1v = h$, where f is commonly a sigmoid squashing function

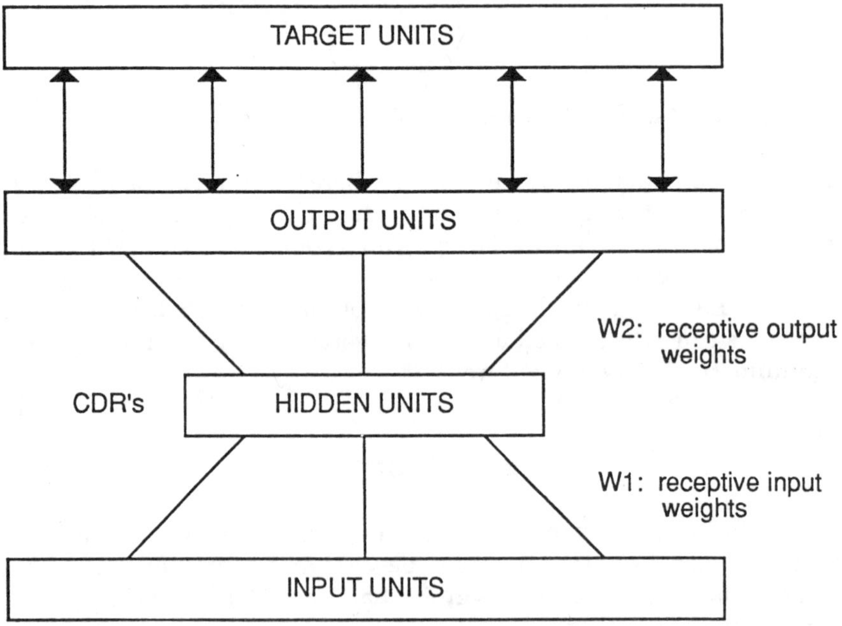

Figure 14.5. A backpropagation network

$1/1+e\text{-}x$. This may be though of as a nonlinear mode of combination (or composition) of the input words.

3. Map the compact distributed representation states onto the output units, which would consist of the semantic information associated with the target word. The mapping is the same as that in Step 2 except that v would now be h and $W1$ would now be $W2$: $f{:}W2h = o$.
4. Compare the output with the target information that was required ($t\text{-}o$) and, if there is an error, apply the backpropagation error-correction procedure (see Rumelhart, Hinton, & Williams, 1986, for details).
5. Iterate the four steps until the net produces some criterion fit to the desired outputs.

Once the net has learned, it can be used for the required task by running it through Steps 1–3 (in other words by omitting the error correction procedure).

There are many advantages of using representations created by variants (such as recurrence) of the learning described here. For example, recent research has shown that CDRs trained by simple variants of this method exhibit functional compositionality (Van Gelder, 1990) and allow structurally sensitive operations (Chalmers, 1990). Furthermore, statistical and geometric analyses of such nets have revealed that they can contain a rich variety of structural and semantic information (cf. Sharkey, in press). Thus they can contain information about the typing of their constituents (Elman, 1989), their syntactic class (Hanson & Burr, 1990), and their semantic class (St. John & McClelland, in press), as well as information about path and long-range dependencies (when trained on finite state grammars; Servan-Schreiber, Cleeremans, & McClelland, 1988). Others (e.g., Elman, 1989; Pollack, 1990; Smolensky, 1990) have also demonstrated how connectionist nets can be trained to develop recursive distributed representations in their CDRs. All of these properties fall out of the learning mechanisms, unlike the early Hinton net that had to be told which were the type markers.

Another important advantage of learning is that the same network can be trained on many different tasks by changing only the weights for the mapping between the CDRs and the output. Thus, for example, a single network could be trained to translate words (contextually) into different languages. Then the upper weights (those that map the CDRs onto the output) could be replaced by a set of naive weights. The same CDRs could then be mapped across a new set of trainable weights to produce a translation into a new language or even to perform a mapping from

English words onto featural representations. Training the same network on different tasks would instill considerable semantic richness and variation into the net. It is by using a variety of tasks that learning could be used to develop a dictionary that is an amalgam of an encyclopedia and a dictionary (cf. Wilks, this volume). Indeed, given the backpropagation learning algorithm, the contextual information (and world knowledge) in the CDRs may go even beyond that required by any of the tasks. This is because the training procedure computes high-order statistical relations in the input set. Unlike standard corpora (e.g., LOB) that exploits pairwise covariances (i.e., second-order statistics), backpropagation can build complex structures by modeling the joint probability distribution of n variables ($n > 2$) using *nth* -order statistics.

Finally, the main advantage of using learned CDRs for the construction of a connectionist MTD is that the representations of words reflect context-dependent differences in meaning. This context sensitivity is the result of the way in which words in an input sentence are mapped onto the hidden unit representations (Steps 1 and 2). Essentially, the input states of a group of words (say a sentence) are mapped onto the hidden unit representations by summing the weights for the words, and then running these sums through a nonlinear output function. Thus, the amount of loading on a hidden unit microfeature for a particular word will vary according to the context in which it occurs. To make these points clearer we report an illustrative simulation in the following, and follow this with a detailed explanation of the dynamics of the compositionality on the CDRs.

3. AN ILLUSTRATIVE SIMULATION

In order to illustrate some of the points made in this chapter, we ran a simple simulation. This is really only a "toy" connectionist MTD, but it serves to demonstrate one way in which a connectionist net could be used to access contextually relevant semantic features of words. The idea was to query the net with a word and, in order to capture the shade of meaning, to provide it with a relevant sentence context. So, for example, if the query word was *ball*, the input to the net might be "Fred hit the ball with the bat. [BALL]." The required response from the net is a set of descriptors such as small, hard, round, solid, and heavy.[3] The same sentence could also be used for a different queries such as, "Mary

[3]Obviously these are not an exhaustive set, as they just as easily describe a cannonball, but they suffice for our current purposes.

hit the ball with the bat. [BAT]". The required response would then be medium-sized, hard, heavy, solid, and wooden.

For inputs, we chose the four words, BAT, CLUB, COACH, and BALL as our target queries both because they are all homonyms and because they can be used in a variety of sentence contexts to indicate subtler shades of meaning, for example, the difference between a soccer ball and a cricket ball. The sheer semantic complexity created by using combinations of the four homonyms can be seen from a close examination of the following example.

> The coach took the ball into the club. The coach went to a ball in the club. The club hired a coach to go to the ball. The coach hit the ball with the club. Fred gave the bat to the coach. Fred chased the bat in the coach.

The difficult task for our toy connectionist MTD was to output a contextually relevant set of descriptors (features), in turn, for each of the probed homonyms in each of the sentences. The output features we used here were sets of descriptors that were collected in a psychological normative study for other purposes in our laboratory. We used these here because they were conveniently available and not because of any theoretical motivation (see the test runs that follow for some examples of the output features).

The connectionist MTD was trained on 25 sentences like those shown in the example with the different homonym probes. Regardless of the "sense" of a particular homonym, it always had the same input representation. For example, the query for the word *ball* was always the same BALL whether referring to a dance or a game. These were distinguished only by their output features. The different senses of the words and their frequency of occurrence in the training sets were danceBALL 4, game-{cricketBALL 2, golfBALL 1, soccerBALL 1, generalBALL 1}, vehicleCOACH 3, trainerCOACH 5, cricketBAT 3, flyingBAT 2, socialCLUB 2, golfCLUB 1.

The net consisted of two layers of weights (as shown in Figure 14.5), 60 input units, 15 hidden units, and 159 output units. The sentences ranged in length from five to ten words. During learning, each sentence plus its query word was coded onto a binary activation vector and input to the net. Similarly, the required output features for each word were coded as a binary activation vector and used as a target for the learning. Using the backpropagation algorithm described earlier, the connectionist MTD learned to output the correct features for 100% of the queries in 1,278 learning trials (with a learning rate = 0.1).

We can illustrate the behavior of the net by examining a sample from a test run after learning. The first query illustrates how our system picks out the "dance" sense of ball from the sentence context.

QUERY1: Cindy danced at the ball. [BALL] ANSWER: fun, expensive, fancy, noisy, posh.

In contrast, Queries 2, 3, and 4 select the "game" sense of ball. However, notice that each of the sentences indicates a different shading of the "game" sense of ball—soccer ball, cricket ball, and golf ball.

QUERY2: Mary kicked the ball at the goal. [BALL] ANSWER: game_object, pastime, inanimate, bouncy, round, soft, medium-sized, rolls, hollow.

QUERY3: Fred hit the ball with the bat. [BALL] ANSWER: graspable, game_object, pastime, inanimate, small-sized, hard, round, solid, heavy, red, rolls.

QUERY4: Cindy hit the ball with the club. [BALL] ANSWER: graspable, game_object, pastime, inanimate, v-small-sized, hard, round, solid, light, white, rolls.

This net also exemplifies the extraction of type information. For example, in Query 5, the context sentence makes it clear the it is the "game" sense of ball that is required. However, the contextual information is insufficient to indicate exactly what kind of ball is being referred to. In the example, we can see that the answer contains the features common to golf, soccer, and cricket balls. This is clearly compatible with the notion of type described earlier for the Hinton (1981) system. The type information is contained in the trainable weights and manifests in the CDRs given an ambiguous context.

QUERY5: The coach took the ball into the club. [BALL] ANSWER: round, game_object, pastime, inanimate, rolls.

The last two queries we discuss pick out two senses of the word bat as in "game" and "flying creature." Query 6 selects the "game" sense of bat and was chosen as an example to illustrate how the same sentence (i.e., from Query 3) could be used for more than one probe word. Query 7 selects the "flying creature" sense of bat.

QUERY6: Fred hit the ball with the bat. [BAT] ANSWER: medium-sized, hard, graspable, game__object, pastime, heavy, solid, wooden, inanimate.

QUERY7: Harry saw the bat at the belfry. [BAT] ANSWER: small, black, furry, squeaky, animate, flying.

In summary, contextually sensitive lexical outputs were developed for four homonyms by training a backpropagation net to associate the relevant set of features with each homonym, dependent on the particular sentence context in which it occurred. The test trials shown here demonstrate how even a connectionist MTD given a very small language sample can learn to discriminate between subtle differences in the senses of words. For our purposes, though, the important point of this discussion is the nature of the CDRs that mediated between the input

```
                          Rescaled Distance Cluster Combine

       CASE    0         5        10        15        20        25
     Label Seq +---------+---------+---------+---------+---------+

danceBALL       -+
danceBALL       -+
danceBALL       -+---------------------------+
danceBALL       -+                           +-------+
                                             I       I
vehicleCOACH    -+                           I       I
vehicleCOACH    -+---------------------------+       I
vehicleCOACH    -+                                   I
                                                     I
personCOACH     -+                                   +-----------+
personCOACH     -+                                   I           I
personCOACH     -+                                   I           I
personCOACH     -+-------------+                     I           I
personCOACH     -+             +---------------------+           I
                               I                                 I
socialCLUB      -+-----+       I                                 I
socialCLUB      -+     +-------+                                 I
socialCLUB      -------+                                         I
                                                                 I
golfBALL        ---+-----+                                       I
typeBALL        ---+     +-------------+                         I
cricketBALL     -+---+   I             I                         I
cricketBALL     -+   +---+             +-------------------------+
soccerBALL      -----+                 I
                                       I
flyingBAT       -+---------+           I
flyingBAT       -+         +-----------+
                           I
cricketBAT      -+-+       I
cricketBAT      -+ +-------+
cricketBAT      ---+
```

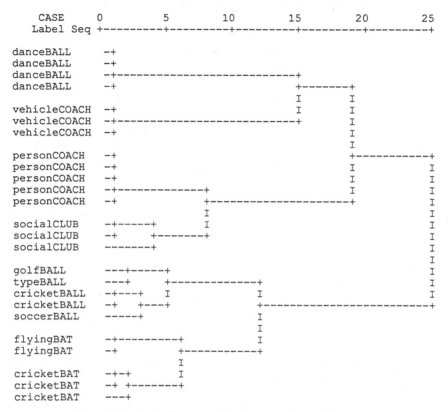

Figure 14.6. A dendogram of the cluster analysis of the CDRs

queries and the output features. One way that we can examine the nature of such context-sensitive representations is by subjecting them to a hierarchical cluster analysis, which we now briefly describe.

The first step in the analysis is to run the net on a trial run with a number of queries that reflect all of the relevant senses of the probe words under investigation. After the presentation of each query, the CDR activation pattern is recorded. At the end of the test the collection of CDRs is analyzed in terms of their Euclidean distance from one another.[4] The distances are then fed into a hierarchical cluster analysis (Everitt, 1978) to produce a dendogram as shown in Figure 14.6.

The main points worthy of note in Figure 14.6 can be seen from an examination of the seven numbered clusters. In the main, the semantic

---

[4]The Euclidean distance between two vectors *v1* and *v2* is given by the length of the first vector minus the second, i.e., $||v1 - v2||$, where length $||v|| = \sqrt{(v.v)}$.

classes of each of the queries are reflected in the clusters. Cluster 1 consists of all four danceBALLs, cluster 2 of vehicleCOACHes, and cluster 3 of personCOACHes. Cluster 4 is slightly odd in that it contains both socialCLUB and golfCLUB. However, this is mainly because there are so few examples, and socialCLUB forms a subcluster of its own. We might expect with more contextual regularity, engendered by a larger training set, that golfCLUB would be closer to cricketBAT. Cluster 5 contains all of the gameBALLs, cluster 6 the flyingBATs, and cluster 7, the cricketBATs. The message here is that the representations of similar query types (e.g., gameBALL) are clustered together in Euclidean space. Thus similar query types will produce similar results. This is the point about generalization that we were making earlier in our description of the Hinton (1981) paper.

4. CONTEXT SENSITIVITY

The context sensitivity of the CDRs, as demonstrated in our illustrative simulation, can now be considered in more detail. As was pointed out earlier, it is the mode of composition of the words in the context sentences and the query words on the CDRs that give the system its representational power.

The dynamics of this nonconcatenative compositionality, to use Van Gelder's (1990) term, can be seen by examination of a commonly used mapping function for backpropagation, a nonlinear (but monotonic) sigmoidal function: $1/1+e\text{-}x$, where $x = S\,wijai + \text{bias}$, wij is the weight from the *ith* input unit to the *jth* hidden unit, and ai is the activation state of the *ith* input unit. Let f be the sigmoid function, x is a vector of the weighted sums of the input activations and biases for a sentence S, and x' is a vector of the weighted sums of the input activations and biases of S - k; that is, the input sentence S with the *kth* word deleted. For example, our sentence S could be "Fred hit the ball with bat [BALL]." Then x would be the input vector representing S , and x' would be the input vector representation of "Fred hit the ball with the bat"; that is, the sentence without the query word. In other words, unit k would be [BALL]. Then the magnitude of the effect, m, of unit k (e.g., [BALL] to the hidden unit vector is given by: $mk = f(x) - f(x')$.

Now in order to understand how the composition is context sensitive, we examine the behavior of a simple net with only one hidden unit, and with the weighted value of the *kth* input unit held constant at 0.5 as shown in Figure 14.7a. To find out how the magnitude of x' affects nk, we can graph the familiar S -shaped sigmoid function, as shown in Figure 14.7b, and then choose a point on the horizontal axis for x', which means that the horizontal coordinate for x is then $x' + 0.5$. Thus if, as is shown on the graph, the point chosen for x' is 1.5, the horizontal coordinate for x is $x' + 0.5$, or 2. Or if the point chosen for x' were 0, the horizontal coordinate for x would be $x' + 0.5$ or 0.5. Reading across, the vertical axis gives us $f(x)$ and $f(x')$. Note that the steepest increase from $f(x')$ to $f(x)$, and hence the largest value of mk, is when $x' = 0$. The size of mk diminishes progressively on both sides of zero. The bell-shaped graph of the derivative $f'(x)$ shown in Figure 14.7c provides an illustration of the diminished size of the magnitude of the effect, m, of unit k on the hidden unit vector when the input x' is greater or smaller than zero.

What all this means for a connectionist MTD is that the output information for a word will vary depending on the context in which it is presented. This is an essential requirement for a connectionist MTD for use in computational semantics. More importantly, when this context sensitivity is combined with the properties of generalization described here, we have an extensible dictionary that not only effectively resolves ambiguities, but is capable of capturing new senses of a word when it is presented in novel contexts.

It would be relatively easy to set up a learning system, following this blueprint, to accept a large corpus of sentences and queries. This could be extremely beneficial in that the larger the sample, the greater the chances of the CDRs picking up a wide range of contextual regularities. Thus, the system could be very general. The hardest part would be in the choice of a sufficient and appropriate set of features for the output answers. What we have provided here is a general framework for the development of connectionist MTDs. The choice of output would depend on a particular researcher's goals. Once trained, such a connectionist MTD could easily be integrated, as a high-speed component, into something like a preference semantics system with a front end parser to carry out the input coding. However, because of its limited size, this

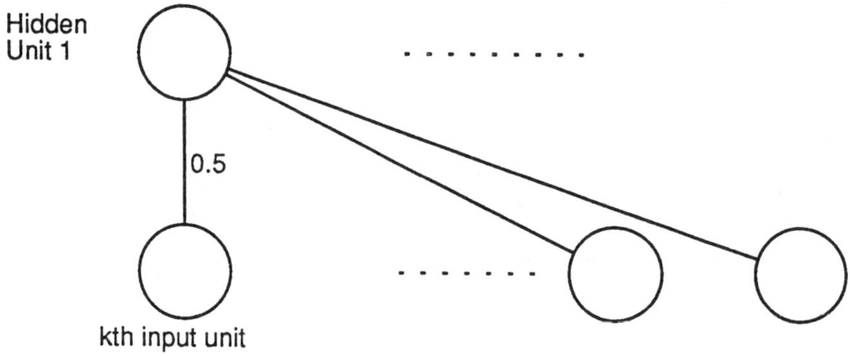

Figure 14.7a. One hidden unit with a weighted value of 0.5 from the kth input unit

simulation only touches on the power of a connectionist MTD, and does not demonstrate either the generalization or property inheritance.

Of course, a network will learn the correct context-sensitive semantic and syntactic information only if it is trained on a sufficiently representative sample of the target language. It is possible to identify three alternative approaches to the problem of finding a representative sample of language: (a) The first method would be to use a massive corpora of real texts for training the system. If this proved impractical (because of the sheer size of a corpus), an alternative method would be (b) to generate the training sets by using a sentence generator. Elman (1989) for instance employed a sentence generator to produce a training set. However, a problem with sentence generators is that they are necessarily theory dependent, because they require a symbolic preanalysis of the language to encode the rules and categories. A final alternative, (c), would be to use an amalgam of the first two approaches, and to use a manageably sized sample of real language, having checked its representativeness. Aspects of the sample that could be checked would include the frequency of particular syntactic constructions, the overall frequency and the conjoint frequency of lexical items.

A final point to be stressed here about CDRs is that they can be manipulated directly without being decoded onto the symbol surface; that is, the CDRs themselves are structure sensitive. This is quite a crucial area for connectionism and research has only just begun. However, what there is (e.g., Chalmers, 1990; Pollack, 1990) shows considerable promise. Why is this important for connectionist MTDs? Well firstly, we have already described many of the advantages of CDRs in terms of both their memory and representational capacity, as well as

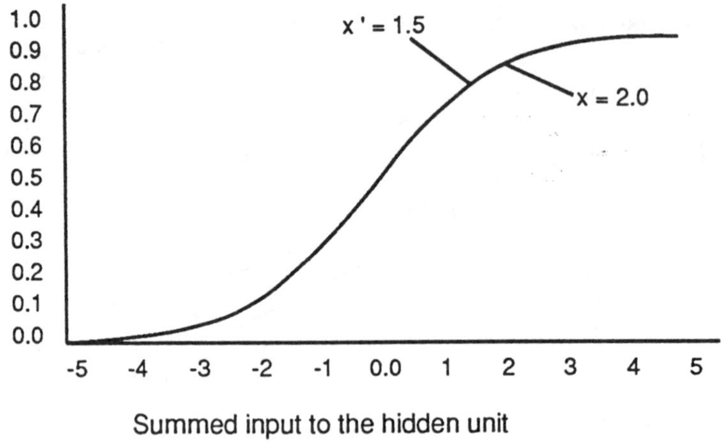

Figure 14.7b. A graph of the sigmoid function for the output of a hidden unit

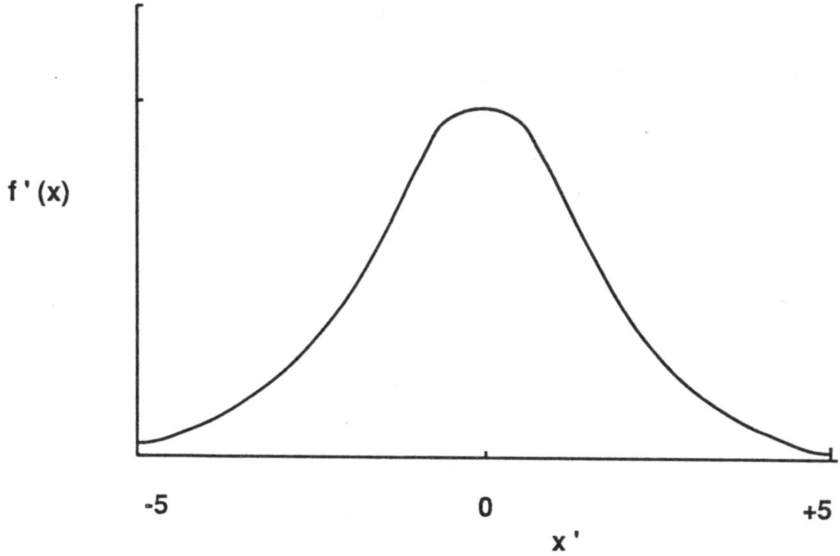

Figure 14.7c. A graph of the derivative of the sigmoid function shown in Figure 14.7b

their built-in generalization properties. Remember that these representations can be a significant reduction in size from the input representations. Thus CDRs are ideal for the sort of high-speed manipulations that would be required of our futuristic connectionist MTDs.

5. CONCLUSIONS

It is one thing to sketch the benefits that would in principle be obtained from a connectionist MTD that consisted of CDRs, and another to flesh them out into reality. We are quite some way from creating a usable connectionist MTD, and even the production of a good pilot version would be a reasonably long-term project. However, what we have tried to show here is that many of the basic principles are in place and that connection science is now in a position to make a start on such a project. The aim of this chapter was to show some of the advantages of taking the connectionist route. These include: (a) efficient compact memory storage and manipulation, (b) fast parallel access, (c) natural content-addressable memory, (d) built-in generalization, (e) automatic cross-referencing, (f) learned representations, (g) extensible and extensional representations, (h) representations capturing high-order statistical relations in language (not just conjoint frequency), (i) representations that combine knowledge of the task world with knowledge about language (a dictionary/encyclopedia amalgam), and (j) context sensitive processing. The time is now ripe to exploit these tools either as a whole or in part to supplement current MTDs.

CHAPTER 15

THE DYNAMIC DATABASE*

B.T.S. Atkins
Oxford University Press

Before considering methodologies for developing large-scale electronic dictionaries, I would like, as a career lexicographer standing outside mainstream research, to express two concerns relevant to this theme. First, I am disturbed by the central role in NLP research currently assigned to existing machine-readable dictionaries (MRDs) as a repository of linguistic fact. To my mind any dictionary intended for human use, which is what these once were, is an inadequate foundation for a knowledge base destined to record a whole language. Second, I am also disturbed by the marginal role in NLP research assigned to professional lexicographers. After years of gathering, classifying, sorting and selecting lexical data, they are the people with the specialized skills crucial to LDB building, yet at present they are certainly not being used to best advantage. Many research projects employ completely untrained staff (graduate students often) to perform lexicographical tasks requiring advanced skills and professional expertise. Existing lexicographers must be retrained. Turning them into computational lexicographers could probably be done in a year of intensive study, whereas making a computational linguist into a lexicographer would take several years of dictionary-compiling practice, for lexicographic skills cannot be acquired through study alone.

It is often asserted that, as Byrd et al. (1987) put it, "There are too many systems requiring too much information about too many words

*This chapter previously appeared in the Proceedings of the International Workshop in Electronic Dictionaries (pp. 162-178) held at Osio, Japan on November 8-9, 1990.

for the manual approach to succeed." On the contrary, there are too many systems requiring too much information about too many words for the manual approach to be ignored. Of course, it cannot be done entirely manually, but neither can it be done by investing the MRD with an authority that it does not, and cannot, possess. Building a large-scale electronic dictionary requires a large-scale collaborative effort.

1. DESCRIPTION OF LEXICAL DATABASE

In this broad description I refer only to the content of the LDB, not to its form, although of course the design of the lexical entry structure is of paramount importance. Interesting work is being done by the EC (ESPRIT) ACQUILEX Project in devising a common lexical entry structure for some of the European Community languages (Calzolari, Peter, & Roventini, 1990).

As to content,[1] language is dynamic, and a lexical database designed to record language must in its own way be equally dynamic. There is no place in our thinking for a fixed, rigid, static LDB. Rather we should be trying to create an organic repository of relevant facts, one that is able to grow and develop as these facts change our perceptions of what language is. The development of this LDB should be seen essentially as a bottom-up process, one that involves a continual redrawing of the ground plan. Those who use online text in lexicography find in their corpus not only information but inspiration. As the LDB grows, new insights will undoubtedly lead to variations in design. For the database to be effective, or even merely adequate, it must be possible to modify its predictive power as new facts are discovered. The database must also be as explicit, systematic, and comprehensive as possible in these main areas:

- Vocabulary coverage: Few English-language MRDs in use in NLP contain even 100,000 lemmas, less than half the number of current English lemmas in the *New Oxford English Dictionary*
- Types of information recorded: Morphological, syntactic, lexico-semantic, collocational, and so on
- Data coverage: All dictionaries are selective and much NLP time and effort goes into filling the gaps

[1]In this discussion I draw all my examples from English, although of course such a database is a core component in the processing of every natural language.

Naturally, the structure and coherence of the LDB will depend on a prior model of linguistic generalizations. This refers not only to the grammatical relationships of the language inherent in the database structure, and the morphological relationships among lexical items there, but also to the lexico-semantic generalizations called *regular polysemy* in Apresyan (1973) and discussed in Pustejovsky (1990) and analyzed (for verbal lemmas) in Levin (in press).

1.1. What is an Objective Lexical Fact?

This term is used to denote a self-evident truth that depends neither on an individual's particular linguistic theory, nor on an individual's particular store of facts about the language (much used in the past for the type of linguistic analysis that relies on introspection). Objective facts must be validated by nonsubjective evidence, and the greatest source of such evidence today is the electronic text corpus. You have to look at language in use by other people in order to get at real hard facts.

It is important to realize that dictionaries do not provide such evidence (Atkins, 1991), because their content results at least partially from the introspection of the editors. Even dictionaries claiming to be based on corpus evidence and thus to provide "real" facts do not do so. Every fact in any dictionary is filtered by the lexicographer's selective process. No humanly selected subset of facts may be relied on to provide an objective and representative reflection of the total situation.

The inadequacy of existing dictionaries is particularly acute when it comes to considering centrality and typicality in language use. How often does a word occur in a particular context? Sense disambiguation may often depend on the comparative frequency of co-occurrence of various lexical items. Furthermore, the language-using computer, in evaluating grammaticality, must be able to distinguish between what is legitimate to decode and what is legitimate to encode, in lexicographical terms. In decoding mode, it must be able to handle the productive use of metaphor and other creative facets of language as used by human beings. On the other hand, if its output is to be credible, in encoding mode it must not use metaphor very much at all. Eventually, therefore, it will be necessary to distinguish which linguistic usages are central and typical from those which are not. Usage is not currently as well-documented as morphology, syntax, semantics, and the other aspects of language that have traditionally been studied and recorded, but facts about what is central and typical are highly relevant to the type of LDB being considered here. Once again, they are to be found not in dictionaries, but in text.

Examples[2] of objective facts relating to one lemma (RISK) and validated by evidence from one corpus (the APHB) are:

1. The verb RISK passivizes (a fact of syntax); for example, "They could not be risked," "In the meanwhile our child's life must be casually risked day in day out?" and so on.
2. The verb RISK is not typically used in the passive voice (a fact of usage). Only 10 out of 810 instances (1.23%) are passive.
3. The noun RISK has the following complementation structures:(syntax) ZERO COMPLEMENT ("A few of them did so surreptitiously at a risk, among them Thomas Jefferson."), CLAUSE ("There is, of course, the risk that a parent might detect a reminiscent familiarity in the technique."). Also (listed here without examples) FOR+NP, IN+GERUNDIAL-VP, IN+NP, OF+GERUNDIAL-CLAUSE, OF+GERUNDIAL-VP, OF+NP, OVER+NP, TO+NP, WITH+NP.
4. The verb RISK occurs with the following common nouns in subject position when its complement is a direct object NP (syntax/collocation):

actors	company	guy	men	ship	superpowers
board	contractor	individual	millions	skipper	teenagers
brigands	doctors	eader	moneymen	society	thane
buyer	fisherman	leadership	mother	soldiers	thief
chaps	fleet	lives	neighbours	son	tournaments
children	girl	man	pilot	soul	typist
civilians	government	manager	prisoners	star	women
companies	governments	members	publisher	stranger	writer

5. Gerundial objects account for 28.4% of all objects of the verb RISK (usage, 230 gerundial objects out of 820 verb citations in the database).
6. The frequency of co-occurrence of TAKE with RISK in a window of six tokens is statistically significant (usage/collocation). The phrase TAKE A RISK accounts for 11.97% of all citations-168 out of 1403-for the noun RISK in this corpus.

1.2. Scope of a Lexical Entry

Because defining the scope of the lexical entry is the responsibility of the theoretical linguist, not the lexicographer, it is sufficient to note at this

[2]These emerge from the analysis of a database of 1770 citations for the lemma RISK, drawn from the 25-million-word corpus provided to IBM Research by the American Publishing House for the Blind, and made available through the courtesy of IBM's Roy Byrd and Slava Katz. This work is partially described in Fillmore & Atkins (1989, 1992).

point that the current basis for the design of an LDB entry is an MRD entry with some or all of the following components:

- Lemma
- Variant form(s)
- Pronunciation
- Inflected form(s)
- Etymology
- Grammatical information: part of speech, complementation
- Senses: semantic classification
- Explanation of meaning: definition, gloss, translation, and so on
- Example of usage, often from citation file or electronic corpus
- Multiword lexeme: idioms and so on, in which the lemma appears
- Labels: information on domain, style, register, region, and so on.
- Network links: cross-references, usage notes, and so on (hyponymy, synonymy, antonymy, collocation relationships)
- Secondary headwords (run-ons): morphologically related lexical items

The dynamic, all-purpose LDB must contain more types of information than those presented in even the most elaborate dictionary. The database should make explicit what a native speaker intuitively knows about a word. However, to ensure that only relevant facts are represented, the presentation must be informed by a theoretical understanding of lexical organization (Atkins & Levin, 1991; Levin, 1991, in press).

2. EXPERT COLLABORATION IN DATABASE BUILDING

The task of defining, identifying, recording, storing, and accessing the essential facts of the language by scrutinizing millions, or even billions of words of text calls for a collaborative effort from the many disciplines with appropriate expertise. Success is possible only if the load is shared.

2.1. Defining the Data Types

In their number the theoretical linguists must include all the appropriate specialisms, from morphology through syntax to at least lexical semantics.[3] Deciding what types of fact are essential to a really useful

[3]I say "at least lexical semantics" because from my lexicographer-worm's eye view of expert activity in the area of LDBs, I can see no common view of what the semantic component of an LDB should or could comprise. Certainly there seems to be no consensus

description of a language demands not only the ability to analyze lexical usage in microscopic detail but also to construct for and out of this analysis a coherent global view of the language. In the course of attempting this, linguists must define concepts such as argument, valency, and complement, and provide adequate criteria for assigning these descriptions to items of corpus data, for without this no lexical analysis will be systematic.

However, above all, linguists and lexicographers, who have to work closely together as the database grows and develops, must be adaptable. Those with rigid preconceptions have no place in this project. A constant, flexible dialogue between these two groups is essential. Together, they have to send the computer into the wilderness of raw text to capture the data; together, they have to evaluate the results and plan the next step. Like all the other contributors to the LDB, they must be prepared to reflect on the facts that emerge from the corpus scrutiny, and modify their world view (and the LDB) accordingly.

2.2. Designing and Building the LDB

This is not an enterprise to be lightly undertaken. Even a one-volume dictionary of some 20 million characters, containing but a small subset of the facts needed by the LDB, will take around 100 person-years to edit if properly researched. For LDB development, the lexicographers will need powerful computational support. They must be given the most sophisticated lexical tools that the theoretical and computational linguists, statisticians, and programmers can build for them. The task of discovering the facts and recording them so that they are accessible to scholars of all theoretical persuasions necessitates a lexicographical workstation that will perform (at least semiautomatically) the massive routine tasks involved.

The design of such a workstation is not trivial. Even the hardware must surpass anything routinely available at present. A single large VDU with a sophisticated window facility is not enough, because the lexicographer's mind will reconfigure as the screen reconfigures. A screen that reconfigures in order to present a listing of data distorts the lexicographer's map of the word. It seems that the dictionary compiler's skill in sorting data depends at least partially on spatial aspects of

on what constitutes an objective semantic fact. For that reason, the LDB described here has no pure semantic component, but restricts itself to the assembly of data relating to morphological, syntactic, and collocational relationships, and to the lexical items instantiating these. Handling semantics is a task to be undertaken subsequently, one that may prove easier, and can hardly prove more difficult, when the research community has at its disposal a larger pool of specific objective facts.

memory. This is most noticeable in the regular assignment of citations to dictionary senses. A compiler working on a lexical item with many major senses and subsenses will remember these senses-perhaps as a hangover from the days of heaps of index cards-in some spatial configuration (Sense 4 is at ten past two, Sense 12 at quarter to nine). As a result, online compiling of a complex lexical entry with a single screen requires constant printouts of each sense grouping. A lexicographical workstation must offer a bank of screens, each with multiple windowing facilities, where subsets of the data may be held in view during compilation.

In the realm of software, the lexicographers need all the help they can get. As well as routine sorting, the workstation must accelerate, systematize, and control their work. Corpus data must be presented to them in the form that best facilitates its processing. Computational routines must be devised to predict their decisions, so that instead of initiating classifications the lexicographers will simply either accept or correct them. The workstation designers must monitor the lexicography in action, enhancing the computational component in order to allow the great mass of text to be scanned (initially by the lexicographers, but progressively more and more by automatic means).

The aim is to make the database to some degree self-generating. Using the workstation tools for textual analysis, the lexicographers will systematically increase the store of structured lexical data in the computer. As the database grows, the tools that it informs will become more intelligent and powerful. In time, computational routines will be developed to bring the data gathering from the initial computer-aided human compiling to the point where raw corpus is routinely processed (Clear, 1988) with the objective of isolating linguistic phenomena that the database can still not account for, facts that the computer cannot recognize. The lexicographers' task may by then be reduced to appending these into the database, perhaps after the linguists have adapted its design to allow this.

Storage of and access to the database, so that it may be maximally used by an NLP community with a multitude of diverse needs and skills, is of course the responsibility of the computer programmers, who will develop routines for automatic online access and controlled enhancement of the database by those who use the data.

Finally, of the experts whose collaboration is essential to the success of the enterprise (perhaps it was not without design that I included amongst these the lexicographical workstation itself), there remains one without whose skill the database would never reach first base-the adminstrator. Here, experience in managing large dictionary projects is highly relevant. The administration of the LDB project must be of the highest order, demanding skills in decision making, large-scale project planning and management, personnel management, compilation monitoring, data control, and all the other tasks on which the success of the project will depend.

3. ACQUISITION OF LEXICAL DATA: METHODOLOGY

Large projects pose large problems. The burden of administration, personnel management and finance beyond a certain point seems to work actively against the success of large projects. On the other hand, building the LDB envisaged here cannot be done without a cooperative effort involving many people. A methodology must be devised to use the talents and abilities of these people without creating a top-heavy project doomed to self-destruct.

It would seem unwise to place in one single location the large group of specialists required, or to plan a multi-institution, multisite undertaking. A better way to build this resource might be to locate the core of the project at one center, and include at specific points in the workflow specific contributions from the theoretical linguists and other experts who would work in their own institutions and meet for discussion when necessary.

There would have to be a core team of lexicographers, but not with the task of compiling this ambitious database from scratch. To do that would require literally scores, perhaps hundreds, of lexicographers. Their task should rather be to integrate into the database data acquired from outside sources, to control the quality of such data, and to supplement it in the areas for which there is no external source of supply. In order to populate the database, we should be looking to the people who already own large amounts of lexical data, that is to say to the publishing houses.

3.1. The Publishers' Dilemma

Before eyebrows are raised at the idea of commissioning lexical data from publishers, it is appropriate to consider three important factors in the current situation that suggest that the development of large-scale lexical resources may both profit from and serve to correct an unfortunate phenomenon in dictionary publishing today.

First, dictionary publishers with the expertise and resources to improve the quality of their books have little commercial incentive to do so. Original research is highly labor intensive, and market forces hold the price of dictionaries too low to allow such research unless other marketing pressures come into play (for instance, a need to extend one's range of titles on the bookseller's shelves or to beat a high-quality competitor). A new dictionary must match the selling price of its competitors, even if the latter are simple reprints of a text that has existed for 50 years or more (there are many such instances). If one were held to cutting one's coat according to one's cloth there would be virtually no original lexicographical research done within publishing houses.

Second, and paradoxically, the lexical material contained in published dictionaries is a fraction of the data developed within publishing houses, though much of this is ephemeral at present. Most dictionaries are still compiled by an age-old method of lexicography that rejects, often because of space constraints, much of what the compiler knows about the word at the point of writing the dictionary entry. With increasingly computerized methods, including electronic text sources and online compiling, the material rejected for human-user dictionaries may be salvaged for computer-user dictionaries, and indeed for LDBs.

Third, the electronically accessed dictionaries of the future will impose no such space constraints on the editors. Online dictionaries will rapidly outgrow the lexical resources at present available to their publishers. When a dictionary could produce at the touch of a key 20 citations of a word in one particular sense, or a listing of near synonyms in disambiguating contexts, then machine-readable versions of paper dictionaries will not be good enough. Larger dictionaries will require larger data resources. At present publishers simply cannot invest enough to produce these resources.

3.2. Shared Needs and Shared Resources

Like the dictionaries of the future, a lexical database of the type we are discussing here also requires large-scale data resources. Those with common needs must in some way supply their common needs by a collaborative effort.

In the U.K., raw text in electronic form has come to be regarded as a precompetitive resource by some publishers, who are currently collaborating to create an electronic text library for public use. This body of text, known as the British National Corpus, is being developed by a consortium led by Oxford University Press, and comprising publishers, two universities, and a national organization, the British Library. The project is partially funded by the British government.

However, publishing houses cannot, and indeed must not, cooperate beyond the limits of commercial competition. Dictionary publishers, willing to share with their competitors electronic sources of lexical evidence, would rightly be unwilling to share the structured body of lexical data from which dictionaries are drawn. LDBs are unlikely to be considered by dictionary publishers as precompetitive, at least not in the immediate future, and getting one publisher to build the database is not a viable option, for no single publisher has the resources to carry out such an ambitious project.

Nonetheless, publishers' expertise in the collection of lexical data must be used in the development of the large-scale LDB needed for NLP research. It seems reasonable to suggest that once the LDB project has acquired access to the very large corpus of electronic texts on which its account of the language is to be based, and has developed its prototype lexicographical workstations and designed its entry structure, then it should commission from publishers the data it needs to populate its database.

3.3. Data Commissioning: Specification and Tendering

As with any commercial call for tenders, an exact specification of the required product must be given. Such a specification for lexical data might be something along the lines of "a listing of the complementation of nouns within a named frequency band together with the relative frequencies of occurrence of the complementation structures" (the data shown earlier on the complementation of the noun RISK, point 4, would be relevant here); or again, "a list of the words (tokens) that occur in the frequency band of 0.2 to 1.5 instances per million words, in a 'balanced'[4] corpus of 1,000 million words at minimum, together with IPA transcriptions for each in British and American English." Publishers in a position to supply such data would then tender for the supply of the data specified.

As is also the case with any commercial call for tenders, the price of the product must adequately recompense the supplier. There is a tendency amongst national and international funding bodies, and the research institutions dependent on them, to believe that a rich market for NLP applications is just around the corner, and that consequently publishers and other language industries will at any moment be motivated to fund large-scale NLP research. However, publishers are reluctant to invest in NLP applications. Their perceived market is still

[4]By "balanced corpus" is meant a body of electronic text that has been carefully designed with the objective of supplying representative lexical data for a specific purpose, in this case that of building a lexical database for NLP research. Establishing what this term implies in the way of corpus design criteria is the subject of current work both within and outside the British National Corpus initiative.

that of paper dictionaries. It is vain for the NLP community to look to publishers for research funding on the scale they need. That is the responsibility of national and international funding agencies. Nor is it fair to see the publisher as a potential benefactor distributing lexical largesse to the research community. This may be an attractive vision for researchers, but it is considered at best unrealistic and at worst suicidal by the publishers themselves.

The interests of publishers and LDB developers could however coincide to the benefit of both. Take for instance the second of the data specifications outlined earlier. A publisher who had assembled for a new dictionary a list of the lemmas in the specified frequency band, with British IPA transcriptions for these words, might very well think it worthwhile to increase the publishing database (and hence future publishing potential) in order to include the American IPA transcriptions, if revenue from the sale of this data to the NLP database were available to offset the additional cost. As a result, not only would the database acquire the data it needed, but a tangible improvement would be wrought in the publishers' own resources, and hence in their dictionaries, both paper and (eventually) electronic.

Although this is not the place to expand on data specification for the population of an NLP database, one point must be clarified before the topic is closed. Much lexical data relates not to the lemma but to one sense of a lemma. For instance, the word *check* in English has many complementation patterns, severally associated with specific dictionary senses. Thus in the *Concise Oxford Dictionary* (1990) we find sense 1b defined as "make sure; verify; establish to one's satisfaction," and exemplified by "checked that the doors were locked," whereas sense 2a is defined as "stop or slow the motion of; curb or restrain," and exemplified by "progress was checked by bad weather." A database for NLP research must hold, for the complementation of the lemma CHECK, more than a flat listing that includes both NP as direct object complement (valid for 1b and 2a) and sentential object complement (1b only). On the other hand, semantic analysis can certainly not yet be said to be objective. Dictionaries vary in the way they handle meaning, and often corpus evidence seems to support incompatible semantic analyses (Atkins, 1991). We do not yet know how to specify objective semantic data.

This should not, however, stop us from developing the rest of the LDB. Specifications for complementation data, ignoring for the moment semantic analysis, might instead call for details of syntactic structures together with a list of the actual words (types) that, in the source corpus, instantiate these (as in point 4 of the RISK data examples given earlier). This would provide a comprehensive body of structured data to feed into linguistic research for analysis by lexical tools. Vital to the development of these tools are the taxonomies and other lexical relationships extracted from existing MRDs (Boguraev, 1989, 1991; Byrd, 1989; Byrd et al., 1987; Calzolari & Picchi, 1988; Chodorow, Byrd, & Heidorn, 1985; Klavans, in press) and the stochastic routines being developed to operate on raw text (Church, Gale, Hanks, & Hindle, 1992; Church, Gale, Hanks, Hindle, & Moon, 1991; Church & Hanks, 1990). In the case of the verb RISK, extrapolation from the data shown in point 4 by means of such tools might show that this verb in active sentences requires, or at least prefers, a +HUMAN marking on its surface subjects.

3.4. Standards and Quality Assurance

Standards must be devised to ensure data compatibility, ideally both within the LDB and among LDBs of many languages. Quality targets must also be defined, to ensure that the data, whether compiled internally or commissioned from external sources, is consistently reliable. These controls must relate principally to the accuracy and comprehensiveness of the material supplied. If, as suggested earlier, the LDB is to be populated solely by objective data, and if part of the definition of objective is "validated by corpus statistics," then the body of electronic texts from which an individual supplier's data is drawn must also conform to certain quality specifications.

It is therefore incumbent on the research community to devise the necessary standards and to ensure that the data in its LDB is representative of the language as a whole, or of the particular subset of that language being recorded at the time. The community must therefore also consider standards for and quality control of corpus design and construction. It is perhaps worth noting that, whether or not it is decided to buy data from external suppliers, the work of harmonizing and quality controlling must still be carried out.

4. CONCLUSION

The quality of the database depends on the quality of the sources of the data with which it is populated. It also depends on the soundness of the theoretical basis of the LDB design, in particular on the criteria established by the theoretical linguists for the various types of lexical data being collated. Such a database cannot be constructed without active participation from the lexicographical community, equipped with powerful workstations, resulting from the cooperation of theorists and practicians from many disciplines. Existing MRDs have a crucial role to play in the development of sophisticated lexical tools but are inadequate as a reliable source of lexical data. Their contents may be used provisionally to populate the database, but if the definition of valid data is based on corpus evidence, then this initial data from MRDs can be only provisional.

Lastly, such an ambitious project cannot be successfully carried out in a vacuum. Publishers have an interest in developing larger and more exact databases from which to construct the more complex dictionaries that online access will require them to supply, but cannot afford the investment that such resources will demand. Developers of large-scale lexical databases have the same needs as the publishers, though multiplied a hundredfold. The time has come for these two contributors to NLP infrastructure to devise collaborative methods of database building that will be to their mutual advantage.

The so-called language industries will, in my view, never have the commercial incentive to construct a sophisticated LDB of the quality and comprehensiveness needed for natural language processing. For this, funding is certainly required at the national or international level. For publishers, LDBs cannot be considered a precompetitive resource, and they cannot therefore offset by cooperation the huge expense involved. However, for political institutions (such as the EC or individual governments) or industrial concerns, LDBs are a precompetitive resource. Reinventing the wheel is a waste of time and money. A single dynamic, reliable, polytheoretical, multifunctional, multipurpose LDB for English should, if it lives up to that description, meet the basic needs of all researchers and provide a launchpad for all English language NLP. Collaboration-between scholars and industrial researchers, between commercial and national funding institutions, and between nations who need the data-will provide the means to achieve that end.

PART II

CONSTRUCTING A MTD FROM LDOCE

Cheng-ming Guo
Computer Science Department
Tsinghua University

CHAPTER 16

INTRODUCTION

Part II of this book presents a detailed account of the author's own attempt at constructing a MTD from a MRD, specifically LDOCE. The research adopted a compositional-reduction approach to obtain a formalized set of definitions of sense entries in a nested predicate form, where all definitions are given in terms of a set of seed senses, to be defined in Section 4. This attempt, then, is a Fregean compositional formalization of LDOCE.

Part II consists of six chapters, 16-21. This chapter presents an overview of the attempt: the nature of the work, its theoretical assumptions, information about the source dictionary LDOCE, and an outline of the processes of constructing an MTD from LDOCE. Chapter 17 looks at previous work done in related research on MRDs. It also discusses other related research, such as studies on semantic primitives and machine learning. Detailed descriptions of the construction processes are presented in Chapter 18. Chapter 19 focuses on one particular aspect of the construction process and presents a microscopic view of the bootstrapping process; that is, the last step of the construction process. A summary of my work is given in Chapter 20, and Chapter 21 contains the conclusion of the book.

1. NATURE OF THE WORK

The nature of the work is interdisciplinary, with emphasis laid on its computational content rather than psychological claims. The work draws on insights from several subject areas-linguistics, psychology, and artificial intelligence (AI) research. The work inherits the computational tradition of preference semantics (Wilks, 1972) in AI and NLP. It is anchored largely in the spirit of cognitive grammar, or space grammar (Langacker, 1974, 1975, 1976, 1978, 1979, 1982; Langacker & Munro, 1975), as it was formerly named. An important theme that runs through the entire discussion is that of learning, especially of machine learning of semantic preference information from LDOCE sense definitions. The work also benefited from earlier research on dictionaries, particularly the work of Sparck Jones (1964, 1967), Amsler (1980, 1984), and that of Boguraev (1986).

2. THEORETICAL ASSUMPTIONS

Essential to the learning of new concepts, new rules, and new domain theories by machine is the existence of a set of hierarchically arranged primitives (Dietterich & Michalski, 1981; Winston, 1975). Here such primitives take the form of semantic primitives (Wilks, 1972, 1977) in a machine learning system that acquires semantic preference information from dictionary sense definitions. Two alternative approaches to the development of a set of semantic primitives exist-the *prescriptive* approach and the *descriptive* approach. In the prescriptive approach, a set of primitives is defined, or *prescribed,* prior to or in the course of designing and developing a system. An example of a prescribed set of semantic primitives is the set of semantic features used as box codes in the electronic version of LDOCE. The descriptive approach (Wilks, 1977, p. 198), on the other hand, allows a natural set of semantic primitives to be derived from a natural source of data such as a dictionary. The set of seed senses mentioned earlier will be identified as such a natural set of semantic primitives to be derived from LDOCE in the *descriptive* approach.

Although the theoretical implications and computational consequences of such a natural set of semantic primitives are difficult to ascertain at this point, these primitives can be compared with the formalized language of pure thought that Gottlieb Frege called the *Begriffsschrift* (Frege, 1960). Frege's system was modeled on the language of arithmetic, such that every thought is composed of the primitive ideas represented by the primitive signs of the *Begriffsschrift*. The natural set of semantic primitives to be derived from LDOCE is itself part of the natural language people use to communicate thought. In terms of compositionality, the two bear a striking resemblance, because every word in LDOCE can be explained as, or is composed of, a sequence of semantic primitives derived from the dictionary. Although any AI system is Fregean in a similar sense, the system primitives in AI systems may not necessarily be all derived from natural data in the descriptive approach.

The fundamental theoretical assumptions underlying the derivation of a natural set of semantic primitives from LDOCE share much in common with the theories of cognitive grammar (Langacker, 1982), namely:

1. Although any interestingly strong version of the Whorfian hypothesis, which essentially claims that language determines thought, is dubious, it is undeniably true that languages embody divergent codifications of conceived reality.
2. The putative difference between linguistic and extralinguistic knowledge, or between a dictionary-type account of the meaning of lexical items and an essentially encyclopedic account, is illusory.

Point 1 necessitates the derivation of different sets of semantic primitives for different languages. A natural consequence of point 2 concerns an understanding that language and knowledge are ultimately inseparable.

3. THE LDOCE DICTIONARY

LDOCE is a full-sized dictionary designed for learners of English as a second language containing over 55,000 entries in normal book form and 41,100 entries in machine-readable form (a typesetting tape). An *entry* is defined as a collection of one or more sense definitions that ends at the next head. The *head* is the word, phrase, or hyphenated word defined by an entry. A single word can be the head of more than one entry if homographs or different parts of speech exist for that word. A *sense definition* is a set of definitions, examples and other text associated with one sense of a head. If an entry includes more than one sense definition, then each sense definition will have a number.

The preparers of LDOCE claim that entries are defined using a *"controlled vocabulary"* of about 2,000 words and that the entries have a simple and regular syntax.

Table 16.1 shows some basic data derived from Plate's analysis (Wilks et al., 1988) of the machine-readable tape of LDOCE (because of a tape error, words that follow alphabetically after "zone" have not been analyzed). The figure of a 2,166-word controlled vocabulary is arrived at as follows. The list of controlled vocabulary given in LDOCE contains 2,219 items. Among them 58 are prefixes and suffixes. Thirty-five other words from the list did not have heads. These are all removed. Furthermore, the analysis shows that some words are not part of the controlled vocabulary yet are used frequently in definitions, for example, the word *aircraft* is not part of the controlled vocabulary yet it is used 267 times in sense definitions. About 30 such words have been added to the list of controlled vocabulary words, giving a total of 2,166.

It is interesting to note from Table 16.1 that the number of senses for words belonging to the controlled vocabulary is extremely high. Although there are only about 2,166 words in the controlled vocabulary, over 24,000 of the 74,000 senses defined in LDOCE are senses of these words (including senses of phrases beginning with a word from the controlled vocabulary). To put this another way, members of the controlled vocabulary are roughly six times as ambiguous as those of the noncontrolled vocabulary. Each controlled vocabulary word has about 12 senses, whereas each noncontrolled vocabulary word has approximately two. The book and tape versions of LDOCE both use a grammatical code of about 110 syntactic categories that vary in generality from noun to noun/count to noun/count/followed-by-infinitive-with-TO.

The machine-readable version of LDOCE also contains box and subject codes that are not found in the book. The box codes use a special set of prescribed primitives such as "abstract," "concrete," and "animate," organized into a type hierarchy. The primitives are used to assign type restrictions on nouns and adjectives, and type restrictions on the arguments of verbs.

The subject codes use another special set of primitives organized into a hierarchy. This hierarchy consists of main headings such as *engineering* and subheadings like electric*al*. The primitives are used to classify words by their subject, for example, one sense of *current* is classified as *geography: geology* whereas another sense is marked *engineering/electrical*.

4. VOCABULARY TYPES IN LDOCE

Important to this study is a four-way distinction applied to all words and word senses contained in LDOCE. Each of these types of words and

TABLE 16.1. Head Counts for Words, Entries, and Senses in LDOCE

Heads	*Words*	*Entries*	*Sense Definitions*
Controlled Vocabulary	2,166	8,413	24,115
Noncontolled Vocabulary	25,592	32,687	49,998
Totals	27,758	41,100	74,113

word senses is a subset of the next set of words and word senses given below. These four types are: (a) *LDOCE words* and LDOCE senses, (b) *controlled words* and controlled senses, (c) *defining words* and defining senses, (d) *seed words* and *seed senses*. They are defined as follows:

- Any word contained in LDOCE is a *LDOCE word*. Any word sense of any LDOCE word is a *LDOCE sense*.
- Controlled words are words from the list of the controlled vocabulary given at the back of the LDOCE dictionary. All the word senses of the controlled words defined in LDOCE are *controlled senses*.
- Defining words are words that are used to define the meanings of all the controlled words in their sense definitions. Note that not every controlled word is used in the definitions of the meanings of other *controlled words*. *Defining senses* are individual word senses of the *defining words* that are used in the definitions of the meanings of the *controlled words*.
- *Seed senses* are natural semantic primitives to be derived from this work on the dictionary. The words that the seed senses are senses of are called the *seed words*.

The subset relationships that exist between these four types of words and word senses are shown schematically in Figure 16.2.

5. OVERVIEW OF THE CONSTRUCTION PROCESSES

The construction of the MTD consists of two main processes: the process of *reduction* and the process of *composition*. Each process consists of two subprocesses. The reduction process involves the determination of the defining senses and the derivation of the seed senses. The compositional process, on the other hand, involves a process of machine learning with the natural set of semantic primitives; that is, the seed senses, obtained through the reduction process to compose formalized sense entries of the MTD called the Fregean Formulae or *FFs* for short. An example of an FF is given in Section 5.2.1.

5.1. The Reduction Process

The reduction process proceeds in two steps. Step 1 involves the determination of the defining senses of LDOCE. Step 2 involves the derivation of the seed senses of LDOCE.

The first step is determining the defining senses of LDOCE; that is, those word senses that are used in the definition of the meanings of 2,137 controlled words of LDOCE (note that the 2,137-word set does not include the 30 or so words like *aircraft* that are added to the controlled vocabulary list). The set of words which the defining senses are senses of constitutes the set of defining words of the dictionary. As mentioned earlier, defining words are a subset of controlled words in LDOCE. There are 2,000 defining words in LDOCE.

The input to Step 1 of the reduction process is a collection of some 17,000 LDOCE sense definitions of the controlled words of LDOCE in single-head entries. The output of this subprocess is the set of determined defining senses of LDOCE. For the lack of more efficient algorithms, human judgment was used to determine which word senses of each controlled word of LDOCE are used in these 17,000 sense definitions. This subprocess produced a set of some 3,800 defining senses of LDOCE.

The second step is deriving the seed senses of LDOCE; that is, a subset of the defining senses of LDOCE, which are sufficient to define the set of defining senses in Step 1. There are 3,280 seed senses in LDOCE. The words that the seed senses are senses of constitute the set of seed words of the dictionary, and there are 1,433 seed words in LDOCE.

The general strategy used in the derivation of the seed senses of LDOCE is first to derive the seed words of LDOCE. Once the seed words are derived, their defining senses, known from Step 1 of the reduction process, automatically become the seed senses of LDOCE.

Another strategy used in the derivation of the seed senses of LDOCE is the use of a hypothesized set, also called the *hunch set*, of seed words of LDOCE. The initial hunch set of seed words contains all defining words with multiple defining senses and a subset of defining words with single defining senses. If the hunch set of seed words is found sufficient to define the meanings of the defining senses of LDOCE, its status of being the confirmed set of seed words of LDOCE is established. The defining senses of these confirmed seed words are then taken as the seed senses of LDOCE.

One more strategy used in the derivation of the seed senses of LDOCE is to allow the use of defining cycles. A defining cycle refers to the process of one group of words defining another group of words, resulting in the second group of words being defined. At each defining cycle, some new words; that is, words outside the hunch set, are defined. These newly defined words join with the hunch set to define more new words at the next defining cycle. The maximum allowable number of defining cycles for the defining senses is three. This means that the seed words must be able to define all the meanings of the defining senses of LDOCE within three defining cycles.

There is a tradeoff between the size of the hunch set of seed words and the number of defining cycles used by the seed words to define all the meanings of the defining senses of LDOCE. The bigger the size of the hunch set, the less the number of defining cycles needed.

A program was written to obtain newly defined words at each defining cycle. The program uses a reference file that initially consists of the hunch set of seed words only. The input to the program consists of the definition text of all the defining senses of LDOCE. Part of the output of the program is a list of defined words. The reference file expands as newly defined words at each defining cycle join with the hunch set of seed words to define more words at the next cycle. If, at the end of the third cycle, the list of defined words coincides with the list of defining words of LDOCE, the hypothesized set of seed words is confirmed. The defining senses of the confirmed seed words become the seed senses of LDOCE. If, on the contrary, some defining words remain undefined at the end of the third cycle, the hunch set of seed words is revised. The details of the revision process are presented in Chapter 5. After the hunch set is revised, the program uses the revised hunch set as the initial reference file to start the first defining cycle again. The process repeats until the hunch set of seed words is confirmed. The seed senses thus generated become the natural set of semantic primitives to be applied to the compositional process of constructing the MTD to be described in what follows.

5.2. The Compositional Process

The goal of the compositional process involves the reformulation of LDOCE sense definitions into FFs. If we could liken the MTD to a forest, each FF would be a tree in the forest. These trees of FFs grow out of the seed, or the primitives, generated through the reduction process. These seeds grow into trees in the sense that the seeds assist the parsing of the sense definitions into parse trees. Each FF contains the parse tree of the definition text of the word sense being defined. In fact the compositional process of constructing a MTD from LDOCE is essentially a process of machine learning with seed senses as primitives. The details of the compositional process are presented in Chapters 4 and 5 although an overview is given later after a discussion on FFs.

5.2.1. The FFs. A FF constitutes an MTD definition of a word sense. It takes the form of a two-place predicate where the first argument is a word sense being defined and the second is a parse tree of its sense definition. Hanging at each terminal symbol of the parse tree is a primitive, or another FF in the case of a nonprimitive leaf. Terminal symbols used in the parser are *n* (noun), *pron* (pronoun), *v* (verb), *adj* (adjective), *adv* (adverb), and so forth. The following is an example. The word-sense definition of a medical doctor as given in LDOCE is:

A person whose profession is to attend to sick people or animals.

The FF for the word sense is shown in Figure 16.1.

Although most terminal symbols on the parse tree have primitives as their leaves, three of them do not. They are "whose2," "whom1," and "attend_to1." Note that in the definition of "whose2," which is "of1 whom1," another nonprimitive leaf "whom1" is encountered. In this case the FF of "whom1" is embedded in the FF of "whose2" in the same way the FF of "whose2" is embedded in the FF of "doctor2."

Two claims are being made about the FFs. First, an FF is an integrated form of representation of both linguistic and world knowledge information about a word sense. In the aforementioned example, if we got rid of all the embedded FFs (those for "whose2," "whom1," and "attend_to1"), and stripped off all the numbers attached at the end of each word sense on the parse tree, we would recover a sense definition as given in an ordinary dictionary.

The FF also contains implicit semantic preference information in the representation. In fact, semantic preference relations exist between many of the word senses in the FF. Three types of semantic preference relations are identified within one FF:

Type A: That between the first argument of the FF (doctor2 in the previous example) and the head of each of the major constituents of the FF. A constituent is a syntactic member of a sentence such as np (noun phrase) or vp (verb phrase). The following is some Type A semantic preference information implicitly contained in the FF.

prefer(doctor2, person1, 1).

prefer(doctor2, profession1, 1).

prefer(doctor2, attend_to1, 1).

Note that the third argument "1" indicates both semantic preference relationship between the two word senses and the truth condition of the relationship. For example, prefer(doctor2, person1, 1) means that the two word senses, "doctor2" and "person1," prefer each other in terms of semantic matching between word senses, and that it is true that a medical doctor is a person.

Type B: That between heads of major constituents in the second argument of the FF. The following are some examples:

prefer(person1, attend_to1, 1).

prefer(profession1, attend_to1, 1).

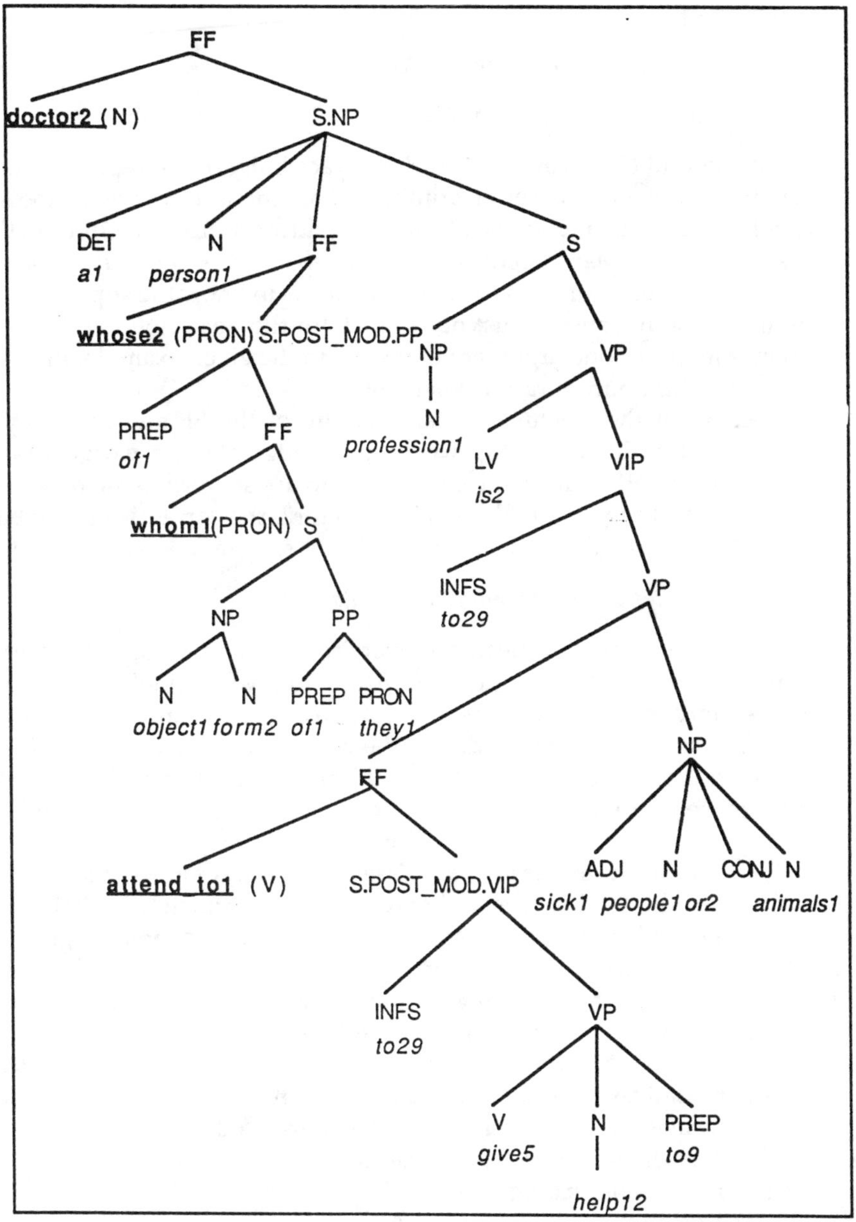

Figure 16.1. An example of an FF

Type C: That within each major constituent, for example, within the vp of the FF:

prefer(attend_to1, people1, 1).

prefer(attend_to1, animal1, 1).

The second claim concerns machine tractability of the representation. On the one hand, the set of primitives hanging at terminal symbols of the FFs are finite and known from the reduction process. On the other hand, the two-place predicate and the parse tree facilitate machine tractability. For example if the machine needs to know the superordinate term of a noun sense, it just has to look for the head noun of the noun phrase in the second argument of the FF. In the given example, the head noun for the noun phrase is "person1."

Because of the machine-tractable nature of the FF and its ability to integrate both linguistic and world knowledge about a word sense in one representation, it can be easily used to assist word-sense disambiguation in NLP. In fact, with the FF of doctor2, the correct senses of both *doctor* and *attend to* can be chosen correctly for the following sentence:

The doctor attends to animals every day.

The word *doctor* can mean a university doctor or a hospital doctor-a PhD or an MD. "Attend_to" can mean "to give help to" or "to direct one's effort and interest to" as in " I have an urgent matter to attend to." In the absence of counterevidence, the parser would select "doctor2" for doctor and attend_to1 for "attend_to" because of the implicit semantic preference information.

5.2.2. From primitives to FFs. Essentially, the compositional process starts with the seed senses and ends with approximately 74,000 FFs of the MTD, with each FF corresponding to a sense definition given in LDOCE. The process proceeds in two steps.

The first step is hand-coding the initial knowledge base for the natural set of semantic primitives derived from LDOCE.

Two alternative methods exist to hand-code the initial knowledge base for the primitives. *Alternative 1* uses a program to elicit semantic preference information from a native speaker informant concerning $n(n-1)/2$ pairs of primitives. For each pair of primitives, the informant will respond "yes" or "no" concerning a semantic preference relation that possibly exists between the two primitives. All positive responses lead to explicit semantic preference information stored in the knowledge base. One obvious drawback of this method is that it is both time consuming and labor intensive. If it took the informant 3 seconds to accomplish one response, the entire project would take about 3 years. However, if compared with the pure hand-coding approach that attempts to hand-code an entire encyclopedia in a period of 10 years using a group of about 30 experts, the hand-coding effort involved in this project would be dwarfed. *Alternative* 2 involves hand-coding the least amount of semantic preference information into the initial knowledge base to start the parsing of LDOCE sense definitions. The goal of this method is only to provide required semantic preference information for the parsing of a collection of sense definition texts and no more. The idea is for the system to acquire as much semantic preference information as it can to avoid hand-coding as much as possible. Both alternatives are tried in this study. Further discussions on hand-coding are presented in Chapter 18.

The second step is bootstrapping from the initial hand-coded knowledge base by parsing LDOCE sense definitions and acquiring semantic preference information from the parse trees.

The main operation of the compositional process involves parsing LDOCE sense definitions into parse trees. These parse trees replace the original LDOCE sense definition of the word sense. The revised sense definitions are stored in the lexical base of the MTD. The purpose of parsing LDOCE sense definitions is twofold. On the one hand, each parse tree produced for the definition of each word sense constitutes an important component of the FF for that word sense. On the other hand, new preference information can be acquired from the parse trees to enable more sense definitions to be parsed later in the bootstrapping process. For examples of acquired semantic preference information, see the previous examples of three types of semantic preference information implicitly contained on the parse tree of the FF for doctor2. In fact the implicit semantic preference information on a parse tree is made explicit through a process of knowledge acquisition during bootstrapping. The explicit semantic preference information in the form of *prefer(wordsense1, wordsense2, 1)* is stored in the knowledge base of the MTD. The lexical and knowledge bases constitute an intermediate or working form of the MTD. Once the FFs of the MTD are constructed, the lexical as well as the knowledge base of the MTD can be discarded.

The relation between Steps 1 and 2 of the compositional process is an important one. Initially both the lexical base and the knowledge base of the MTD are empty. An empty knowledge base is, of course, detrimental to the parsing of sense definitions, because the parser would have no way to disambiguate multiple word senses. In order to prepare the system for parsing LDOCE sense definitions, semantic preference information concerning the primitives is hand-coded into the knowledge base. After the initial hand-coded knowledge base is constructed, the bootstrapping process follows.

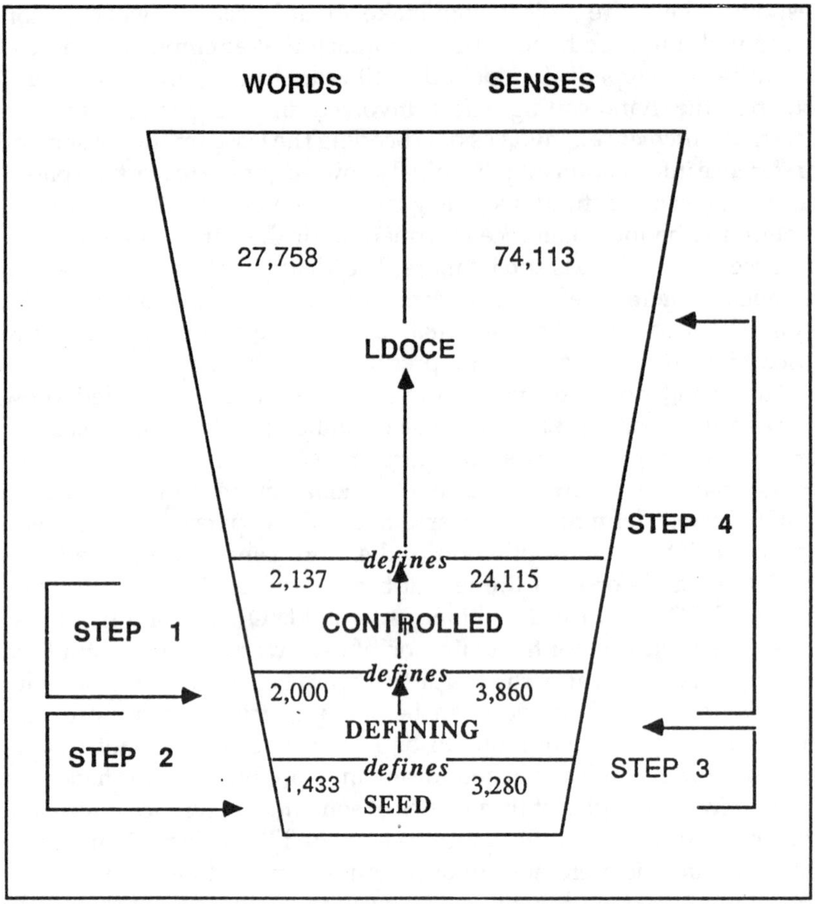

Figure 16.2. Schematic representation of the project

Step 1 of the construction process has been completed. A total of 3,860 defining senses have been determined. Step 2 of the construction process has also been completed. A total of 3,280 word senses are found to be the seed senses of LDOCE. These seed senses are taken as a natural set of semantic primitives derived from the dictionary. The feasibility of Steps 3 and 4 of the construction process have been demonstrated with implemented examples. What remains to be accomplished is to complete Steps 3 and 4 to build a full-size MTD from LDOCE using as guidelines the results of initial implementation of the two steps. A schematic representation of the 4-step construction process is shown in Figure 16.2.

CHAPTER 17

PREVIOUS WORK

This chapter reviews relevant work from three related areas: (a) the study of MRDs, (b) the literature on semantic primitives, and (c) the research on human and machine learning.

1. THE STUDY OF MRDS

Three excellent surveys have been written in the area of MRD research, one by Amsler (1984), one by Boguraev (1986), and most recently one by Evens (1989).

The body of work on MRDs could be approached in several ways. We could either look at each MRD research center and see what MRD-related research has been, and is being done. We could also look at the theoretical issues involved in MRDs, or we could set up useful dimensions and examine individual studies in the light of each of these dimensions. Most of these approaches have been adopted by previous surveys. To avoid redundancy, the emphasis of this review is on the extraction of information from MRDs.

Most MRDs contain at least the following four types of information: phonological, morphological, syntactic, and semantic. Roughly speaking, the first three types of information belong to lexical properties, and the last lexical meaning (Boguraev, 1986). More often than not, information concerning lexical properties is coded explicitly in MRDs. Retrieving such information does not present much difficulty. The more interesting problem in information extraction from MRDs involves extracting information concerning lexical meaning. The focus of this review is on the extraction of semantic information from MRDs.

Research on the extraction of semantic information from MRDs has had two active areas: the extraction of semantic hierarchies of genus terms and the determination and the use of defining patterns found in dictionary definitions.

1.1. Semantic Hierarchies

In the mid-1970s, Amsler became interested in the construction of a complete lexical classification of the English language based on the content of an MRD. While working with White at the University of Texas at Austin, he supervised the complete semantic disambiguation of all the head nouns and verbs in the definitions of nouns and verbs from the MRD (Amsler & White, 1979). This work was performed by manually disambiguating specially created concordance output containing all the definition texts indexed by their nouns and verbs. The information of nouns and verbs was then assembled into two gigantic data structures to form two taxonomic-like semantic networks. Amsler (1980) demonstrated that additional structures could be imposed on a dictionary by making certain assumptions about the ways dictionary definitions are constructed. Among these assumptions is that definitions consist of a genus term, which identifies the superordinate concept of the defined word and a differentia that distinguishes this instance of the superordinate category from other instances. Amsler's work presents conclusive evidence that a dictionary contains a nontrivial amount of information that can be semiautomatically structured into a semantic hierarchy of defining concepts.

Following Amsler (1980), Chodorow et al. (1985) created procedures to automate the genus extraction and disambiguation processes. Two head-finding heuristics were found: sprouting and filtering. The sprouting procedure works interactively with the user. It uses the results of a head-finding procedure as raw material. For each new word, all of its hyponyms are added to a tree that keeps sprouting until no further words are found to be added to the tree. The filtering procedure also works interactively with the user. The output of the procedure is a list of words bearing a certain property (e.g., [+ human]). The work represents an attempt to explore ways of easing the construction of a large lexicon for systems capable of processing unrestricted English input.

Similar efforts to automate the locating of superordinates (genus term extraction) without having to invoke a full-scale natural language analyzer include Ahlswede (1983), Cowie (1983), Calzolari (1984), Alshawi, Boguraev, and Briscoe (1985), and Alshawi (1987). A unique feature of Alshawi et al. (1985) is that they have taken advantage of the 2,000-word restricted definition vocabulary used in LDOCE. "This largely disposes of the need for genus terms disambiguation and has made it possible to parse the LDOCE definition of a word sense in the restricted vocabulary" (Boguraev, 1986, p.17).

An important issue related to the extraction of semantic hierarchies of the genus terms is the extraction of a minimum set of semantic primitives from a monolingual dictionary. The role of semantic primitives in natural language processing was demonstrated by Wilks (1972). Good and bad arguments about them are discussed extensively in Wilks (1977). Recourse to using ordinary dictionary definitions as a source of material for the enumeration of semantic primitives received little attention until Amsler (1980). He suggested a technique for identifying semantic primitives from his hand-disambiguated tangled hierarchies of English nouns and verbs obtained from the MPD definitions (p. 97). Detailed discussion on semantic primitives is given in the next section.

Three recent projects in this area have been reported. They are Guthrie, Slator, Wilks, and Bruce (1990), Copestake (1990), and Vossen (1991). Guthrie et al. (1990) described a heuristic procedure that automatically locates genus terms for nouns in LDOCE with the help of LDOCE semantic category codes and subject codes. Copestake (1990) described how taxonomical information is obtained from LDOCE semi-automatically by the use of a parser. The emphasis of the study was on using the constructed taxonomy to structure a lexical knowledge base based on the notion of default inheritance. Both Guthrie et al. (1990) and Copestake (1990) represent the continuation of early efforts in constructing semantic hierarchies from dictionary definitions.

Vossen (1991) compares taxonomies constructed from Dutch and English monolingual dictionaries. The research represents part of the effort to construct a common multilingual knowledge base using taxonomical information extracted independently from monolingual dictionaries of English, Dutch, Italian, and Spanish. In order to build such a multilingual knowledge base, individual taxonomies derived from the individual monolingual dictionaries have to be mapped onto each other. Vossen (1991) uses a Dutch-English bilingual dictionary as a bridge to realize the mapping. For example,

Dutch		*English*
middle < means>	< – >	substance
genotmiddle < stimulant >		
chocolade	< – >	chocolate

Chocolade is the Dutch equivalent of the English *chocolate*. Going up the hierarchy from *chocolade* in Dutch, we first hit *genotmiddle* and then *middle,* whereas on the English side, the word *chocolate* belongs directly to *substance.* Hence the English chocolate-to-substance hierarchy can be mapped onto the Dutch chocolade-genotmiddle-middle hierarchy.

Vossen (1991) used three dictionaries: the Van Dale Dutch monolingual dictionary, the LDOCE monolingual dictionary, and the Van Dale Dutch-English bilingual dictionary. He compared the taxonomical information extracted from the Van Dale Dutch monolingual with that extracted from LDOCE, using the Van Dale Dutch-English dictionary as the bridge.

In order to do the mapping, Vossen had to compare two pairs of word lists-one Dutch pair and one English pair. One of the two Dutch word lists comes from the Dutch monolingual dictionary, and the other from the Van Dale Dutch-English bilingual. One of the two English word lists comes from LDOCE, and the other comes from the Van Dale Dutch-English bilingual dictionary. What is interesting about comparing the two English word lists was that only 60% of the words in LDOCE found a match in the English translation of the Dutch words in the Van Dale Dutch-English bilingual dictionary, and only 28% of the English translation of the Van Dale bilingual found matches in the LDOCE word list.

Vossen (1991) compared the taxonomies of *substances* extracted from the Van Dale Dutch monolingual dictionary and from LDOCE, respectively. Figure 17.1 and Figure 17.2 show examples of both equivalent partial taxonomies and nonequivalent partial taxonomies concerning substances based on the definitions in the Dutch Van Dale monolingual dictionary.

Although the hierarchy as shown in Figure 17.1 cannot be identical to the English taxonomy of *substances* extracted from LDOCE (e.g., *tear* in English is *liquid,* not necessarily *eye liquid*), these words more or less end up in a similar classification scheme as their English equivalents. It is interesting to note that in Dutch there is no such term as *chemical* so that *silicone* belongs directly to *substance.*

As can be seen from this, not all LDOCE *substances* end up in the *substantie-stof* node in the Van Dale taxonomy. All the words here are either directly or via some intermediate node related to the word *middel* (equivalent to the English *means*), which is defined as "anything that can be used to achieve a goal."

The comparison of semantic hierarchies obtained from monolingual dictionaries of various languages is a fairly recent phenomenon. Further studies in this area should give a better understanding of how to correctly handle differences in the semantic structures of different languages. It may have profound significance as to what can be done to avoid cultural chauvinism in our design of multilingual MTDs.

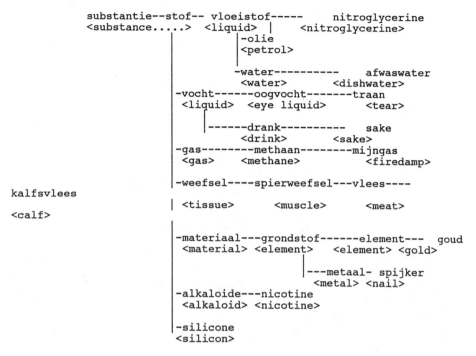

```
substantie--stof-- vloeistof-----      nitroglycerine
<substance.....>  <liquid>  |     <nitroglycerine>
               |            |-olie
               |            |<petrol>
               |            |
               |            -water----------     afwaswater
               |             <water>        <dishwater>
               |-vocht------oogvocht-------traan
               | <liquid>  <eye liquid>       <tear>
               |     |
               |     |------drank----------   sake
               |             <drink>        <sake>
               |-gas--------methaan--------mijngas
               | <gas>     <methane>          <firedamp>
               |
               |-weefsel----spierweefsel---vlees----
kalfsvlees
               | <tissue>      <muscle>       <meat>
<calf>
               |
               |-materiaal---grondstof------element---  goud
               | <material> <element>   <element> <gold>
               |                      |
               |                      |---metaal- spijker
               |                        <metal> <nail>
               |-alkaloide---nicotine
               | <alkaloid> <nicotine>
               |
               |-silicone
               <silicon>
```

Figure 17.1. Equivalent piece of *substance* taxonomy based on Van Dale Dutch monolingual

1.2. Defining Formulae

Dictionary definition texts are a specialized form of ordinary natural language text. However, they are neither a formal logical language nor normal descriptive English. Consequently, they can be parsed with less effort than any other form of text (Amsler, 1980). One way to take advantage of this specialized form of text is to make use of the significant recurring patterns (defining formulae) in the definition texts. This syntactic approach is motivated partly by the genus terms extraction effort discussed earlier, and partly by the more ambitious desire to construct lexical entries automatically from information available in MRDs.

Twenty-three years ago, Olney et al. (1967) noted the use of *defining formulae* found in dictionary definitions. Amsler (1980) discussed three common definition formats: single text, synonymous cross-reference, and a combination of single text and synonymous cross-reference. Smith (1981) studied the defining formulae in a selection of adjective

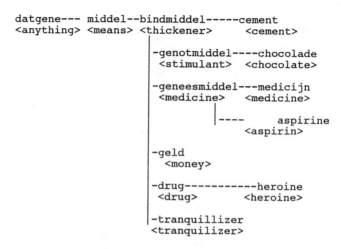

```
datgene--- middel--bindmiddel-----cement
<anything> <means> <thickener>     <cement>
                   |
                   |-genotmiddel----chocolade
                   | <stimulant>  <chocolate>
                   |
                   |-geneesmiddel---medicijn
                   | <medicine>   <medicine>
                   |          |
                   |          |----     aspirine
                   |              <aspirin>
                   |
                   |-geld
                   |  <money>
                   |
                   |-drug-----------heroine
                   | <drug>       <heroine>
                   |
                   |-tranquillizer
                   <tranquilizer>
```

Figure 17.2. Nonequivalent piece of *substance* taxonomy based on the Dutch Van Dale monolingual

definitions from *Webster's Seventh Collegiate Dictionary (W7)*. Ahlswede and Evens (1988) identified defining formulae in noun, verb, and adjective definitions from *W7*. Perhaps the most recent and most interesting works in this area are Ahlswede (1985) and Markowitz, Ahlswede, and Evens (1986).

Ahlswede (1985) described a set of interactive routines that were used to create a 2,000-word strong lexicon for a small medical expert system. An important feature of the lexicon produced by this system was that it was based on lexical semantic relations such as synonymy, antonymy, taxonomy, part-and-whole, and so on. The data structure of each lexical entry consists of name, sense, class, definition text, semantic attribute list, predicate calculus definition, case structure table, and semantic relation list. A major intent of the study was to use this interactive lexical builder and its associated data structure as the basis for a fully automatic lexical builder in contemplation. The contemplated automatic lexical builder will use Sager's linguistic string parser (LSP) to parse definitions from an MRD into a relational network based on Werner's (1978) MTQ (Modification-Taxonomy-Queuing) schema.

Werner's MTQ schema is a model of simplifying semantic relations. Only three relations are identified: modification, taxonomy, and queuing. All other relations are expressed as compounds of these relations and of lexical items. Werner's concept of modification and taxonomy reflects a popular belief in Aristotle's model of the dictionary definition as consisting of species, genus, and differentia. Taxonomy links the species to the genus, and modification links the differentia to the genus. The reason why Sager's LSP is chosen to parse dictionary definitions is that in a definition following the Aristotelian structure, taxonomy and modification can be identified by purely syntactic means. In a definition, a core word is modified directly or indirectly by all the other words. The core word is linked to the defined word by taxonomy, and all the other words are linked to the core word by modification. LSP is geared toward an analysis of sentences and phrases in terms of centers or cores with their modifying adjuncts, which suits exactly the needs of parsing dictionary definitions into a relational network based on the MTQ schema. It is unclear at this point how well this syntactic approach will manage in the automatic construction of lexical entries.

The goal of Markowitz et al. (1986) is straightforward. They intend to automate the process of lexical construction from information available in the machine-readable version of *W7*. It is assumed by their study that NLP systems require the following information: lexical semantic relations, selectional restrictions, and verb categories. The paper describes methods for finding taxonomy and set-membership relations, recognizing nouns that ordinarily represent human beings, and identifying active and static verbs and adjectives. A common feature of all these methods is the use of defining formulae in the analysis. Here are some examples: Taxonomical relations between nouns are suggested by the pattern "Any-NP;" the set-membership relations are indicated by the pattern "A-member-of-NP"; and the pattern "Act-of-Ving" of nouns is an indicator of action verbs.

Although the study demonstrates the usefulness of defining formulae in determining some semantic relations, the power of these formulae in analyzing various types of definition texts remains a puzzle. It does not seem to be the case that defining formulae dispel the issue of word-sense resolution in the analysis of dictionary definitions. Word-sense resolution processes conceivably associated with the genus terms are unclear in most of the studies on defining formulae. The question of word-sense disambiguation of the genus terms and of the differentia remains an interesting one. With or without defining formulae, word-sense resolution stays as the central issue in the extraction of semantic information from MRDs.

1.3. On Slator (1988)

An important recent work that makes extensive use of research results in the above two areas of MRD research is Slator (1988). It represents a more direct approach to the use of LDOCE in NLP. The suppositions of the approach are two: (a) that LDOCE contains sufficient information to serve as a knowledge resource for text analysis, and (b) that information can be processed in an effective way by programs.

Slator (1988) did two things. On the one hand, he designed and implemented a series of programs for extracting semantic information from LDOCE, with this semantic information put into a form suitable for use by a subsequent semantic analysis program. Also, he designed and implemented a semantic analysis program that accepts short English text and creates a corresponding representation from it. The resulting representation is intended to be suitable for use as a knowledge source for other AI programs. An interesting aspect of this study is the way in which semantic information is extracted from dictionary definitions for either of these two tasks.

The semantic information contained in LDOCE can be both explicit and implicit. Explicit semantic information contained in the electronic version of LDOCE consists of box and subject codes. The subject codes are yet another set of primitives that classifies the subject area in which a certain word sense is most likely used. An example of the main headings of subject codes is engineering with subheadings like electrical. Extraction of the explicit semantic information from LDOCE is relatively trivial. Box and subject codes contained in LDOCE provide some basic semantic information for Slator's frame-knowledge structures. What is nontrivial is the extraction of implicit semantic information contained in the text of LDOCE word-sense definitions. Slator (1988) uses the implicit semantic information extracted from word-sense definitions to enrich the basic frames constructed from a straightforward process of semantic information extraction.

A chart parser was modified by Slator to accept LDOCE definitions as Lisp lists and produces parse trees. The chart parser is driven by a context-free grammar of about 100 rules and has a lexicon derived from the controlled vocabulary of LDOCE. It is important to note here that the chart parser does not have a semantic component. The derived lexicon from the LDOCE controlled vocabulary may contain some explicit semantic information contained in the electronic version of LDOCE. However, it is not claimed by Slator (1988) that the lexicon has enriched frame-knowledge structures. The parse trees produced by the chart parser are passed to an interpreter for matching and inferencing.

The first step of the tree interpreter picks off the dominating phrase, and after restructuring it into GENUS and FEATURE components (by reference to the currently active grammar version), inserts it into the current basic frame under a GENUS slot. According to Slator (1988), further strategies for patterning-matching are being developed to extract more detailed differentia information, beyond the GENUS and FEATURE modifiers. Let us forget the more detailed differentia information for the moment and look more closely at only the GENUS information that could possibly be obtained. At this point, what puzzles this author is how the correct word sense of a potential genus term appearing in the parse tree passed from the chart parser is selected. This is because LDOCE has a defining vocabulary of 2,000 words. Although half of these words have single defining senses (i.e., only one word sense of these words is used in the word-sense definitions of the LDOCE controlled vocabulary), the other half, about 1,000 strong, have at least two defining senses.

Slator realized the problem. One example cited to show the problem is the word *instrument.* It has two defining senses: one as a tool, the other as a musical instrument. A scheme, although not implemented, was worked out with the intention of solving the problem. The scheme involves looking up the definition of the genus term and then selecting the correct one on the basis of matching the semantic and pragmatic codes of the genus term with the codes associated with the senses of its definitions. Slator predicted two immediate problems:

1. The semantic codes are often too general, and the subject codes are too often missing for this scheme to be completely effective.
2. The program code for this will be slow, requiring an operating system context switch, which makes it cumbersome to jump out and access the dictionary at will.

He concluded that this scheme is, at best, a partial solution to the problem. This conclusion is an honest one, and merits both respect and attention.

It should be clear from the above review of Slator (1988) that, although LDOCE provides some explicit semantic information that is useful for processing natural language text, more semantic information is needed to process LDOCE word-sense definitions in order to obtain implicit semantic information contained in LDOCE word-sense definitions. The big question is whence the needed semantic information ?

1.4. Knowledge Extraction from MRDs

Knowledge extraction from MRDs is by no means without controversy. Two questions keep haunting researchers in the area:

1. Do dictionaries contain knowledge of the world at all beyond word-sense definitions?

2. Is it possible at all to obtain world knowledge from dictionaries if the answer to the first question is in the affirmative?

Different researchers have different responses to these questions. Amsler said the following in a position paper at TINLAP-3:

> For several years now, I have been concerned with how artificial intelligence is going to build the substitute for human world knowledge needed in performing the task of text understanding. I continue to believe that the bulk of this knowledge will have to be derived from existing machine-readable texts produced as a byproduct of computer typesetting and word processing technologies which have overtaken the publishing industry.

Commenting on the difficulty of extracting world knowledge from these sources, he continues: "However, there are many obstacles to the acquisition of world knowledge from text."

Bran Boguraev said at the same conference, "There is a wealth of information relevant to a range of natural language processing functions available and extractable from the definitions of words found in obvious places like dictionaries."

However, at the same conference, Hobbs made his opposing voice heard. The example he cited in support of his negative view of world knowledge contained in dictionaries concerned the recursive definitions of the words *left* and *right;* that is, the word *left* is defined in terms of *right* and the word *right* defined in terms of *left*. When asked about how he handles the concepts of *left* and *right* in his system, he openly admitted that his system did not have a way to handle it at all. Later at the conference, Hobbs' strong opinion was softened, and he said that he was ready to yield to Amsler's opinion on the matter. Personally, I have very high opinions of dictionaries as sources of general and specific world knowledge. It is just a natural consequence of one of the working hypotheses of this study that language and knowledge are not ultimately separable.

In spite of the fact that Hobbs gave in on his opinion about world knowledge contained in dictionaries, the issue he raised about the recursiveness in dictionary definitions was an important one. There are two schools of thought on the issue. Some people, like Sparck Jones (1964), accept the recursive definitions as they are, but use them as clues to obtain lists of English synonyms. These lists are then used in NLP tasks. Other people are less tolerant of the recursiveness in dictionary definitions, and would like to see every word-sense definition bottom out to some primitives. One of the intended objectives of the natural set of semantic primitives derived from LDOCE is to avoid recursiveness in word-sense definitions.

To end the discussion on the first question, it does not seem to be exaggerating to say that most researchers do believe that dictionaries contain an abundance of world knowledge useful to NLP.

The difficulty in extracting world knowledge from dictionaries is universally recognized. No one claims that it is easy. The difficulty stems from the lack of world knowledge computers need to understand dictionary definitions, as was pointed out in Slocum and Morgan (1987):

> The state of the art does not yet permit the parsing of definition texts and the processing of their usage examples, after all, the knowledge contained in them is required for the parsing itself—and this is precisely where most information resides in general dictionaries intended for human consumption. (p. 8)

Slator's (1988) experience with parsing LDOCE sense definitions provides testimony to the need for hand-coding some minimum amount of world knowledge in order for parsing to succeed in some cases. His predicament was that only about half of the words in the LDOCE controlled vocabulary have single defining senses; that is, only one word sense of these words is used in the definitions of the controlled vocabulary. The other half have at least two defining senses. He found it hard for his system to select the correct word senses for these words in parsing the definitions.

Despite the difficulty involved, the present approach is not to avoid parsing dictionary definitions. The exact opposite is true. To overcome the lack of world knowledge needed for the parsing process, a natural set of semantic primitives is derived from the dictionary first , and then hand-coded semantic preference knowledge concerning these primitives is used to start the bootstrapping process.

2. SEMANTIC PRIMITIVES

In the preceding review of previous work, the term *semantic primitives* has been mentioned several times without being defined and explained. This section examines the goals and history of semantic primitives as well as other issues of concern such as the NP-completeness issue associated with extracting a minimum set of semantic primitives from a monolingual dictionary.

2.1. The Goals of Semantic Primitives

> A 'PRIMITIVE' (or rather a set of primitives plus a syntax, etc.) is a reduction device which yields a semantic representation for a natural

language via a translation algorithm and which is not plausibly explicated in terms of or reducible to other entities of the same type. (Wilks 1977, p.184)

There is widespread agreement that primitives are like words used in dictionary definitions. Zwicky's (1973) hypothesis that every semantic primitive can appear as a surface word in a natural language was supported by Wilks. Wilks also accepts Sampson's (1973) view about primitives being comparable in role to English pound notes with the inscription "I promise to pay the bearer on demand the sum of one pound." The currency promises gold but in fact one only gets more currency for it, never gold. Wilks comments that, "In the same way, primitives may seem to promise access to something else, but all one ever gets by way of explanation of their meaning is more primitives" (p.196).

Although up to this point no set of semantic primitives has ever been derived from a dictionary, having actual English words as primitives does not seem to be a controversial issue to start with. In the final chapter of this book, some of the theoretical aspects of semantic primitives will be reexamined, and the natural set of semantic primitives derived from LDOCE will be evaluated in terms of some well-known criteria.

2.1.1. Research history. Semantic primitives did not come out of thin air. They were part of the results of some persistent and painstaking efforts to build machine translation (MT) systems in the 1950s and 1960s. A review of these efforts up to a point where the emergence of semantic primitives was seen may be helpful to the understanding of the purpose, as well as some desirable properties, of semantic primitives.

One of the major problems that was holding up the development of MT systems at that time, and still hinders the development of many NLP systems now, is lexical ambiguity. The following is a presentation in chronological order of some of the suggestions put forward by some well-known researchers in the field to resolve the problem.

2.1.1.1. Warren Weaver (1949). Warren Weaver is the author of a historic document in MT literature. His *Translation* kindled widespread interest in the possibility of automatic translation all over the United States. The question he formulated to solve the lexical ambiguity problem was as follows: "What minimum value of N (number of words on both sides of a central word) will, at least in a tolerable fraction of cases, lead to the correct choice of meaning for the central word?" (p. 21).

Weaver suggested that the answer to this question lies in the statistical semantic character of language. It was emphasized in his *Translation* that statistical semantic studies should be undertaken as a necessary preliminary step in resolving ambiguity.

2.1.1.2. Victor Yngve (1955). One of the greatest difficulties that researchers in MT found in the early 1950s was that one input word could have several meanings in the output language. According to Yngve, most researchers proposed to resolve the problem by submitting alternate meanings for the input words, and instructing either the reader or a posteditor to chose the appropriate one.

Yngve suggested that the information necessary for the resolution of multiple-meaning problems resides in the context and that a context of about one sentence should be considered. Yngve believed that some knowledge of the lexical as well as the contextual information allows the output words to be found in a dictionary.

2.1.1.3. Erwin Reifler (1955). Reifler, another pioneer in MT research, wrote that the simplest form of MT would be one with pre-editing, in which the pre-editor determines the meaning indicated by each context and denotes it by special graphic symbols that are added to the conventional written form in all instances involving multiple meanings (p. 141). He also argued that the burden of semantic interpretation could also be put on the customer; that is, those who want foreign works mechanically translated (p. 142).

2.1.1.4. Ross Quillian (1962). Quillian emphasized the importance of understanding on the part of the computer in MT. In his opinion, MT programs would be able to solve certain problems, for example, the resolution of multiple meanings, only by storing the meaning of natural language words in a medium and format providing properties similar to those of human understanding. He described the general characteristics of human meaning as follows:

1. The universe of human meaning is composed entirely of measurements on mental measuring standards.
2. Human meaning is simultaneously present in different, overlapping levels called "wholeness levels."

The tasks confronting a MT researcher who wishes to equip the computer with an understanding are as follows:

1. One must establish an adequate medium of element scales for the presentation of meaning, and an intraword syntax for building up constellations of readings on those scales.

2. One must code the meanings of natural language words into such constellations.
3. One must arrange all this information into a semantic dictionary. (p. 24)

2.1.1.5. Michael Zarechnak (1965). In an effort to resolve syntactic ambiguity on the semantic level, Zarechnak explored possible solutions from applied radical semantics, the study of the basic semantic elements (BASES) of word roots (RADICES) in terms of their properties and their relations with other radices. The study concentrates on nonsyntactic, semantic regularities. The focus of the study was of a nontheoretical, experimental, and operational nature (pp. 90-91).

Subject identification within a two-place predicate structure was presented as an illustration of the resolving power of applied radical semantics. Consider the example below:

Kislorod dostavljaet k kletkam krov

This has two interpretations: (a) oxygen supplies to the blood cells, or (b) oxygen is supplied to the cells by the blood.

The first and the last word of the sentence are nouns that are normally interpretable both nominatively and accusatively. There is nothing in the given example either on the morphological or on the syntactic level that would help to resolve the ambiguity. Intuitively, according to Zarechnak, the last word is the subject. The first word is the object of the verb.

Zarechnak tried to break the word roots (RADICES) into their BASES. This is shown in Table 17.1.

Given a list of nouns with the accompanying codes for the BASE description, Zarechnak proposed a set of rules for identification of the subject function within the two-place predicate structure. One of these rules reads:

> If one noun is *liquid* and not *air,* and the other noun is *solid* or *fluid* , the noun with the BASE *liquid* is the subject. Thus *kislorod (fluid*) dostavljaet k kletkam krov (*liquid*) means "Oxygen is carried to the cells by the blood."
> The notion underlying these procedures is that word structure in a natural

TABLE 17.1. Word Roots and Their Bases

English Word	*Russian Words*	*Bases*
oxygen	kislorod	fluid motion gaseous
cell	kletki	solid container living operand
blood	krov	liquid animal

> language is considered as a cluster of BASES among which certain relations hold. This concept is an important one for MT because for meaning transfer from source to target language one has to operate on the level where the invariant minimal units are accessible for machine handling. (p. 93)

To justify the approach, Zarechnak continued, "In modern science it is customary to consider any object under observation as having multi-dimensional structure, and among these dimensions there are invariant properties and relations around which different objects are built" (p. 93).

Zarechnak further remarked that if the procedures suggested were developed sufficiently to reach the point of using them for the coding of the entries of a sizable (say 50,000 entries) dictionary, the procedures could have immediate relevance for various areas including MT, where the language built around BASES is an approximation of a logical artificial language and correspondence between two languages with BASES coding could be established on an intermediate level.

2.1.1.6. Karen Sparck Jones (1965). The Cambridge Language Research Unit explored the possibility of using the thesaurus for resolving ambiguity in MT. It was suggested that words in a thesaurus are classified under different conceptual headings corresponding to the ideas that the words may express. Thus, if a word has different uses, this fact will be represented by the occurrence of the word in a number of sections under different headings. By looking for a word meaning appropriate for a particular context, ambiguity may be resolved.

Experiments were carried out in the research unit using the Penguin edition of *Roget's Thesaurus of English Words and Phrases.* These experiments were only moderately successful. It seemed that no existing thesauri would be adequate for the purpose of machine translation. The question of constructing a better thesaurus for MT purposes was considered, which would involve (a) better analysis of word uses, and (b) checking the headings.

Of the two considerations, the first one is essential and still in need of much effort.

2.1.1.7. Yorick Wilks (1968). Wilks gave a clear definition of ambiguity resolution when he wrote: "What I am referring to is a procedure for getting a computer to do what human beings do naturally when they read or listen, namely, to interpret each word in a text in one and (usually) only one of its possible senses" (p. 59).

He described a system for the online semantic analysis of texts of up to a paragraph in length. The intermediate purpose of the analysis was to resolve the word-sense ambiguity of the text. His working hypothesis was that many word-sense ambiguities cannot be resolved within the bounds of the conventional text sentence because there simply is not enough context available. For example, the word *post* in "I'll have to take this post after all," can either mean a job or a stake, depending on the larger context of the sentence.

The system Wilks developed was in fact a system for the representation of the content of texts. Its use as an ambiguity resolution procedure is some test of its ability to represent texts for subsequent interrogation as part of a more general information system, because representation of content involves disambiguation, essentially.

Important to his content representation is his coding system, in which a word with multiple senses is put under different category markers. For example, the word *salt* may be an old soldier or the substance sodium chloride. MAN will be the category marker for *salt* as an old soldier, and STUFF will be for *salt* as the substance sodium chloride. In his system, fragments of a text are assigned semantic patterns called templates. More than one template may be attached to some text fragment. By specifying rules that relate templates together to correspond to a proper sequence of text fragments, the number of templates attached to a particular text fragment is reduced to one. For example, the sentence, "The old salt is damp, but the cake is still dry," may have the following two template sequences:

1. MAN + BE + KIND and STUFF + BE + KIND
2. STUFF + BE + KIND and STUFF + BE + KIND

In the absence of any overriding considerations, a rule of template sequence could take the second (and correct) sequence in preference to the first on the basis of the repetition of the marker STUFF.

The semantic clues Wilks provided for his system are the category markers. Other formal means employed are text fragments, templates, and template-sequence rules. By imposing templates on fragments of a text, conventional syntactic processing is replaced by semantic processing.

The category markers became the forerunners of semantic primitives in Wilks' (1975a, 1975b, 1978) systems. The term primitive is also used to describe Schank's (1972) primitive ACTs in the conceptual dependency (CD) representations. The call for the derivation of a natural set of semantic primitives in the descriptive approach was made more than a decade ago in Wilks (1977).

2.1.2. The NP-completeness issue. Dailey (1986) claims that the extraction of a minimum set of semantic primitives from a monolingual dictionary is NP-complete. The problem was stated as follows:

> Given a dictionary, we seek to rewrite that dictionary, substituting definitions for words freely so as to minimize that portion of the lexicon occurring as members of defining strings. That is, what is the smallest number of words in the lexicon such that all other words may be defined from this select set? (p. 306)

This is exactly what is being done in deriving the seed senses from LDOCE. These seed senses, as mentioned before, are intended to be the natural set of semantic primitives derived from the dictionary.

There is no argument about the problem of extracting a minimum set of semantic primitives from a monolingual dictionary being NP-complete. Using a so-called restriction technique (Garey & Johnson, 1979), Dailey showed us that the problem is equivalent to a well-known NP-complete problem in graph theory. In fact, as Litkowski (1988) put it, Dailey has transformed the classic problem of the vicious cycle or circle into the neoclassical paradigm of NP-completeness. No disagreement is observed in the literature with Dailey's conclusion as regards the nature of the problem.

However, two issues are open to discussion: the problem of circularity of definitions, and the problem of whether it is possible to reduce the size of the problem so as to make it tractable. Dailey seemed to be concerned with both problems. Litkowski, on the other hand, argued that by reducing the size of the problem, the extraction of a minimum set of semantic primitives from a monolingual dictionary can be made tractable. Litkowski characterized his solution as follows:

> The definienda and definitions of a monolingual dictionary can be mapped into a graph theoretic structure with nodes corresponding to definienda(as Dailey does), but with links going from a word occurring in a definition to the word being defined (opposite to Dailey's direction). The problem of finding semantic primitives in this model is then equivalent to finding what is called in digraph theory the point basis of a digraph, i.e., those nodes from which all others in the dictionary are reachable. (p. 52)

Using the above algorithm, Litkowski holds, the size of the problem can be reduced considerably. Litkowski (1978, 1980) actually reduced an initial set of 20,000 verbs to 4,000 more primitive verbs.

Litkowski continues:

> After applying such "gross" techniques for pruning, the problem is more tractable and it is possible to take advantage of special features of the problem at hand. In particular, it is possible to develop many heuristics which take into account many of the characteristics of a dictionary as well as many semantic considerations. These heuristics make it possible to reduce the problem even further, moving closer to semantic primitives. (p. 52)

This statement was found true in this study. In fact, LDOCE has a controlled vocabulary of about 2,000 words. The controlled vocabulary is equal to what could be achieved using Litkowski's algorithm to reduce the entire LDOCE vocabulary to a more primitive subset. The processes of first finding out the defining senses of LDOCE, and then deriving the seed senses are part of the heuristics employed in this study to arrive at a reasonable set of semantic primitives for the LDOCE dictionary. Note that the natural set of semantic primitives derived from LDOCE as the seed senses of the dictionary is not meant to be a minimum set of semantic primitives for the dictionary because, after all, the method is only an approximation to the solution of an NP-complete problem.

3. HUMAN AND MACHINE LEARNING

The derivation of a natural set of semantic primitives from LDOCE is not the end in itself, but a means to the end of building a MTD from the MRD. These semantic primitives are used to represent world knowledge that facilitates the parsing of dictionary definitions. These semantic primitives are also used in acquiring semantic preference knowledge from the parse trees. The process of parsing dictionary definitions and acquiring semantic preference knowledge from them is, in fact, what is called the bootstrapping process. Essentially, the process of bootstrapping is a process of machine learning of semantic preference knowledge from dictionary definition text. The following section reviews relevant literature in both human and machine learning.

3.1. Definition of Learning

Of all definitions of learning in the field of AI, two are most appropriate to quote in this context, one from Simon (Michalski, Carbonell, & Mitchell, 1986), the other from Michalski (Michalski et al., 1986). The one by Simon reads: "Learning denotes changes in the system that are adaptive in the sense that they enable the system to do the same task or tasks drawn from the same population more efficiently the next time" (p. 10).

The one given by Michalski sounds more cognitively oriented: "Learning is constructing or modifying representations of what is being experienced" (p. 10).

The two definitions seem to emphasize two different but equally important aspects of learning: visible behavioral changes vs. invisible changes in the memory structure. In fact, the two definitions reflect two developmental stages in our understanding of the nature of learning.

Michalski's characterization of learning reflects his concern with the inductive learning paradigm where new concepts are added to the database by induction. It says nothing, though, about the performance criterion of learning. On the contrary, Simon was overtly concerned about behavioral criteria, but made no explicit mention of what exact changes he meant could take place in the system.

Minsky's (1985) definition is intermediate: "Learning is making useful changes in our minds." This definition suffers from vagueness, and he himself realized that such a definition was too broad to be of any use.

My own definition of learning is this: Learning refers to changes in the behavior or behavioral potential of a system (a man or machine), brought about by processing environmental information that results in the change of the system's memory.

The intent is to provide a definition comprehensive enough to accommodate all aspects of learning by both man and machine. Changes in a system's memory include those in knowledge representations.

3.2. Human Learning

Research in human learning has had a 100-year history. Over a considerable part of this time, behaviorist principles prevailed. Changes in animal or human behavior were taken as the sole indicator of possible changes in the brain. Psychologists infer from their observations of behavior what could have happened in the brain, considered a black box. Their theories on various types of conditioning stimulated research on learning in the behaviorist vein. This lasted until about 30 years ago when cognitive psychology began to take over. That change was a change in philosophy. Both schools have their merits and there is no reason for one to perish for the survival of the other. In fact, one remarkable resemblance exists between the two. Neither school seems to have offered any adequate answers to the age-old question of the physiological basis of memory and learning. In other words, up to the present, mechanisms in the brain that are involved in processes associated with learning are largely unknown.

People interested in computer simulation are often encouraged to appreciate the beauty of another branch of psychology–mathematical psychology, where emphasis is laid on the formal and quantitative aspects of the study of human behavior.

One can hardly talk about mathematical psychology without talking about Dr. W. K. Estes, one of its founders. Over a period of more than 40 years, Estes dedicated his efforts to the study of learning. His explorations of the relationships between learning and performance led him in modifying and elaborating his working models to a more and more formal and adequate theory of learning. His interest in mental representations prepared him for his ready reconciliations with the views of cognitive psychology.

Important influences on Estes in his research philosophy can be traced to three men, B. F. Skinner, C. L. Hull, and E. C. Tolman. To Skinner, under whom Estes received his early training, learning was simply the modification of behavior as a consequence of reinforcement. For Hull, a distinction between learning and performance was important, but the result of learning was still the modification of stimulus-response connections. In Tolman's theory, the distinction between learning and performance was basic: Learning resulted in changes in mental states and it was not directly related to behavior. To Estes, Tolman (1932) and Hull (1937, 1943) were much closer to his own aspirations toward more general and more powerful theories. In his later studies, Estes showed clear tendencies toward a cognitive approach to the study of learning. The human organism is hypothesized as an information processor and decision maker. Rather than being driven by information feedback from the consequences of his behavior, the information processor "is seen as actively sampling the alternative courses of action available in a choice situation, generating expectations about the probable consequences of the actions based on his past experience, and tending to select the response yielding the higher expectations of success" (Estes, 1982, p. 80).

3.3. Machine Learning

3.3.1. Do computers learn? One question that often haunts the minds of machine-learning researchers is whether computers ever learn. The answer to the question really depends on the philosophical view one adopts with respect to learning. An empiricist would probably answer yes, whereas a nativist would say no. I personally adopt an eclectic view, and my answer is in the affirmative.

Learning has been a matter of deep concern to philosophers, who are interested in the analysis of knowledge and that of the nature of our mental life. Epistemology is what they call the study of knowledge. In fact, learning can be called experimental epistemology because learning and knowledge seem related. Within the theory of knowledge, two opposing views exist-empiricism and nativism. The two views differ in their understanding of the relationship between experience and the organization of the mind. According to empiricism, experience is the only source of knowledge. Sense data, memory, and ideas are associated together in the mind through experience. In the computer analogy, a machine can be programmed so that it learns to accumulate experience. Nativism, on the other hand, holds that knowledge is innate. Sense data do not constitute the basis of knowledge. The most extreme form of nativism was that stated by Plato: All knowledge of any importance was alleged to be innately recorded in the human mind. The point of experience was to merely bring out that knowledge in explicit form. To these extreme nativists, computers could hardly learn because they do not have the innate knowledge to start with. Noam Chomsky would be a good example of such a nativist.

3.3.2. Research history. According to Cohen and Feigenbaum (1982), machine-learning research underwent three stages up until 1982. The first stage was characterized by optimistic exploration of self-organizing systems. These systems were supposed to modify themselves to adapt to their environments. Various computational analogues of neurons were developed and tested, the foremost of which was the Perceptron (Rosenblatt, 1957). Unfortunately, these early attempts failed to produce any convincingly intelligent systems.

The beginning of the 1970s saw a renewal of interest in learning with the publication of Winston's influential thesis "Learning Structural Descriptions from Examples." Research efforts went two ways. Some workers studied simple learning tasks in depth (such as learning simple concepts). Some others built learning systems that incorporated large amounts of domain knowledge (such as the Meta-DENDRAL and AM programs) so that the system could discover high-level concepts.

The third stage of learning research, motivated by the need to acquire knowledge for expert systems, was underway by 1982. The author believes that we are still in this third stage, but energetically seeking ways and means to enrich knowledge bases for a new generation of computing technology.

3.3.3. Types of machine learning. Cohen and Feigenbaum (1982) advocated a simple but encompassing model of machine learning. The model consists of four parts. In order of the sequence of data flow, these four parts are (a) the environment, (b) the learning element, (c) the knowledge base, and (d) the performance element. The environment and knowledge base are bodies of information. The learning element and the performance element are procedures. The environment supplies information to the learning element and the learning element uses this information to make improvements in an explicit knowledge base. The performance element uses the information to carry out its task. Finally, feedback information gained during attempts to perform the task goes back to the learning element. Depending on the type of information supplied by the environment to the learning element, there exist five different learning strategies. These are rote learning, learning by instruction, learning by deduction, learning by analogy, and learning by induction. Learning by induction further divides into learning from examples and learning by observation and discovery.

In rote learning, the information supplied by the environment is more or less directly accepted by the learning system. The strategy is elementary, and not powerful enough to accomplish intelligent learning on its own, but it is an "inherent and important part of any learning systems" (Cohen & Feigenbaum, 1982, p.335).

Learning by instruction was originated by McCarthy (1958) when he proposed the creation of an advice-taking system that could accept advice and make use of it to plan and execute actions in the world. Few serious attempts were made at this technique until recent years when the problem of converting expert advice into expert performance became real. The steps for automatic advice-taking proposed by Hayes-Roth, Klahr, and Mostow (1981) are:

1. Request: requesting advice from the expert
2. Interpret: assimilating advice into internal representations
3. Operationalize: converting representations into useful form
4. Integrate: integrating representaions into knowledge base
5. Evaluate: evaluating resulting actions of the performance element

In deductive learning, the learning element draws deductive, truth-preserving inferences from the knowledge given, and stores useful conclusions. In inductive learning, information provided by the environment is too detailed and specific. The learning element must infer general rules from examples, observations, or discoveries.

Learning by analogy is deductive and inductive learning combined. In learning by analogy, descriptions from different domains are matched to determine a common substructure, which serves as the basis for analogical mapping. "Finding the common substructure involves inductive inference, whereas performing analogical mapping is a form of deduction" (Michalski et al., 1986, p. 15).

3.3.4. Pitfalls in machine learning. One important issue in machine learning concerns its possible undesirable consequences.

The first problem is so-called predictive opacity (Michalski et al., 1986). That is, it is much more difficult to predict behaviors of machines that learn inductively than to predict behaviors of machines without such an ability.

Another serious problem associated with inductive learning is that knowledge acquired by generalization from specific observations or by analogy to known facts cannot in principle be proven correct, though it may be disproven. This stems from the fact that inductive inference is not truth preserving, but only falsity preserving (Michalski, 1983).

3.3.5. Machine learning of natural language. In the machine-learning literature, very few studies have been conducted on machine learning of natural languages. Among those that were found on machine learning of natural languages, Berwick's (1985) The *Acquisition of Syntactic Knowledge* attracted the most attention. Generalizing from this study, which involves learning grammar rules from several hundred positive examples, Berwick arrived at the so-called subset principle (Michalski et al., 1986). It was claimed that "the subset principle heuristic drives language acquisition through its stages" (p. 627). What is the subset principle?

Intuitively, it is a strategy of timid acquisition: If possible guesses can be arranged in a subset relationship, then the learner should make the smallest possible guesses about what it should learn consistent with the evidence it has seen so far.

The motivation behind this heuristic is that in learning from positive-only examples, overgeneralization easily occurs because there is a lack of a discrimination process that helps to push back overgeneralizations and reveal the concept boundary. The subset principle serves to restrain the power of generalization so that rules or concepts generated are free of overgeneralizations. Unfortunately, the subset principle finds it difficult to account for the basic facts of second-language acquisition. In acquiring a second language, people, especially adults, are not timid at all. Bold contrastive-analysis (CA) errors and overgeneralizations are frequently observed in second-language-learning situations (Lado, 1957). An otherwise timid person may boldly throw a bunch of English words together, in an order strange to a native speaker, but consistent with the syntactic structures of his or her own mother tongue. They may get by without being corrected, but when comprehensibility becomes an issue, they are almost always corrected. It was fine for Berwick to do learning from positive-only examples. However, it would be very hard to generalize it to a general constraint in language acquisition.

3.3.6. Comparisons with related work in machine learning.

3.3.6.1. Lehnert (1987). Lehnert (1987) describes a pseudoconnectionist sentence analyzer called ELAN (Episodic Language Acquisition Network) that learns to parse sentences into case- frame-meaning representations by acquiring a case-based memory for syntactic/ semantic relationships. ELAN has a network structure that represents the search space of possible interpretations of a sentence. A relaxation algorithm is applied during parsing to identify a preferred interpretation with the network representation of ELAN. ELAN acquires the case-based memory during a training mode. The emphasis of the system is on learning.

Knowledge is represented in ELAN by means of integration maps, or simple associations between individual syntactic constituents and their related conceptual case-frame slots. All integration maps are deduced by ELAN during training. The following is an example of an integration map.

When ELAN is trained on the sentence "John gave Mary a book," the target case-frame representation is "event ATRANS actor John object book recipient Mary." ELAN derives an integration-map sequence of the form (NP / actor VP / event NP / recipient NP / object). If ELAN ever sees another sentence that can be segmented into the sequence (NP VP NP NP), it may consider using this integration-map sequence as a source of slot-filling preferences.

ELAN utilizes supervised-learning trials in order to construct episodic memory structures for sentence analysis. Each sentence input to ELAN is accompanied by a target case-frame structure in terms of Schank's CD representations. The following is an example of representations for the sentence "John gave Mary a kiss on the cheek."

EVENT = move, ACTOR = John, OBJECT = lips part John,

DESTINATION = cheek part Mary < = = result = =
PHYSCONT (lips part John, cheek part Mary)

ELAN walks through a three-step training session with each training item: (a) segmentation, (b) consolidation, and (c) integration.

First the input for the training session is segmented into local constituents. No global syntactic structures are produced. This frees the system developer from the worries of PP-attachment or other semantic disambiguating tasks. The segmentation task assumes the existence of a lexical dictionary and a simple syntactic grammar. The first step produces a single segmentation, for example, NP1 V1 NP2 NP3 PP1 for the example sentence "John gave Mary a kiss on the cheek."

Consolidation is a process of matching syntactic constituents against conceptual case-frame slots. For example the head noun of an NP is matched against some slot filler in some target frame representation. If the number of syntactic constituents matches the number of case slot-value pairs in the target representation, the training will proceed to Step 3. If the numbers are not equal, ELAN opts to retreat from further matching.

During integration, ELAN modifies its memory structures with successful matching operations of Step 2. If such matchings do not exist in ELAN's memory, ELAN adds in the new integration maps. In the present example, the following integration map is added to ELAN's memory:

NP -> ACTOR V -> NIL NP -> DESTINATION NP -> EVENT

PP -> DESTINATION

The ACTOR is *John* , the nil verb is *gave* , the first NP representing destination is *Mary* , the NP representing the EVENT is *kiss* , and the PP showing DESTINATION is *on the cheek*. Most of these integration maps are indexed under specific verbs or key nouns.

To use the memory structures ELAN constructed during training, ELAN enters into the test mode. The input is a sentence to be analyzed. The output is a case-frame meaning representation for that sentence. The test process proceeds in four steps: (a) segmentation, (b) network construction, (c) network relaxation, and (d) frame instantiation.

Segmentation for the test mode is identical to that conducted during training. The output is a small number of syntactic segmentations of the input sentence.

During network construction, a network is constructed so that each instance of an integration map that can be applied to a given syntactic constituent becomes a node in the network. Constructing such a network is part of the process to identify a preferred segmentation along with a unique integration map for each constituent in that segmentation. Both syntactic constituent information and case role-binding information are used to eliminate competing syntactic segmentations and their associated integration maps. To reduce the search space, ELAN uses a dictionary that keeps an account of all the case frames associated with each word. ELAN uses the dictionary as a filter to eliminate less possible integration maps. The principle of preference semantics (Wilks, 1975a) is applied to the process to select a preferred segmentation and its associated integration map, although some of the well-established strategies, for example, the use of semantic primitives, are not. ELAN associates previous slot fillers with specific integration map sequences. Preference for case-frame alternatives is found by giving stronger credibility to concepts that have played these roles before. For each integration map within an indexed map sequence, prior role bindings are examined. The integration map is ranked either with a 1 or 0 depending on the bindings returned. This information is then added to the network by creating context nodes. Each context node is associated with a candidate map sequence retrieved from memory. Note that only the context nodes have activation links connecting them to all the integration maps in the network that fit the map sequence. This results in a network where some nodes do not have links to the context nodes.

Step 3 of the test mode is network relaxation. All map nodes are initialized with an activation level at 0. The algorithm for initializing context nodes is to take (10 x (the number of confirmed case/slot instantiations) / (the total number of case slots)) where a case/slot instantiation is confirmed when a word is recorded as appearing in a certain case/slot before. A relaxation algorithm is then applied to the initialized network. The relaxation process terminates when the network completely stabilizes. Possible paths are identified, along with varying degrees of credibility for each path. In case no unique path of maximal activation is found, the sentence is taken as ambiguous.

The last step is frame instantiation. At Step 4, conceptual knowledge associated with the top-level event is applied to the instantiation process. Given a generic frame associated with the top-level event, the approximate case-frame representation generated by the network is used to guide the instantiation to produce a complete case-frame representation.

Lehnert's (1987) research is related to this study in many ways. First, ELAN was not designed with concern for language acquisition only. It was designed for sentence analysis. In other words, learning is not for the sake of learning or validating some empirical data, but for the practical purpose of natural language processing. Learning in the MTD project is also an important component of the process of constructing a MTD from a MRD. After the MTD is constructed, the same learning mechanism is intended for knowledge acquisition from general unrestricted text.

Secondly, both ELAN and this study apply semantic preference principles to the process of sentence analysis, the difference being that ELAN uses the number of confirmed case/slot instantiations as a basis for making preference decisions, whereas the present study applies the well-known semantic preference strategy of using semantic primitives.

Thirdly, both studies represent some progress, or rather some alterations, in the general scheme for natural language processing from the semantic primitive traditions of the 1970s and early 1980s. In ELAN, the CD representation with semantic primitives such as ATRANS and PTRANS is not the only representation that the system uses. Some syntactic information together with some simple form of constituent analysis became an important part of the learning and analysis mechanisms. In ELAN the tendency to incorporate some of the research results in connectionism is obvious, for example, the use of some connectionist algorithms in sentence analysis.

The present study maintains the tradition in the use of primitives in NLP but develops a different set of semantic primitives; that is, a descriptive set of semantic primitives (Wilks, 1977) from an MRD. These descriptive semantic primitives are then used in both language learning and language analysis.

3.3.6.2. Michalski (1983). According to Dietterich and Michalski (1981), the process of inductive learning can be viewed as a search for plausible general descriptions (inductive assertions) that explain the given input data and are useful for predicting new data. Discussed here is Michalski's INDUCE program (Michalski, 1983) to show, through an example, how inductive learning is conducted in the system.

The task of INDUCE is to induce rules. For example, INDUCE generalizes rules that could be used to determine whether a train is eastbound or westbound. To accomplish the task, INDUCE must, first of all, have a description language to characterize input examples to the system. For instance, each car of the train may be described as being long or short, as having a particular shape, or color. These are called the descriptors of the system. Descriptors can be hierarchically arranged, for example, shape over triangle, square, and polygon. Initial input to INDUCE consists of a set of observational statements about each example. There are also rules of generalization for INDUCE to apply so as to develop more general descriptions from the initial statements. An example of these rules might be turning constants into variables (e.g., replacing *red* by *any color*). The inductive learning algorithm focuses on various single positive examples and contrasts them with negative examples. First a *seed* example is randomly selected from the category of positive examples. Then this seed is described in terms of the descriptors in various alternative and general ways. In the process of generating such candidate descriptions, all kinds of generalization rules are applied. Descriptions that are consistent and complete are retained. A description is consistent if it does not apply to any negative examples, and complete if it applies to all positive examples. If a description is found to cover all positive examples, the examples are removed from the original set, and a new seed is selected from the remaining examples. The process repeats until a solution is found in a single conjunction or a disjunction of such descriptions.

The inductive learning that occurs in the present system both resembles and differs from the inductive learning in INDUCE in the following ways:

1. Both systems use a set of primitives. The present system uses a set of about 3,000 primitives. The descriptors used in INDUCE are, in fact, primitives that the system uses in forming rules of generalization. They differ not only in size but also in coverage. The 3,000 primitives in the present system cover the English language (at least LDOCE English), whereas primitives in INDUCE cover task domains.

2. Inductive learning in both systems produces some generalizations. The present system produces generalized semantic preferences to allow new word senses the system never encountered before to be chosen in the semantic disambiguation process (see Section 6.1). INDUCE produces some structural description for a set of examples.

3. Although both systems are engaged in some inductive learning, the actual process of learning differs. INDUCE generalizes within some search space of rules to arrive at some generalized description that fits all members of a set of positive examples. The present system makes use of existing semantic preference knowledge and analyzes dictionary definition text to see whether the semantic preference relation concerning a word sense can be generalized (or specialized to its genus term).

3.3.6.3. De Jong (1981, 1982). Another popular approach to machine learning is Explanation Based Learning (EBL). The technique, once called explanation schema acquisition, has two main features:

1. EBL is capable of one-trial learning. The schema acquisition process does not depend on correlational evidence.
2. EBL is heavily knowledge-based; that is, a great deal of background knowledge must be handcrafted into the system in order for learning to take place.

The schema acquisition process proceeds in the following three steps:

1. The new input is understood.
2. The input is evaluated to see if schema formation is warranted.
3. The input is generalized to a schema.

The following brief story may serve to illustrate the acquisition process.

John, a bank teller, discovered that his boss, Fred, had embezzled $100,000. John sent Fred an interoffice memo saying he would inform the police unless he was given $15,000. Fred paid John the money.

To understand the story, the system constructs a causally complete representation of the story. This means that any crucial information missing from the story must be inferred and that the causal relations between components can be discovered and made explicit.

If the representation fits some schema available in the system, that schema would be used to process the story. If not, the constructed representation would be evaluated in terms of the following five criteria:

1. Is the main goal of a character achieved?
2. Is the goal a general one?
3. Are the resources needed by the goal achiever generally available?
4. Is this new method of achieving the goal at least as effective as the other known volitional schemata to achieve this goal?
5. Does the input match one of the known generalizable patterns?

If any of the criteria does not hold, no new schema would be constructed.

To generalize a new schema from the constructed representation of the input story, the specific objects and events that occurred in the story would be replaced by more abstract entities. In the given example, a BLACKMAIL schema is constructed as the result of the learning process.

The learning that occurs in this study is similar to learning in the EBL paradigm in several ways. First, both need prior hand-coded knowledge in order for learning to take place. EBL needs a great number of schemata representations in the system with goals, actions, objects, and inference links. The present study also requires hand-coded semantic preference knowledge concerning the seed senses to be present in the knowledge base of the MTD in order for learning to occur in the bootstrapping process (see Section 5.3). Secondly, learning occurs in the present study in one trial also. It does not need any correlational data either. Each time the definition text of a certain word sense is parsed, some new semantic preference knowledge is acquired, and the knowledge base of the MTD enriched. One important difference between learning in the present study and EBL is that EBL does not operate on a set of semantic primitives as the present study does. In the present study, general world knowledge about a word sense resides in its semantic preference relations with other word senses. It does not require complex and delicate knowledge structures for learning to occur. This is both its strength and weakness. The strength of the representation lies in its simplicity, which results in a less laborious process of learning. The weakness is that no explicit causal links are built into the system. As a result of this weakness, the sentence analyzer has to pass what it obtains at the sentence level to a discourse analyzer before a coherent analysis of some text can be achieved.

CHAPTER 18

CONSTRUCTING A MTD FROM LDOCE

Constructing a MTD in the present approach involves two major subprocesses: the process of reduction and the process of composition. The process of reduction reduces LDOCE sense definitions to a group of seed senses. These seed senses are then applied in the process of composition as a natural set of semantic primitives derived from the dictionary. The final form of the MTD consists of a whole collection of FFs (Fregean Formulae), with each FF being the definition of one word sense. All FFs are composed of seed senses or embedded FFs. During the compositional process, the MTD keeps two working databases: a lexical base and a knowledge base. The lexical base consists of LDOCE sense definitions in the form of Prolog clauses. The knowledge base contains semantic preference information concerning word senses defined in the lexical base. Each of the two major subprocesses proceeds in two steps. The overall construction process proceeds in four steps with the two steps of the reduction process being the first and the second and the two steps of the compositional process being the third and the fourth. This chapter presents a full account of the four-step construction process. The construction process will be presented in four sections. At the beginning of each section is a flowchart showing the input, output, and processes involved in a particular step of the construction process. Section 5 of this chapter discusses issues concerning scaling up the scope of the project.

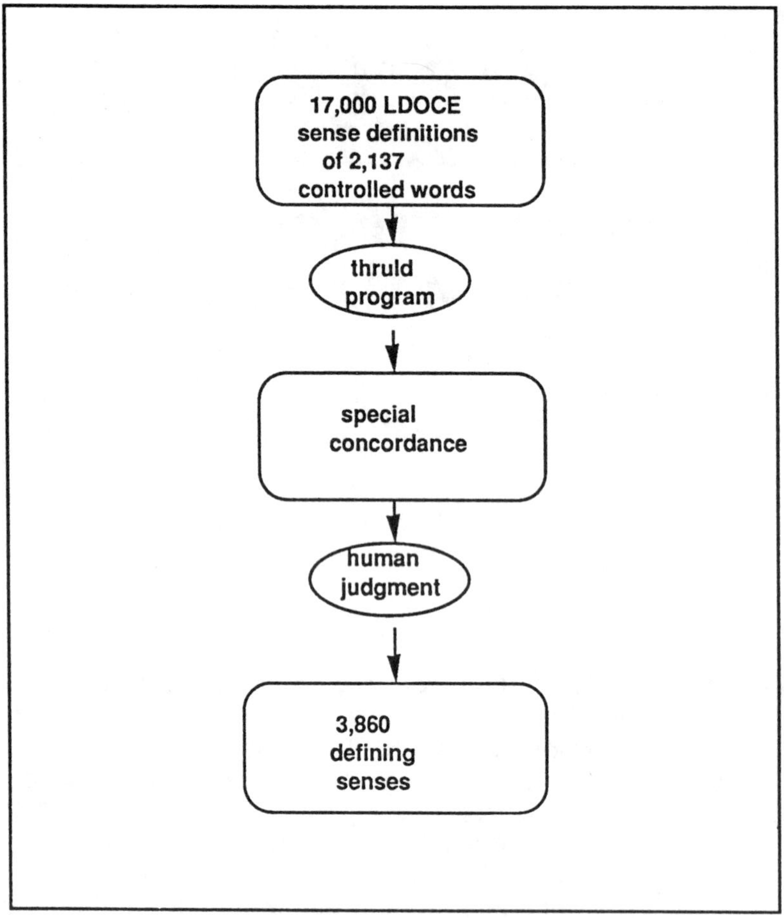

Figure 18.1. Flowchart of Step 1

1. STEP 1: DETERMINING THE DEFINING SENSES

1.1. Preprocessing of LDOCE

Preprocessing a MRD so that each word-sense entry adopts a form required by some computer language is not my invention. Boguraev (1986) has Lispified the entire LDOCE. For the purpose of this study, a program has been developed by the author to turn each LDOCE word-sense entry into a Prolog clause. The following is an example of such Prolog clauses produced by the program:

proldoce(farm, n, 1, ['ag'], ['n'], [], [], [an, area, of, land, ', ', together, with, its, buildings, ', ', concerned, with, the, growing, of, crops, or, the, raising, of, animals], [a, pig, farm, '|', we, work, on, the, farm]).
proldoce(farm, n, 2, ['ac'], ['n', 'x'], [], [], [farmhouse], []).
proldoce(farm, v, 0, ['ag'], ['h', 'n'], ['t1', ';', 'i'], [], [to, use, '(', land, ')', for, growing, crops, ', ', raising, animals, ', ', etc, '.'], [my, friend, is, farming, in, wales]).

The three Prolog clauses listed above represent three word senses of the word *farm.* Two of them are noun senses and one is a verb sense. Within each Prolog clause, the first argument is the word. The second argument is the part of speech of the word sense. Next is the numbering that word sense has within the part of speech. The following four arguments contain codes of some syntactic and semantic information. Some of these codes do not appear in the book version of LDOCE, for example, subject codes (the fourth argument) and the box codes (the fifth argument). The subject codes indicate the subject area where the word sense is used. Box codes give additional semantic information about the use of a word sense, for example, what semantic type of words a verb sense usually takes as its subject or object. The eighth argument is the definition of the word sense. The last argument provides examples of how that word sense is used.

After the defining senses are determined in a process to be discussed in Section 3.1.2., three more arguments are coded in by hand. As a result of the addition, each Prolog clause now has 12 arguments. These three arguments now occupy the fourth, fifth, and the sixth positions within the Prolog clause. The first, second, and third arguments remain the same as before. The fourth argument, the first added argument, represents the serial number of a word sense in all word senses of that word. Note that the serial number for the verb sense of *farm* is now 3. The fifth argument indicates whether a certain word sense is a defining sense or not. A zero indicates "yes," and 1 means "no." The sixth argument shows whether the word is used alone or as part of a phrase. A zero indicates a single word, and 1 means a phrase. The actual phrase then appears in the definition section of the Prolog clause. After the hand-coded information is added to the three Prolog clauses of *farm,* they look as follows:

proldoce(farm, n, 1, 1, 0, 0, ['ag'], ['n'], [], [], [an, area, of, land, ', ', together, with, its, buildings, ', ', concerned, with, the, growing, of, crops, or, the, raising, of, animals], [a, pig, farm, '|', we, work, on, the, farm]).

proldoce(farm, n, 2, 2, 1, 0, ['ac'], ['n', 'x'], [], [], [farmhouse], []).
proldoce(farm, v, 0, 3, 1, 0, ['ag'], ['h', 'n'], ['t1', ';', 'i', '-'], [], [to, use, '(', land, ')', for, growing, crops, ', ', raising, animals, ', ', etc, '.'], [my, friend, is, farming, in, wales]).

1.2. Determining the Defining Senses of LDOCE

LDOCE has a list of 2,137 controlled words. For each of these words, a special concordance file was created of all occurrences of the word in the definition text of all the controlled words, using Plate's thruld program. The program reads through the entire LDOCE dictionary, looking for occurrences of a certain word in the definition text of word senses. For the lack of adequate computational techniques, human judgment is used in determining what senses of each controlled word are the defining senses of LDOCE. The human judge, the author in this case, looks at each special concordance file created for each controlled word, and determines what senses of the controlled word are being used in defining the meanings of any of the 2,137 controlled words. Below is an example of a file of all occurrences of the word *father* in the text for the definitions of all the senses of the 2,137 controlled words.

aunt(0,1): the sister of one's father or mother, the wife of one's uncle, or a woman whose
brother or sister has a child
by(1,16): having (the stated male animal, esp. a horse) as a father
get(0,17): to become the father of | BEGET
grandfather(0,0): the father of someone's father or mother
grandmother(0,0): the mother of someone's father or mother
parent(0,1): the father or mother of a person
uncle(0,1): the brother of one's father or mother, the husband of one's aunt, or a man
whose brother or sister has a child
uncle(0,3): a man who takes the place of a father, esp. in relation to the children of a
woman who is or was married to someone else

The word *father* can either be a noun or a verb. LDOCE provides eight senses for *father* as a noun. In the pervious example, only the "male parent" sense of *father* is used to define the word senses of other controlled words. Hence "a male parent" (father(1,1), i.e., the first sense of the first homograph of *father*) is recorded as the defining sense of the word in LDOCE. This process repeats itself until the defining senses of all the defining words are determined. A total of 3,860 word senses of

2,000 controlled words have been determined as the defining senses of LDOCE. About half of these 2,000 words have single defining senses, whereas the other half have multiple defining senses.

It was found during the process of determining the defining senses of LDOCE that 137 controlled words do not participate in defining the word senses of the controlled words because nonempty concordance files could not be constructed for these 137 words using Plate's thruld program. In effect, there is a reduced set of 2,000 controlled words. In this study this reduced set is called the defining words of LDOCE. The word senses of the defining words that are used in the sense definitions of the 2,137 controlled words are the defining senses of LDOCE.

2. STEP 2: DERIVING THE SEED SENSES OF LDOCE

The following is a description of how the seed senses of LDOCE are derived:

1. A hunch set of the seed words is first developed, containing all defining words with multiple defining senses and and some defining words with single defining senses. Frequency of occurrence criteria are applied to the selection of hunch set seed words with single defining senses. The selection of defining words with single defining senses for the initial hunch set is done by intersecting four lexicons. These four lexicons are the 4,000 most frequently used words in all sense definitions in LDOCE as found in Plate's word frequency study of LDOCE (Wilks et al., 1988), the 850 words of basic English used in *The General Basic English Dictionary* (Ogden, 1942), the 500 most common words in Kucera and Francis (1967), and 1,051 defining words with single defining senses. The underlying concept here is that it is highly unlikely for words that appear in all these lexicons to be a nonseed word of LDOCE.
2. The hunch set is then tested in terms of its capability for having all the defining senses accounted for within three defining cycles. A defining cycle refers to the process of one group of words defining another in a dictionary, resulting in the second group of words being defined. A defining sense is accounted for if its definition text contains only words from the hunch set and/or words whose defining sense have been defined. At the end of a cycle, those words whose defining senses have been accounted for join with the words that define their meanings to define more words at the next cycle.
3. If the hunch set is capable of having all the defining senses accounted for within three defining cycles, the words in the hunch set

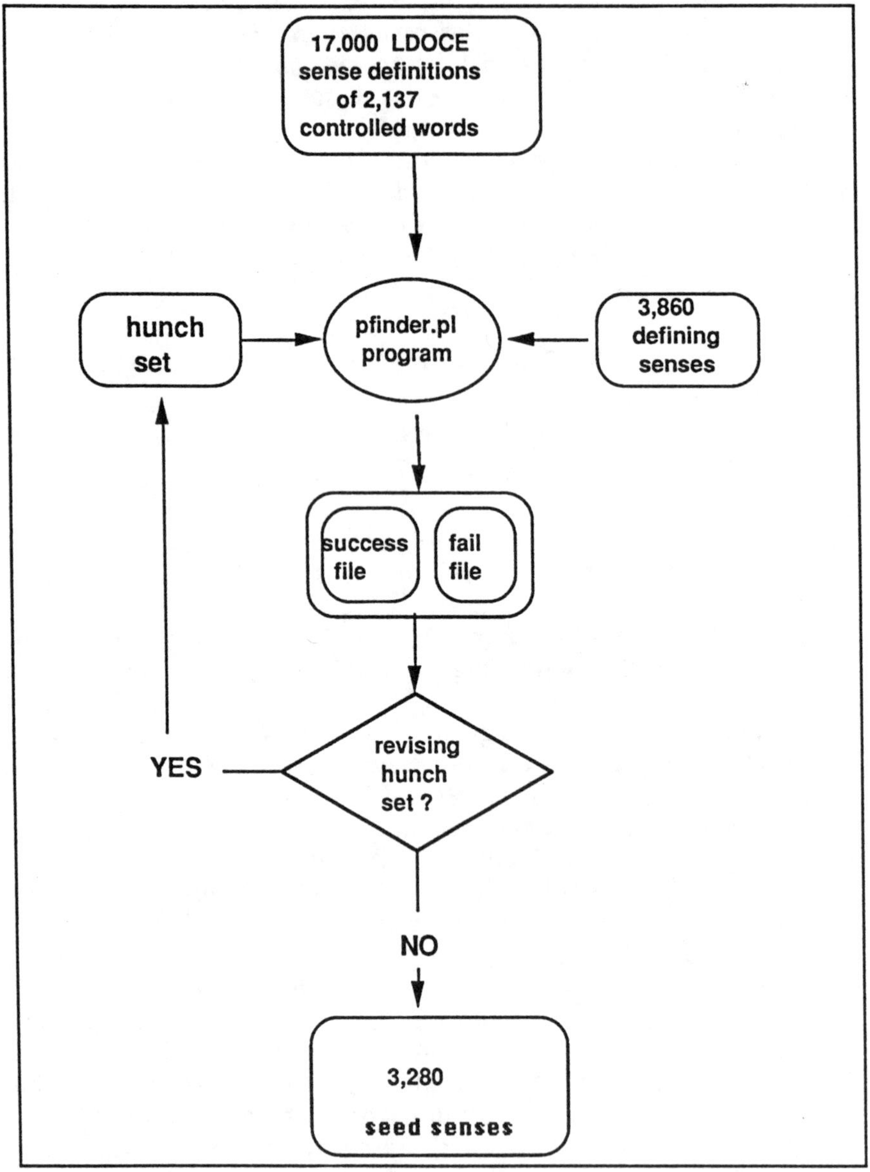

Figure 18.2. Flowchart of Step 2

become the seed words. Otherwise, the hunch set is revised and Process 2 above is repeated.

A computer program was developed to keep records of words that are accounted or unaccounted for at each defining cycle. The program looks at each word in the definition text of each of the defining senses to see whether it is a word from the hunch set. If all the words in the definition text of a defining sense are from the hunch set, the defining sense becomes a candidate to be entered into a "success" file. The word senses that are not accounted for enter a "fail" file. The fail file keeps a record of both the word senses that are not accounted for, and all the problematic words in the definition that cause the word senses to be unaccounted for. At the end of the first defining cycle, words that have been defined join with the hunch set to start the next cycle. Notice that the hunch set of seed words remains unchanged at this moment although the number of words that enter the second defining cycle increases. The program starts checking again for the second defining cycle. It examines every word in the definition text of the defining senses that are yet to be accounted for to see whether the word is from the hunch set or the added set of words that have been accounted for at the first defining cycle, then builds another success file and another fail file. If the 3,860 defining senses are not all accounted for at the end of the third defining cycle, the hunch set is revised to include some problematic words that were found to have caused some of the word senses to be unaccounted for. The process repeats itself until all the defining senses are accounted for at the end of the third cycle.

An issue involved in the revision of the hunch set is how large of a hunch set is preferable. The maximum number of words that can be put in the hunch set equals the number of the defining words. However, a look at the fail file created for each defining cycle would reveal that certain words are more problematic than others; that is, more frequently recorded in the fail file as causing some word senses to be unaccounted for. Preferably, only the more problematic words would be used to expand the hunch set.

Before the hunch set is expanded, a check is run on all new candidate hunch set words to make certain that they were not recorded in any success files. Any candidate new hunch set words that are found recorded in the success files are deleted. The deletion helps to reduce the size of the seed words without causing any defining sense to be left unaccounted for at the end of the third defining cycle. The process of deriving the seed words for LDOCE is an empirical process of trial and error. However, each time the hunch set is revised, the chance of confirming the hunch set as the seed words increases.

The final results of the derivation process show that the confirmed hunch set of seed words has 1,433 words. At the first defining cycle, 433 more words, or rather their defining senses, are defined by the hunch set. These 433 words join with the 1,433 seed words to define more words at the next cycle. At the second defining cycle, 128 more words (their defining senses to be exact) are defined. By the end of the third cycle, all defining senses of all defining words outside the hunch set of 1,433 seed words are defined. It takes one more defining cycle to have all controlled words defined.

3. STEP 3: HAND-CODING THE INITIAL KNOWLEDGE BASE

Two alternative ways of hand-coding semantic preference information into the initial knowledge base exist. For the sake of discussion, they are called here the generous hand-coding method and the thrifty hand-coding method. Generous hand-coding involves massive hand-coding of semantic preference information between all possible pairs of the semantic primitives derived at Step 2. Thrifty hand-coding attempts to minimize the load of hand-coding by hand-coding as much semantic preference information as is needed by the bootstrapping process. Pilot studies on both alternatives have been conducted. These studies reveal some of the strengths and weaknesses associated with each method.

3.1. The Generous Hand-Coding Method

A computer program was developed to massively elicit semantic preference information from native speaker informants. A list of 33 seed words with a total of 68 seed senses was used in the pilot study. The informant chosen for the pilot study was a male psychology major who had strong background in both linguistics and computer science. The program asks the informant whether a semantic preference relation exists in some context between pairs of the seed senses. The informant responded to the program 68*(68-1)/2 (= 2,278) number of times. On the average, it took the informant about 3 seconds to accomplish one response. A total of 838 positive responses were recorded. They are stored in a knowledge base as 838 pieces of semantic preference information between the 68 seed senses.

The elicited semantic preference information was then plugged into a parser to assist the semantic disambiguation process. In most of the cases, the parser turns out correct parses—a testimony to the usefulness of the semantic preference information elicited. However, the elicited

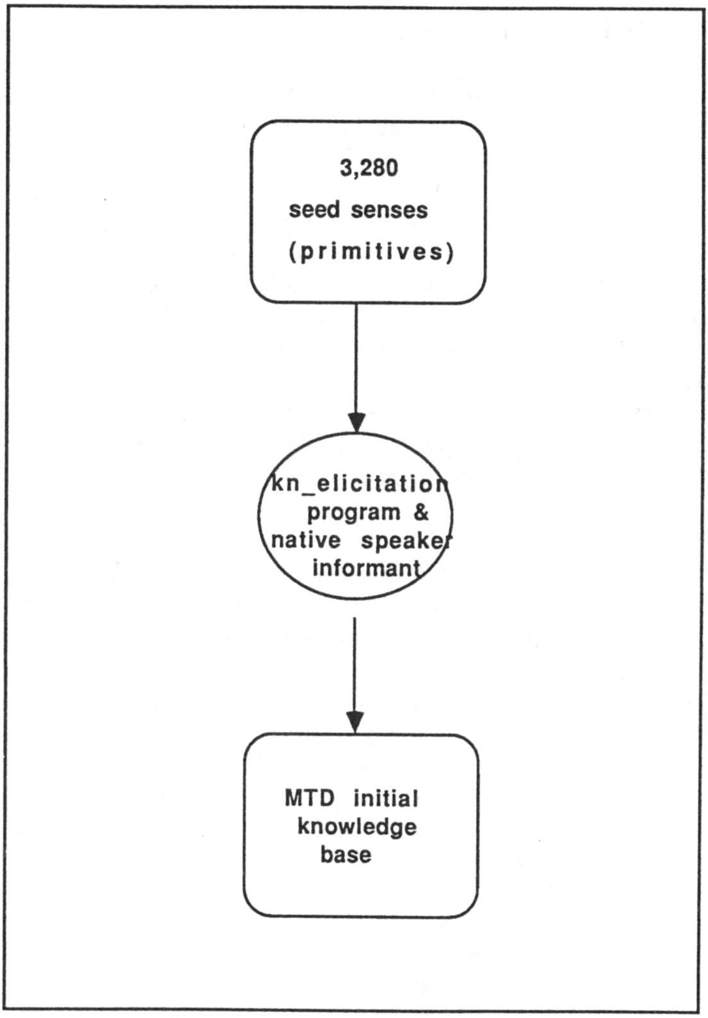

Figure 18.3. Flowchart of Step 3—generous hand-coding

semantic preference information sometimes allows too many parses, although these parses might all be correct. Because dictionary definition text is typically short with limited context, parsing the definitions with massively elicited semantic preference information about the seed senses has fairly high risk of getting into the mire of multiple parses. Owing to this drawback associated with the generous hand-coding method, the elicited semantic preference information produced by the method was not used in the bootstrapping example to be discussed in Section 3.4.

3.2. The Thrifty Hand-Coding Method

The thrifty hand-coding method involves minimum hand-coding of semantic preference information between a set of seed senses for the parsing of a collection of dictionary definitions. In the example for the bootstrapping process to be discussed in Section 3.4, a total of 338 seed senses are involved in parsing 16 word-sense definitions during a bootstrapping process aimed at processing two noun senses of *nurse*. The details of the bootstrapping process are presented in the next section. A pilot study was conducted on the thrifty hand-coding method to hand-code the minimum amount of semantic preference information for the parsing of 16 word-sense definitions. It turned out that the initial knowledge base hand-coded using the thrifty method has only 74 pieces of semantic preference information in it. These 74 pieces of semantic preference information are the minimum number needed for the correct word-sense selection in parsing the 16 word-sense definitions. They were created as follows.

First, a file consisting of word-sense definitions to be parsed in the bootstrapping process is produced. It consists of sense definitions of nonseed words found both in the definition text of two noun senses of *nurse* and in those of the nonseed words found in the two noun sense definitions of *nurse*. A file of 16 word-sense definitions to be bootstrapped is thus produced. These 16 word senses are whom1, them1, whose1, whose2, attend_to1, attend_to2, especially1, especially2, typically1, typically2, typically3, hospital1, doctor1, doctor2, nurse1, and nurse2.

Secondly, a human judge, in this case the author himself, went through each of the sense definitions in the file, identifying four types of semantic relations in each of the sense definitions. These four types of semantic relations are agent–action relationship, action–patient relationship, attribute–object relationship, and semantic relationships involving prepositions.

Thirdly, for each identified semantic relationship involving a pair of words, identify the correct word senses of the two words involved, and hand-code the semantic preference information in the initial knowledge base of the MTD. Thrifty hand-coding for a collection of word-sense definitions to be bootstrapped is completed when all identified semantic relationships in all the sense definitions to be bootstrapped have relevant semantic preference information asserted in the knowledge base.

For example, typically1 is a nonseed word found in the sense definition of nurse1. Its sense definition, *in a typical manner,* is included

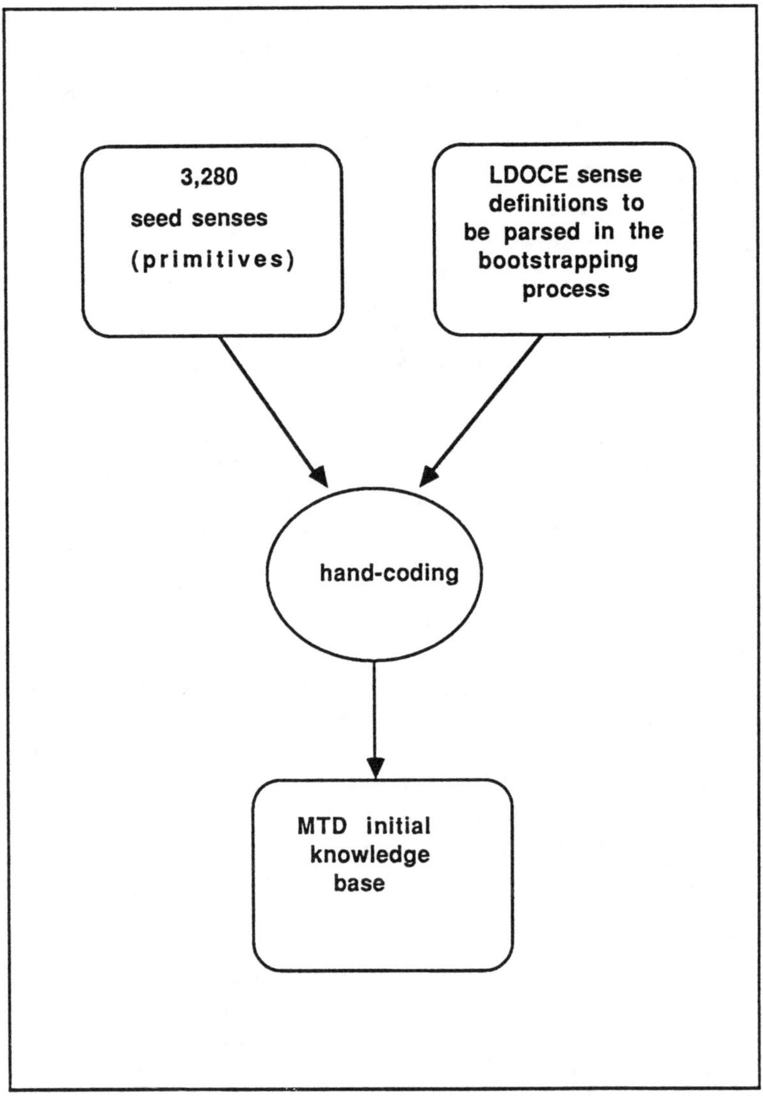

Figure 18.4. Flowchart of Step 3: Thrifty hand-coding

in the file for bootstrapping. A semantic matching relation involving the preposition *in* and the noun *manner* is identified. Another semantic relationship (attribute–object) is also identified between *typical* and *manner*. For each word involved in the two semantic relations, a required word sense is selected by the human judge for the word. The word sense selected for *in* is "in13" and that for *manner* is "manner1." The word sense selected for *typical* is "typical1." Hand-coded in the knowledge base is the following semantic preference information:

prefer(in13, manner1,1). prefer(typical1, manner1,1).

One important advantage of the thrifty hand-coding method is that it helps to produce single deterministic parses. The parse trees produced during bootstrapping are shown in the next section.

4. STEP 4: BOOTSTRAPPING FROM THE INITIAL HAND-CODED KNOWLEDGE BASE

Bootstrapping refers to a process of parsing dictionary definitions and acquiring semantic preference knowledge from the parse trees using an initial hand-coded knowledge base. The initial knowledge base contains hand-coded semantic preference information between a set of semantic primitives derived at Step 2.

A sentence analyzer has been developed by the author to demonstrate the feasibility of the bootstrapping process. Two main subprocesses are involved: the process of language analysis and the process of semantic preference acquisition. Language analysis of dictionary definition text involves both syntactic and semantic analyses. The input to the process is dictionary definition text. The output of the analysis is a parse tree with numbered word senses. These parse trees replace the original LDOCE word-sense definition given in words, thus expanding the lexical base of the MTD. Semantic preference acquisition involves assigning semantic preference relations to pairs of related word senses found on the parse tree. The acquisition is carried out by the acquisition module. The input to the module is a parse tree and the output is a newly acquired piece of semantic preference knowledge. For example, when a semantic preference relation is established between the head noun of the object and the main verb in the parse tree, a piece of new semantic preference knowledge like the one shown below is acquired by the acquisition module.

prefer(wordsense1,wordsense2,1).

The acquired semantic preference knowledge goes to enrich the knowledge base of the MTD.

The process proceeds in accordance with a bootstrapping schedule that fits the defining cycles of the dictionary. The bootstrapping schedule is concerned with which word senses are to be processed first, and which later. The need for the bootstrapping schedule stems from

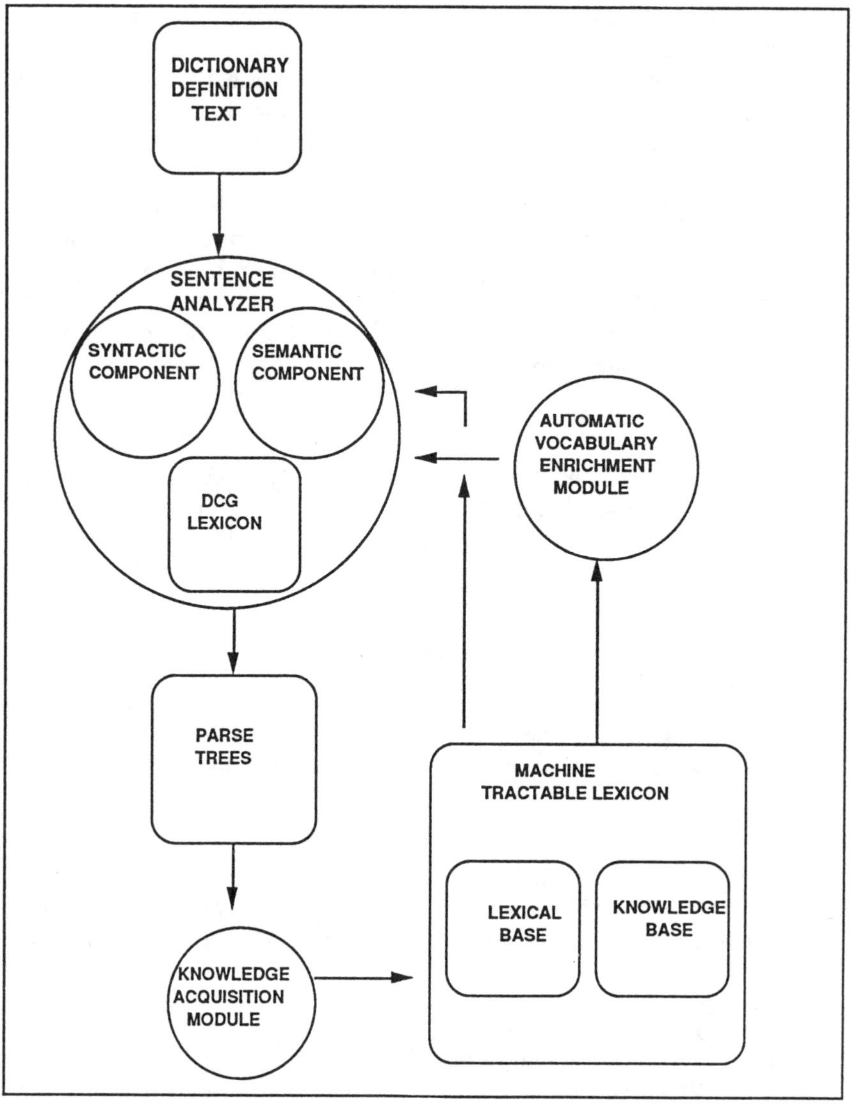

Figure 18.5. Flowchart of Step 4

the fact that both lexical and world knowledge concerning the words used in the definition text of a word sense have to be present in the MTD before the definition text of that particular word sense can be analyzed and new lexical and world knowledge acquired. Lexical and world-knowledge information acquired from analyzing the definition text of a word sense scheduled for earlier processing assists the analysis of the definition text of word senses scheduled for later processing. The success files discussed earlier are records of which word senses are defined at which defining cycle. These files provide an adequate basis for the establishment of an accurate bootstrapping schedule. The bootstrapping process for the entire LDOCE terminates when a MTD is built for all the word senses defined in LDOCE.

Following is an example showing the general process of bootstrapping associated with two defining senses of *nurse* as a noun. The semantic preference information required by the bootstrapping example was created by the thrifty hand-coding method.

The electronic version of LDOCE provides the following definitions for the two noun senses of *nurse*:

Sense 1:

proldoce(nurse, n, 1, [a, person, typically, a, woman, who, is, trained, to, take_care_of, sick, hurt, or, old, people, esp, as, directed, by, a, doctor, in, a, hospital]).

Sense 2:

proldoce(nurse, n, 2, [a, woman, employed, to, take_care_of, a, young, child]).

The bootstrapping process produces word-sense definitions given in terms of word senses with explicit word-sense numbers attached.

Sense 1:

proldoce(nurse, n, 1, [a1, person1, typically1, a1, woman1, who2, is2, trained9, to29, take_care_of1, sick1, hurt1, or2, old2, people1, especially2, as9, directed3, by5, a1, doctor2, in1, a1, hospital1]).

Sense 2:

proldoce(nurse, n, 2, [a1, woman1, employed1, to1, take_care_of1, a1, young1, child2]).

In what follows, we will show how the bootstrapping process produces word-sense definitions with explicit word-sense numbers attached. The semantic preference information contained in the initial knowledge base takes the form "prefer(seedsense1, seedsense2, 1)."

The seed words involved in the process are the following:

a, above, all, and, animal, as, be, belong_to, by, case, child, condition, cure, degree, different, direct, effort, employ, example, form, from, give, great, have, help, high, hold, hurt, ill, in, interest, manner, object, occasion, of, old, one, or, other, particular, people, person, place, profession, should, sick, special, stay, such, take_care_of, that, the, they, to, towards, train, treatment, typical, university, very, way, where, which, who, woman, young.

Step 1: At Step 1, the definitions of the following words are parsed and new semantic preference knowledge concerning these words acquired:

attend_to, them, whose.

The following are the parse trees produced for each of the senses of each of the above words:

1. attend_to
   s(post_mod(vip(infs(to29), vp(v(give5), np(n(help12), s(post_mod(pp(prep(to9)))))))))
   s(post_mod(vip(infs(to29), vp(v(direct5), np(adj(one's),n(effort2), conj(and1), np(n(interest1), s(post_mod(pp(prep(towards1))))))))))
2. them
   s(np(n(object1), s(np(n(form2), s(post_mod(pp(prep(of1), pron(they1))))))))
3. whose
   s(post_mod(prep(of1), conj(or2), ingf(belonging_to1), np(pron(whom1))))
   s(post_mod(pp(prep(of1), pron(which6))))
   s(post_mod(pp(prep(of1), pron(whom1))))

Step 2: At Step 2, the definitions of the following words are parsed and the new semantic preference knowledge acquired:

doctor, hospital, especially, typically.

The following are the parse trees produced for the sense definitions of the above words:

1. doctor
   s(np(det(a1), n(person1), ingp(ingf(holding6), np(pron(one22), pp(prep(of1),np(pre_mod(det(the1), adj(high5)), n(degree3))), pastp(given5), pp(prep(by5),det(a1), n(university1)), pp(prep(such_as1), np(det(a1), n(phd), n(dsc), n(dlitt),adv(etc1)))))))
   s(np(det(a1), n(person1), pron(whose2), s(np(n(profession1), s(vp(lv(is2), vip(infs(to29), vp(v(attend_to1),

np(adj(sick1), n(people1), conj(or2), np(n(animals1)))))))))))

2. hospital
   s(np(det(a1), n(place1), conj(where3), np(pre_mod(adj(ill1)), n(people1)), v(stay4), conj(and1), v(have5), n(treatment1), pron(which7), v(should5), v(cure1), np(pron(them1))))
3. especially
   s(post_mod(pp(prep(to8), np(pre_mod(det(a1), adv(very4), adj(great3)), n(degree1)))))
   s(post_mod(pp(prep(above7), pron(all22))))
   s(post_mod(adv(in_particular1)))
4. typically
   s(post_mod(pp(prep(in13), np(pre_mod(det(a1), adj(typical1)), n(manner1)))))
   s(post_mod(pp(prep(in18), np(pre_mod(adj(typical1)), n(condition1)))))
   s(post_mod(pp(prep(on5), np(pre_mod(det(a1), adj(typical1)), n(occasion1)))))
   s(post_mod(pp(prep(in19), np(det(a1), pre_mod(adj(typical1)), n(case1), conj(or2), np(n(example1))))))

Step 3: At Step 3, the two noun senses of *nurse* are parsed and semantic preference knowledge regarding each of the senses acquired. The following are the parse trees for each of the two senses of *nurse*:

s(np(det(a1), n(person1), adv(typically1), np(pre_mod(det(a1)), n(woman1)), s(np(pron(who2)), vp(lv(be2), pastp(trained9), vip(infs(to29), vp(v(take_care_of1), np(pre_mod(adj(sick1)), pre_mod(pastp(hurt1)), conj(or2), pre_mod(adj(old2)), n(people1)), adv(especially2), conj(as9), pastpp(pastp(directed3), pp(prep(by5), det(a1), n(doctor2))), pp(prep(in1), det(a1), n(hospital1)))))))))

s(np(det(a1), n(woman1), pastp(employed1), vip(infs(to29), vp(v(take_care_of1), np(pre_mod(det(a1), adj(young1)), n(child2))))))

In the course of the bootstrapping process, one more learning module is at work. It is the automatic vocabulary enrichment module (AVEM). The function of AVEM is to update the lexicon for the DCG parser. The input of the module is lexical entries in the lexical base of the MTD. For example:

proldoce(nurse, n, 2, [a, woman, employed, to, take_care_of, a, young, child]).

The output of AVEM is a lexical entry required by the DCG parser. For example:

n(n(nurse2)) – > [nurse].

The module is needed for creating new DCG lexical entries during the bootstrapping process. Every time a new word or new word sense needs to be bootstrapped, that is, its definition text needs to be parsed and relevant semantic preference knowledge needs to be acquired, its lexical entry is lacking in the DCG lexicon of the parser. The problem is taken care of automatically by AVEM.

Table 18.1 represents a summary of how the word senses involved in defining the two noun senses of *nurse* are defined. Most of these senses are seed senses. Semantic preference information concerning these word senses is hand-coded into the lexicon. They are identified by a "+" sign in the SEED SENSE column of Table 18.1. Some are defined at the first defining cycle; that is, by the seed words. They are "especially2," and "typically1," indicated by a "+" sign in the "First D(efining)C(ycle)" column of the following summary table. Others are defined at the "Second D(efining) C(ycle)"; that is, by the seed words plus words defined at the first defining cycle. Doctor2 and hospital1 belong to this group. Note that the word given after a "-" sign in the summary table is the word that keeps the word sense in question from being defined at a particular point during the bootstrapping process; for example, "attend_to" that appears in the definition text of the second word sense of *doctor* ("doctor2") keeps the word sense from being defined until the second defining cycle.

Newly acquired semantic preference information enters the knowledge base in the form of new Prolog assertions. The following are some of the Prolog assertions from processing the definitions of the two noun senses of *nurse*:

prefer(nurse1,hospital1,1).

prefer(nurse2,child2,1).

The acquired semantic preference information is used later on in the bootstrapping process for the semantic disambiguation of word senses.

5. SCALING UP

This section discusses issues of concern in scaling up the scope of the project to build an MTD for the entire LDOCE. This involves the execution of Steps 3 and 4 on a large scale.

5.1. Stages of Execution

The execution of Steps 3 and 4 for the entire dictionary will proceed in two main stages. The task of the first stage is to construct MTD in part

TABLE 18.1. The Bootstrapping Process With Two Noun Senses of Nurse

Word Sense	*seed sense*	*First DC*	*Second DC*	*Third DC*
a1	+	–	–	–
as5	+	–	–	–
by5	+	–	–	–
child2	+	–	–	–
directed3	+	–	–	–
doctor2	–	–attend_to	+	–
employed1	+	–	–	–
especially1	–	+	–	–
hopital1	–	–them	+	–
hurt1	+	–	–	–
nurse1	–	–	–	+
nurse2	–	–	–	+
in1	+	–	–	–
is2	+	–	–	–
old1	+	–	–	–
or2	+	–	–	–
people1	+	–	–	–
person1	+	–	–	–
sick1	+	–	–	–
to1	+		–	–
to9	+	–	–	–
take_care_of1	+	–	–	–
trained2	+	–	–	–
typically1	–	+	–	–
who2	+	–	–	–
woman1	+	–	–	–
young1	+	–	–	–

for the 2,137 controlled words of LDOCE. The task of the second stage is to build a MTD for the rest of LDOCE words to produce a complete MTD from LDOCE. Within the first stage, two main substages exist. The first substage is dedicated to the 17,000 single-head sense entries of the 2,137 controlled words. The second substage is dedicated to additional 7,000 multiple-head entries of the 2,137 controlled words. An example of a multiple head is *deal with* where two controlled words instead of one serve as the head of the entry.

5.2. The Execution of Step 3

The thrifty hand-coding method will be applied to the 17,000 single-head sense entries of the 2,137 controlled words. The hand-coding process is discussed in the following.

For each sense definition, four possible types of semantic relations are identified. For each identified semantic relation, a seed sense is determined by a human judge for each of the words involved in the semantic relation. A semantic preference assertion is then entered into the initial knowledge base of the MTD concerning the two seed senses. These semantic preference assertions will be used by the semantic component of the sentence analyzer in the process of word-sense disambiguation to produce parse trees for the sense definitions.

Firstly, hand-coding for 433 sense definitions that were found defined at the first defining cycle by the seed senses will be done. Secondly, hand-coding for an additional 128 sense entries that were found defined at the second defining cycle will follow. Thirdly, hand-coding for the sense definitions of the rest of the defining senses will be executed. Hand-coding for the sense entries of all the nondefining senses will be done last. Hand-coding at this stage is still necessary because the thrifty hand-coding method produces only a minimum amount of semantic preference information required for parsing sense definitions of the defining senses. It could well be the case that some required semantic preference information for the parsing of sense entries of the nondefining senses may still be lacking in the knowledge base constructed by hand-coding and automatic acquisition through Steps 1–3. Although the total time required for the hand-coding of these 17,000 word senses will not be in terms of man-years, it would still take a considerable amount of time to have the work done.

5.3. The Execution of Step 4

The bootstrapping process, which involves parsing sense definitions and acquiring semantic preference information from the parse trees, accompanies the execution of hand-coding at each of the four stages already discussed. Each time hand-coding is done on a collection of sense definitions, bootstrapping follows. After that particular collection of sense definitions is parsed and semantic preference information is acquired from the parsing trees, hand-coding for the next collection of sense entries begins.

Bootstrapping for the rest of the sense entries, that is, sense definitions other than the 17,000 single-head controlled word entries (approximately 57,000 sense definitions), will be executed without prior hand-coding. However, the bootstrapping process will not be clear sailing. Occasionally, the bootstrapping process may be suspended due to lack of a particular piece of semantic preference information, in which case the lacking semantic preference information will have to be hand-coded into the knowledge base of the MTD. It remains an empirical question, at this point, as to how to ensure a smoother process of bootstrapping for these 57,000 sense entries.

5.4. Other Issues

First, a full-fledged parser is needed for the bootstrapping process. Two alternatives exist. One alternative involves the development of a semantic component for Slator's chart parser (Slator, 1988), the other involves upgrading the mini-parser developed by the author in the process of implementing the bootstrapping example. The development of the parser will accompany the steps of the bootstrapping process. When the process terminates for the entire LDOCE, a full-fledged parser should have been developed.

Another important issue related to the process of bootstrapping concerns 895 words in the sense definitions of the 17,000 single-head entries that are not part of the 2,137 controlled words, per se. These 895 words fall into three categories. Words like *amusement* are derivations of some LDOCE controlled vocabulary words. Words like *Africa* are outside the LDOCE controlled vocabulary. Some words like *unmix* do not have entries in LDOCE at all. For those words in the 895-word set for which LDOCE provides sense entries, stacking could be a processing solution. This means putting noncontrolled words hit during the bootstrapping process on a stack on a first-in-last-out basis so that the sense definitions of these words are processed first before resuming parsing a particular sense definition. For those words in the 895-word set whose definitions are not given in LDOCE at all, some additional hand-coding of relevant information into both the lexical and knowledge bases seems inevitable.

CHAPTER 19

THE BOOTSTRAPPING PROCESS

The example given in the last chapter about the two noun senses of *nurse* is intended to present a macroscopic view of the bootstrapping process. The task of this process is to parse LDOCE definitions, tagging explicit word-sense numbers to the end of each word in the definition text, and acquiring semantic preference information from the definitions. An important principle used in the derivation of explicit word-sense numbers is the principle of semantic preference, due to Wilks (1972). Semantic preference refers to the behavioral tendency of words where more semantically related word senses prefer to stay with each other. For example, it is common knowledge that "a doctor in the hospital" probably refers to a medical doctor. In other words, the sense of *doctor* as a medical doctor *prefers* , so to speak, the sense of *hospital* as *"a place where ill peop*le stay and have treatment that *should cure them.*" The definitions with machine-tagged word-sense numbers become part of the lexical base of the MTD, and the acquired semantic preference information becomes part of the knowledge base of the MTD. Although there could be solid arguments for semantic preference ratings derived on a statistical basis with real number values, the original strategy of using only "0" and "1" in semantic preference ratings (Wilks, 1972) is followed in this study.

This chapter presents a microscopic view of the bootstrapping process as a process of machine learning. Two types of machine learning are involved: the acquisition of semantic preference information from parsing dictionary definition text, and the inductive learning of generalized semantic preferences from the acquired knowledge of semantic preferences. Both types of knowledge enrich the knowledge base of the MTD, facilitating a continuing process of bootstrapping. The example given in this chapter concerns the definitions of "take_care_of." LDOCE provides two senses for the expression "take_care_of," which are:

1. be responsible for
2. beat; kill

The following is intended to show:

1. How the system parses its definitions and acquires semantic preference knowledge from parsing the definitions
2. How the system makes inductions about generalized semantic preferences of a word sense when a certain required piece of semantic preference information is lacking in the knowledge base
3. How the system handles semantic preference violations found in unrestricted general text or utterances

1. MACHINE LEARNING OF SEMANTIC PREFERENCE INFORMATION

The acquisition of semantic preference information *is* machine learning for two reasons. First, dictionary definitions do not explicitly tell the reader what the semantic preferences of a word sense being defined are. The machine has to obtain such information through analyzing the definition text. Of course, LDOCE does provide some box codes in terms of some 30 semantic features. The semantic information contained in these box codes is, however, extremely general. In many cases, it does not provide enough disambiguating power that similar word senses can be differentiated from each other. An example in point is the word *marry,* which has three verb senses. The box codes for the preferred agents and preferred patients (direct objects) of all three senses of *marry* are all "H" (human).

Secondly, the acquisition of semantic preferences either from parsing definition text or inducing over acquired knowledge conforms to well-known definitions of machine learning such as the one given by Michalski: "Learning is constructing or modifying representations of what is being experienced" (Michalski et al., 1986, p. 10).

Through parsing the definitions, the system detects semantic preference information implicitly contained in the definition text, and saves it in some form of representation in the knowledge base of the MTD. The common-sense knowledge thus acquired enables the system to parse more definitions and acquire more semantic preference information in the bootstrapping process of constructing the MTD.

In what follows, examples are presented to illustrate the process of semantic preference acquisition and that of making inductions about generalized semantic preferences over the acquired knowledge.

The first "take_care_of" that the system has to parse is found in the the example sentence given under take_care_of1: "*Take care of the baby while I am out*." Because it is given as an example of the first sense of *take care of*, the *take care of* in the example is, by definition, take_care_of1. The system would produce a parse tree, from which it acquires the semantic preference information of "you1" as the preferred agent, and "baby1" as the preferred patient. Following the bootstrapping schedule, the system parses more definitions and acquires more semantic preference information about "take_care_of1." By the time the system finishes parsing the definition of "nurse1" (a person, typically a woman, who is trained to take care of sick, hurt, or old people, esp. as directed by a doctor in a hospital), the knowledge base has the following as the preferred agents of take_care_of1:

men, woman

It has the following as the preferred patients of take_care_of1:

baby, someone, children, horse, appearance, aircraft, sports field, garden, something

In parsing the definition of "nurse1," the parser uses the semantic preference information acquired thus far in its word-sense disambiguation process. It has no difficulty in taking woman or, woman1 to be exact, as the preferred agent of take_care_of1.

Sometimes the knowledge base of the MTD does not contain a required piece of semantic preference information. The system has to make inductions about generalized semantic preferences of a word sense in order to carry on the parsing process. This concerns the word *people* in the definition. In the knowledge base of the MTD, people1 is not recorded as the preferred object or patient of take_care_of1. What the system does at this point is to form hypotheses about what generalized preferred patients of take_care_of1 could be. It generalizes from *baby, someone,* and *children* to person1 as the generalized preferred patient of take_care_of1. Person1 is exactly the superordinate of "people1." In the absence of counterevidence, "people1" is accepted, by way of induction, as the generalized preferred patient of take_care_of1. With this piece of induced knowledge added to the knowledge base of the MTD, parsing of *take care of* is biased toward its first sense. In making generalized semantic preference inductions, two general constraints similar to those employed in Michalski's INDUCE system (Michalski, 1983) are important. They are the constraints of *consistency* and *completeness*. In Michalski's system, a description is consistent if it does not apply to any members of the contrast set (i.e., it has no counterexamples). A description is complete if it applies to all members of the target category. These constraints, in principle, apply to machine learning of natural language, but not without modifications. The constraint of *consistency* should work for natural language simply because language operates on the principle of distinctiveness. Word-sense definitions are given in such a way that the word senses are made distinct from each other. However, the difficulty with natural language is that the distinction between word senses can be based on more than one level of description. Two word senses are distinct from each other on syntactic, semantic, or pragmatic grounds. The general constraint of consistency is applicable to the process of induction only when two word senses are distinguished from each other on one level of description. *Take care of* is an example in point. Take_care_of1 is distinct from take_care_of2 on the semantic level; that is, in meaning. The generalized action of take_care_of1 (be_responsible_for1)should never be the same as the generalized action of take_care_of2 (beat1 or kill1). The constraint of completeness, when applied to inductive learning of semantic preference situations, becomes a relative notion. A generalized preferred agent does not necessarily have properties that apply to all members of the category of preferred agents of a verb sense. Generalizations made on a subset of all instances of preferred agents are permissible. This is exactly how person1 was induced as the generalized preferred agent of take_care_of1. As is well known with the properties of natural categories, there is no single property that is necessary, and no set of properties that is sufficient. Family resemblance becomes the criterion. It provides the underlying principle for a relative conceptualization of the constraint of completeness in connection with machine learning of generalized semantic preference information.

2. ACQUIRED VERSUS INDUCED SEMANTIC PREFERENCES

One way to contrast and compare semantic preference information as acquired from parsing dictionary definitions versus that induced from acquired semantic preference information is to examine the two types of semantic preference information in terms of levels of generality. Contrary to the intuition of most people, semantic preference information acquired from parsing dictionary definition text can be very general. For example, the definition of *look after* provides very general information concerning the preferred patients of take_care_of1; that is, *someone* or *something*. *Someone* or *something* covers practically all possible instances of preferred patients of take_care_of1. Of course, in most cases, semantic preference information acquired from parsing dictionary definitions is not as general as that acquired from the definition of *look after*. Often, individual example sentences provide particular instances of semantic preference information from which generalizations can be made.

Inductive learning of generalized semantic preferences is both necessary and useful when some piece of required knowledge information is lacking in the system. In the "the pilot took a direct course," for example, the system may have no information about the semantic preferences of various word senses of *course*. In that case, the process of word-sense selection of the correct word sense of *take* and the correct word sense of *course* will not be a simple process of matching with some available information in the knowledge base of the MTD, for example:

prefer(take14,course2,1).

The system would have to make generalizations or specializations from available information to make the best guess about which word sense of *take* could possibly prefer which word sense of *course*.

The process of inductive learning of semantic preference relations proceeds in three steps. At Step 1, the inductive learning module looks through the knowledge base for possible pieces of information by which some induction could be made. For the sake of illustration, suppose the system has the following piece of information:

prefer(take14,path1,1).

At Step 2, the system looks through the lexical base of the MTD and examines the sense definitions of the word (*course* in the present example) for which semantic preference information is missing. The system tries to locate the genus in each sense definition. The genus of a particular word sense is the superordinate word sense identified in its definition. In this example, the genus of course1 is movement1, and that for course2 is path1, and so forth.

At Step 3, the system goes back to the knowledge base of the MTD and looks for a match between any sense of *take* and any genus of any word sense of course. In this example, the system found a match between take14 and path1. The learning module then induces from the matching information, and decides that a semantic preference relation could exist between take14 and course2, for course2 has path1 as its genus and the knowledge base says that take14 prefers the genus term. This induction is then provided to the semantic component of the sentence analyzer to allow the two word senses (take14 and course2) to be chosen.

Although overgeneralization of sense preferences is likely to be rare, the overgeneralization of truth conditions tends to be more common in the inductive learning process. For example, the knowledge base of the MTD says that bird1 as meaning "a creature with wings and feathers" prefers fly1 as meaning "to move or be moved through the air by means of wings or a machine." When parsing the sentence "Do ostriches fly?" the system will induce from the available information (prefer([bird1,fly1,1).) and decide that ostriches could also fly because the definition of *ostrich* says that it is "a type of very large African bird." As a result, a wrong induction would be made about *ostriches* being able to fly. This kind of overspecialization is quite common in humans, let alone machines. The important thing is how to correct them. When processing the answer to the question "No. Ostriches do not fly," we get rid of the contradictory information previously asserted in the knowledge base by changing the 1 in the third argument to 0:

prefer(ostrich1,fly1,0).

Note that 0 does not indicate the absence of a semantic preference relation between the two word senses. Rather it denotes the truth value of the assertion. In other words, what it says is that it is simply not true to assert that ostriches fly. The presence of the above piece of knowledge facilitates rather than prevents the selection of ostrich1 and fly1 the next time the same sentence "Do ostriches fly?" is parsed. The system takes the 0 simply as a positive 1 in terms of the semantic preference relationship between the two word senses. This explains the importance of the third argument in the "prefer" predicate. Without it, it would be hard for the system to make wrong inductions, and then correct them.

3. SEMANTIC PREFERENCE VIOLATIONS

In Guo (1991), an interactive vocabulary acquisition system was presented that uses semantic preference violations as signals of the need to learn new word senses. The mechanism is an important one in that the same mechanism can be applied to learning situations with an MTD. It is especially important considering that:

1. Ill-formedness is a very common phenomenon in general unrestricted text and utterances.
2. Incompatibility between dictionary definitions can best be detected through the detection of semantic preference violations of word senses.

Successful handling of the incompatibility problem between dictionaries would enable us to start with one MTD and acquire an abundance of knowledge from a whole collection of other dictionaries. Detailed research on this topic is beyond the focus of this study.

In the process of bootstrapping to construct the MTD from LDOCE, semantic preference violations occur frequently. However, they are not as revealing as those detected while parsing general unrestricted text with a completed MTD. This is due to the fact that during the bootstrapping process, every time a semantic preference violation is detected, it would have already been known that the definition or the example sentence of a new word sense is being parsed. Also, all the defining senses used in LDOCE are defined in the dictionary. Technically, there should be no real semantic preference violations if a well-controlled bootstrapping schedule is maintained.

The usefulness of semantic preference violations with regard to machine learning of semantic preference information entirely diminishes when possible semantic preference violations are indicated in the dictionary by *fig,* meaning figurative use of a certain word sense. For example, LDOCE has the following example for the figurative use of the first sense of *marry:*

> She married money. (meaning she married a rich man)

However, in parsing general unrestricted text with a constructed MTD, semantic preference violation would mean one of two things in the absence of spelling errors:

1. The figurative use of a word sense; for example, He married books;
2. A possible new word sense is encountered; for example, The star is real bad.

CHAPTER 20

SUMMARY AND EVALUATION

This chapter summarizes my work on constructing a MTD from LDOCE. Following the summary is an evaluation of the natural set of semantic primitives derived from LDOCE in terms of Wilks' (1977) membership restrictions for a set of semantic primitives.

1. WORK ACCOMPLISHED

The process of constructing a MTD from a MRD, LDOCE in this case, consists of two main subprocesses: the process of reduction and the process of composition. Each subprocess proceeds in two steps. The entire construction process consists of four steps. A schematic representation of the construction process was shown in Figure 16.2. Step 1 involved the determination of the defining senses of LDOCE. Step 2 involved the derivation of the seed senses as a natural set of semantic primitives for LDOCE. Step 3 involved hand-coding the initial knowledge base for the seed senses of Step 2. Step 4 involved constructing lexical and knowledge bases for the rest of the controlled words and all the other words in LDOCE.

Step 1 of the construction process has been completed. A total of 3,860 defining senses have been determined. These word senses are used in the definitions of all the senses of the 2,137 controlled words in LDOCE. Currently these defining senses are being compiled into an independent dictionary called *Mini-LDOCE* by Longman Dictionaries, where the definitions of these word senses are given in terms of these defining senses themselves (see Appendix A).

Step 2 of the construction process has also been completed. A total of 3,280 word senses are found to be the seed senses of LDOCE. These seed senses are taken as a natural set of semantic primitives derived from LDOCE. The seed senses act as a reduction device such that every sense definition of LDOCE can be represented in their terms by means of Fregean Formulae to be constructed through Steps 3 and 4.

Step 3 is a preparatory step for parsing LDOCE sense definitions and acquiring semantic preference information from the parse trees. The goal of Step 3 is to construct an initial knowledge base for the parser so that the hand-coded semantic preference information in the knowledge base can be used by the parser in the semantic disambiguation of word senses. The step is an important one in the sense that its omission would disable the semantic analysis of LDOCE sense definitions. Two alternative methods exist: the generous hand-coding method and the thrifty hand-coding method.

The generous hand-coding method requires the elicitation of semantic preference information from one or more native-speaker informants concerning a total of (3,280 * (3,280-1))/2 = 5,377,560 pairs of semantic primitives. An advantage of this method is that it helps to create a large knowledge base of semantic preference information that enables the semantic analysis of a large corpus of data. However, a natural consequence of building such a large semantic preference knowledge base is that the parser easily produces multiple parses for sentences of limited context. Because dictionary definitions are typically short with limited context, multiple parses are unavoidable. Another disadvantage associated with the method is that it is extremely labor intensive. Due to these disadvantages, results of a pilot study using the generous hand-coding method were not applied to the bootstrapping example concerning the two noun senses of *nurse.*

Another alternative, the thrifty hand-coding method, requires minimum hand-coding of semantic preference information for the parsing of a specific collection of dictionary sense definitions. The advantage of this method is that it reduces the effort of hand-coding to a minimum. Only relevant semantic preference information with respect to the bootstrapping process of Step 4 is hand-coded in the initial knowledge base. Judging in terms of the laziness principle, the second alternative seems to be much better than the first. The thrifty hand-coding method is recommended for Step 3 when the scope of the project is scaled up.

For Step 4 of the construction process, a sentence analyzer for parsing LDOCE word-sense definitions has been developed. The parser has both syntactic and semantic components. It was written in Quintus Prolog currently running on the Sun workstations.

To sum up, Steps 1 and 2 of the construction process have been completed. The feasibility of Steps 3 and 4 of the construction process has also been demonstrated with implemented examples. What remains to be done is to complete Steps 3 and 4 of the construction process using as guidelines the results of initial implementations of the first two steps.

2. EVALUATION OF THE PRIMITIVES DERIVED FROM LDOCE

The adequacy of the natural set of semantic primitives derived from LDOCE forms the cornerstone of the entire study presented here. It is scrutinized here in terms of Wilks' 5-point membership restrictions for any set of semantic primitives (Wilks, 1977). The natural set of semantic primitives derived from LDOCE is examined by way of contrast and comparison with the prescribed set of semantic primitives as used in LDOCE.

The first restriction, finitude, requires that (a) names of the natural numbers are not contained in the set, and (b) the set should be considerably smaller than the set of words whose meanings it is to encode. Both sets seem to be acceptable. The prescribed set has a total member of 33 primitives, with 16 generic ones and an additional 17 produced by logical functions AND, OR, and NOT. These 33 semantic primitives provide semantic codings for 74,113 word senses. The natural set, 3,280 strong, constitutes less than 5% of the total number of word senses whose meanings it is to encode.

The second restriction concerns comprehensiveness; that is, the set should adequately express and distinguish the senses of the word set whose meanings it is to encode. This is largely true of the natural set but hardly true of the prescribed set. For example, three senses are given for the word *marry* in LDOCE: (a) to take (a person) in marriage, (b) *to perform the ceremony of marriage for (two people)*; and (c) *to cause to take in marriage*. As mentioned earlier, the expected subjects as well as the expected objects of the three senses of *marry* are all given as "H" (human) in the machine-readable version of LDOCE. These semantic codes do not, and cannot, express and distinguish the three senses adequately. Systems that uses such primitives could have difficulty parsing the sentence "The father married the young couple," for the semantic codes for the two senses of *father*; that is, *parent* father and *priest* father, are both "H," and that for *couple* is also "H." Semantically, any of the three senses of *marry* would satisfy the selectional restrictions. As a result, the word-sense disambiguation process is subject to error. One solution that readily suggests itself is to enlarge constantly the prescribed set of semantic primitives every time an inadequacy is spotted: a heuristic not totally without merit, but that serves only to prolong the agony of endless error correction.

The natural set of primitives derived from the dictionary represents a much richer set of semantic relations, and is capable of handling much finer sense distinctions as required by NLP. In the aforementioned sentence, the expected subjects of the three senses of *marry* are distinct from each other. Marry1 has person1, marry2 has priest1, and marry3 has parent1. The expected objects of the three senses of marry also differ. Marry1 has person1, marry2 has people1, and marry3 has child1. Parsing the sentence "The father married the young couple," should present no major problems to the natural set of semantic primitives. The inherent semantic hierarchies that exist between the natural set of semantic primitives facilitate inductive learning of generalized semantic preferences, an example of which was given in Section 2.

The third restriction concerns what is called independence; that is, "there should not be a marker *X, Y, Z* in the set so that there is some function *F* such that *X* = *F(Y, Z)*." Unfortunately this rule is stretched for both the prescribed set and the natural set derived from LDOCE. More than half of the prescribed set (17 out of 33 primitives) is produced by some logical functions over 16 generic primitives. Although the natural set does not explicitly use any logical functions to produce new primitives, its hierarchical arrangement facilitates such operations, or more frankly, it is the result of such operations performed not by any conscious human being, but by the inner workings of the English language. Such embarrassment was anticipated by Wilks (1977) when he wrote, " This will not be so easy to achieve if the members are hierarchically organized" (pp. 183-184)

*Non*circularity, the fourth restriction, is an easy one for the prescribed set. There are no two primitives in the set that are mutually defined. However, for the natural set, noncircularity poses a severe test. This is because the natural set is derived from a dictionary, and dictionaries in general are notorious for their circular definitions of word senses.

Related work in the literature is Sparck Jones' (1967) study on dictionary circles. Note that Sparck Jones (1967) and this study share similar assumptions, one of which is that useful semantic information can be obtained from analyses of dictionary definitions for purposes of text analysis in general. Sparck Jones (1967) aimed at finding the "relational and classificatory structure" of the English vocabulary (p. 5). Various approaches and methods were discussed to determine interesting dictionary circles. It is important to note that in Sparck Jones (1967) two-word circles were deemed as "quirky and uninteresting" (p. 13), and consequently, were completely disregarded. In the present study, however, two-word circles receive special attention in the process of deriving the natural set of semantic primitives. Mutually defined semantic primitives reduce machine tractability and are harmful to the MTD for which the natural set of semantic primitives is intended. An effort is made in the knowledge base of the MTD such that no such circles are possible within the natural set of semantic primitives. For example, in LDOCE a *trip* is defined as a *journey*, and a *journey* as a *trip*. One way to overcome the circularity is to include just one of the words as a seed word, but not the other. In this particular case, *trip* is included in the set of seed words, and *journey* excluded from it. The first sense of *trip* as a noun, which is a seed sense, becomes a member of the natural set of semantic primitives derived from LDOCE.

The last restriction calls for primitiveness; that is, no marker subset should be plausibly replaced by a smaller defining set. Again neither the prescribed set or the natural set is satisfactory. On the one hand, the prescribed set has a smaller defining set of 16 primitives. The remaining 17 primitives are produced by some logical functions. On the other hand, the natural set is hierarchically organized and the primitives sitting at the top of the hierarchies may well form a plausible smaller defining set.

To sum up, both the natural set and the prescribed set are cleared for Restrictions 1 and 4 (finitude and noncircularity); neither one strictly abides by Restrictions 3 and 5 (independence and primitiveness); and on Restriction 2 (comprehensiveness) the natural set seems to operate much better than the prescribed set. Because semantic primitives are means of expression and distinction of word senses, the advantage of the natural set over the prescribed set on Restriction 2 is nontrivial.

CHAPTER 21

CONCLUSION

This book has presented the views of a multinational assembly of 20 researchers on the design and construction of MTDs. The author's own work on constructing a MTD from LDOCE has also been presented. The presentations touched on almost all important aspects of two fundamental issues in designing and constructing MTDs:

1. In what form should natural language be represented in the lexicon such that NLP tasks on general unrestricted text can be supported?
2. In what way can the production of such lexicons be automated?

As the author and editor of the book, I am constantly amazed by the fact that the breadth of the issues covered in this book outran the depth of the investigation of any one of them by such large margins. Interested readers could easily entertain themselves with a collection of such issues without much difficulty. In a way, this book serves as an initiator of what is hopefully a dialogue on the design and construction of MTDs among all interested parties in the international community.

If we could liken the book to a large expanse of shallow waters on Lake MTD, the water is by no means calm. Tension between the introduction by Robert Amsler and the rest of the book constitutes the major source of energy that created many waves. Every single paragraph of the introduction can be viewed as an indcator of at least one such wave. Frictions in view between the chapters gave rise to no less excitement. For example, if most chapters in this book assume a readiness to recognize the well-established boundaries between word senses given in a dictionary, Pustejovsky's chapter tends to negate such assumptions as having serious problem.

The differences between researchers in the representation of language form-linguistic information at the orthographical, phonological, morphological, and even syntactic levels-are largely negligible. The differences between them in the representation of language meaning are far from being resolved. The difficulties stem from the fact that the adequacy of the representation of language meaning not only rests on the adequacy of the representation in accommodating the needs of computer programs to accomplish NLP tasks, but also rests heavily on whether or not the representation can be constructed automatically from machine-readable sources. For example, most researchers seem to support the idea that certain meaning structures such as verb case roles are important. However to obtain case roles automatically from machine-readable sources is a nontrivial task. Syntactic correlates are not always reliable. In "The wind opened the door," the subject of the sentence, *wind* , is not the agent but the instrument. If it were the case that simpler meaning structures are difficult to obtain automatically, what chance do we have in generating more complex meaning structures from machine readable sources in an automatic fashion?

If the problem of automating the generation of meaning representations remains insolvable, we might be forced to seek alternative computing processes that require less expensive meaning structures, for example, computing on various types of associative networks, where the links are numbered for strength instead of labeled for meaning. Then less expensive means of analysis on natural language data could be employed to produce the numerical information required for such computing processes. It is widely believed that uninterpreted links may be less accurate, and therefore, may find less applications than interpreted links in AI and NLP. The accuracy of the analysis is certainly affected by the language data being used for the analysis. The most recommendable type of data involves the use of fully disambiguated text in large quantities, where all words in the text are tagged explicitly with word-sense numbers. In tagging word-sense numbers to texts, it should make sense if dictionary definition texts are done first, followed by entries in encyclopedias, and then finally on unrestricted text corpora. The *Mini-LDOCE* project under way at Longman represents effort in this direction.

Apoint of intense interest recorded during the discussion was on the concept of a neutral lexicon. So far no one has denied that at the technical level neutral lexicons do not exist. Good NLP programs are always built on good theories, and their lexicons are, by no means, theory neutral. John McNaught of UMIST, who is currently directing several lexicon projects, has the following to say:

> Neutrality does not technically exist. We must have some kind of interpretation of the data in terms of some theory. If we can achieve mappings to other theories, then in a sense, the original one chosen for the lexicon is indeed neutral in some respect. I now prefer to talk in terms of a "reusable resource." The problem then becomes one of being able to state mappings adequately. This can be done in several ways, depending on how you view the desirability or feasibility of setting up some large resource. For example:
>
> one-to-many: one reusable resource that can map to many application-dependent lexica.
> one-to-one: two resources simply exchanging lexical data via some standard exchange mechanism.
>
> The first solution is perhaps the ideal one. It is clearly an expensive and time-intensive enterprise.
> The second solution is the general case of which the first one is the special case. That is, we now talk about bilateral exchange (or of course just one way) of lexical data. (Mc Naught, 1991)

Following McNaught's argument, neutrality in the lexicon really amounts to how well a lexicon can be mapped to a theory-bound lexicon. MTDs can thus exist at two levels: one at the machine-tool level and one at the applicational level. Although MTDs at both levels are important for NLP, the one at the machine-tool level together with a set of mapping procedures (tools) is more sought after today.

Work on MTDs has just begun. The future of this fast developing area remains an empirical one. It largely depends on the outcome of some serious lexicon projects, known or unknown to the public, that are underway in the United States, Europe, and Japan, including the Psych Project at MCC under Lenat, the Lexical Database project at IBM under Byrd and Boguraev, the Japan EDR project, and the lexical projects of the EC (Acquilex, Multilex, Genelex, and Eurotra-7).

Currently we are still a long way from being able to develop sophisticated MTDs that can support complex language processes such as reasoning and inferencing. It is high time, though, for computational linguists, lexicographers, cognitive scientists, AI researchers, theoretical linguists, psychologists, philosophers, logicians, statisticians, and publishers to put heads together and work across national boundaries with official support from each participating country to realize what Atkins called a "dynamic database" that eventually makes everyone of us a winner.

REFERENCES

Ahlswede, T.E. (1983). A linguistic string grammar of adjective definitions from the Webster's Seventh Collegiate Dictionary (master's thesis). Chicago, IL: Illinois Institute of Technology.

Ahlswede, T.E. (1985). A tool kit for lexical building. Paper presented at the 23rd Annual Meeting of the Association for Computational Linguistics, Chicago.

Ahlswede, T.E., & Evens, M. (1988a, June). *Parsing vs. text processing in the analysis of dictionary definitions*. Paper presented at the 25th Annual ACL, Buffalo, NY.

Ahlswede, T.E., & Evens, M. (1988b). Generating a relational lexicon from a machine-readable dictionary. *International Journal of Lexicography*,1, 214–237.

AJCL. (1983). Special issue on processing ill-formed input. The American Journal of Computational Linguistics, 9.

Allen, J.F. (1987). *Natural Language Understanding*. Menlo Park, CA: Benjamin Cummings.

Alshawi, H. (1987). *Processing dictionary definitions with phrasal pattern hierarchies*. Cambridge, UK: University of Cambridge.

Alshawi, H., Boguraev, B., & Briscoe, T. (1985). Toward a dictionary support environment for realtime parsing. *Proceedings of the Second European ACL* (pp. 171–178).

Amsler, R. (1980). *The structure of the Merriam-Webster Pocket Dictionary* (PhD thesis). Austin, TX: University of Texas.

Amsler, R.A. (1981). A taxonomy for English nouns and verbs. *Proceedings of the 19th Annual Meeting of the Association for Computational Linguistics* (pp. 133–138). Stanford, CA.

Amsler, R.A. (1984). Machine-readable dictionaries. In M.E. Williams (Ed.), *Annual review of information science and technology* (Vol.19, pp. 161–209). White Plains, NY: Knowledge Industry Publications for the American Society for Information Science.

Amsler, R., & White, J. (1979). Development of a computational methodology of deriving natural language semantic structures via analysis of machine-readable dictionaries (TR MCS77–01315). Austin, TX: University of Texas, Linguistic Research Center.

Apresyan, J.D. (1973). Regular polysemy. *Linguistics*, 142.

Apresyan, Y.D., Mel'cuk,I.A., & Zolkovsky, A.K. (1969). Semantics and lexicography: Towards a new type of unilingual dictionary. In F. Kiefer (Ed.), *Studies in syntax and semantics* (pp. 1–33). Dordrecht, Netherlands: Reidel.

Atkins, B.T. (1991). Building a lexicon: Beware of the dictionary. In L. Bates & R. Weischdel (Eds.), *Challenges in natural language processing*. Cambridge, UK: Cambridge University Press.

Atkins, B., Kegl, J., & Levin, B. (1988). Anatomy of a verb entry. *Journal of Lexicographic Research*, 1.

Atkins, B.T., & Levin, B. (1991). Admitting impediments. In U. Zernik (Ed.), *Lexical acquisition: Exploiting on-line resources to build a lexicon.* Hillsdale,NJ: Erlbaum.

Barwise, J., & Perry, J. (1983). *Situations and attitudes.* Cambridge, MA: Bradford Books.

Berwick, R.C. (1985). *The acquisition of syntactic knowledge*. Cambridge, MA: The MIT Press.

Bloksma, L., Bolhuis, A.v., Eijk, P.v.d., Hacken, P.t., Herklots, J., Heylen, D., Pijnenburg, H., Sesink, F., Teeuw, A-M., Tombe, L.d., & Wouden, T.v.d. (1990). *Ndict: Final report* (Tech. rep. Eurotra-NL). Utrecht, Netherlands: University of Utrecht.

Boguraev, B.K. (1986). Machine-readable dictionaries and research in computational linguistics. Presented at the *Workshop on Automating the Lexicon*. Grosetto, Italy.

Boguraev, B. (1991). Building a lexicon: The contribution of computers. In L. Bates & R. Weischdel (Eds.), *Challenges in natural language processing*. Cambridge, UK: Cambridge University Press.

Boguraev, B., & Briscoe, T. (1989). *Computational lexicography for natural language processing.* London: Longman.

Boguraev, B., & Pustejovsky, J. (1990). A richer characterization of lexical entries. *Proceedings of the 13th International Conference for Computational Linguistics*. Helsinki.

Byrd, R.J. (1989). Discovering relationships among word senses, dictionaries in the electronic Age.*Proceedings of the Fifth Annual Conference of the UW Centre for the New OED*. Waterloo, Canada.

Byrd, R.J., Calzolari, N., Chodorow, M., Klavans, J., Neff, M., & Rizk, O. (1987). Tools and methods for computational lexicology.*Computational Linguistics*, 13 (3–4), 219–240.

Calzolari, N. (1984). Detecting patterns in a lexical database. *Proceedings of COLING-84* (pp. 170–173).

Calzolari, N., Peters, C., & Roventini, A. (1990). Computational model of the dictionary *entry. ACQUILEX Deliverable, 1.*

Calzolari, N., & Picchi, E. (1988). Acquisition of semantic information from an on-line dictionary. *Proceedings of the 12th International Conference on Computational Linguistics*, Budapest.

Carpenter, R. (1990). Typed *feature structures: Inheritance, inequality, and extensionality.* Paper presented at the Workshop on Inheritance in Natural Language Processing, Tilburg, Netherlands.

Carpenter, B., & Pollard, C. (1990). *Solving feature structure constraint equations*. unpublished manuscript.

Carver, D.J. (1974). *Collins English dictionary*. Birmingham, UK: Collins Publishers.

Cater, A.W.S., Guo, C-M., & Matthews, P. (1990). *Lexical requirements of natural language processing* (ESPRIT BRA 3030, ACQUILEX Deliverable No. 3). Dublin, Ireland: University College Dublin.

Chalmers, D.J. (1990). Syntactic transformations on distributed representations. *Connection Science*, 2(1).

Charniak, E. (1981a). *Passing markers: a theory of contextual influence in language comprehension* (Tech. Rep. TR CS-80). Providence, RI: Brown University, Department of Computer Science.

Charniak, E. (1981b). Six topics in search of a parser: an overview of AI language research. *Proceedings of the IJCAI-81* (pp. 1079–1087). Vancouver.

Chodorow, M.S., Byrd, R.J., & Heidorn, G.E. (1985). Extracting semantic hierarchies from a large on-line dictionary. In M. William (Ed.), *Proceedings of the 23rd Annual Meeting of the ACL* (pp. 299–304). Chicago.

Church, K., Gale, W., Hanks, P., & Hindle, D. (1991). Using statistics in lexical analysis. In U. Zernik (Ed.), *Lexical* acquisition: *Using online resources to build a lexicon*. Hillsdale, NJ: Erlbaum.

Church, K., Gale, W., Hanks, P., Hindle D., & Moon, R. (1992). Substitutability. In B. Atkins & A. Zampolli (Eds.), *Computational approaches to the lexicon*. Oxford, UK: Oxford University Press.

Church, K., & Hanks, P. (1990). Word association norms, mutual information, and lexicography. *Computational Linguistics, 16*(1).

Clear, J.H. (1988). Trawling the language: Monitor corpora. *ZuriLEX '86 Proceedings*. Berlin: Francke Verlag.

Cohen, P.R., & Feigenbaum, E.A. (1982). *The handbook of artificial intelligence*. Stanford, CA: Morgan Kaufmann.

Copestake, A. (1990, August). *An approach to building the hierarchical element of a lexical knowledge base from a machine readable dictionary*. Paper presented at the First International Workshop on Inheritance in NLP, Tilburg, Netherlands.

Cowie, J. (1983). Automatic analysis of descriptive texts. *Proceedings of Conference on Applied Natural Language Processing* (pp. 117–123).

Dailey, D.P. (1986). The extraction of minimum set of semantic primitives from a monolingual dictionary is NP-complete. *Computational Linguistics*, 12, 306–307.

Date, C.J. (1981). *An introduction to database systems*. Reading, MA: Addison-Wesley.

DeJong, G. (1981). Generalizations based on explanations. *Proceedings of IJCAI-81*. (pp. 67–70).

DeJong, G. (1982). *Acquiring schemata through understanding and generalization plans*, unpublished manuscript.

Dietterich, T.G., & Michalski, R. (1981). Inductive learning of structural descriptions. *Artificial Intelligence , 16*, 257–294.

Dowty, D.R. (1989). On the semantic content of the notion of 'thematic role'. In G. Chierchia, B.H. Partee, & R. Turner (Eds.), *Properties, types and meaning II: Semantic issues* (pp. 69–130). Dordrecht: Kluwer Academic Publishers.

Dowty, D.R., Wall, R.E., & Peters, S. (1981). *Introduction to Montague semantics*. Dordrecht, Netherlands: Reidel.

EDR. (1990a). *An overview of the EDR electronic dictionaries* (TR-024). Tokyo, Japan: EDR.

EDR. (1990b). *Japanese word dictionary* (TR-025). Tokyo, Japan: EDR.

EDR. (1990c). *English word dictionary* (TR-026). Tokyo, Japan: EDR.

EDR. (1990d). *Concept dictionary* (TR-027). Tokyo, Japan: EDR.

EDR. (1990e). *Bilingual dictionary* (TR-028). Tokyo, Japan: EDR.

Elman, J.L. (1989). *Representation and structure in connectionist models* (Tech. Rep. TR 8903, CRL). San Diego: University of California.

Estes, W.K. (1982). *Models of learning, memory, and choice*. New York: Praeger.

Evans, R., & Gazdar, G. (1989). Inference in DATR. *Proceedings of the 4th European Conference on Computational Linguistics* (pp. 66–71). Manchester, UK.

Evens, M.W., Markowitz, J., Ahlswede, T., & Rossi, K. (1987). Digging in the dictionary: Building a relational lexicon to support natural language processing applications. *Issues and Developments in English and Applied Linguistics* (Vol. 2, pp. 33–44).

Fass, D. (1988). *Collative semantics: A study in the discrimination of meaning* (Tech. Rep. CSS/LCCR 88–24). Burnaby, BC, Canada: Simon Fraser University, Center for Systems Science.

Fillmore C. (1968). The case for case. In E. Bach & R.T. Harms (Eds.), *Universals in linguistic theory* (pp. 1–90). Chicago: Holt, Rinehart & Winston.

Fillmore, C.J., & Atkins, B.T. (1989, July). Towards a frame-based lexicon: The semantics of RISK and its neighbor.*Paper presented at the NSF Symposium on the Organization of the Lexicon*.

Fillmore, C.J., & Atkins, B.T. (1992). Risk: The challenge of corpus lexicography. In Atkins & A. Zampolli (Eds.), *Automating the lexcion II*. Oxford, UK: Oxford University Press.

Fodor, J.A., & Pylyshyn, Z.W. (1988). Connectionism and cognitive architecture: a critical analysis. *Cognition*, 28, 2–71.

Fox, E. A. (1980). Lexical relations: Enhancing effectiveness of information retrieval systems. *ACM SIGIR Forum, 15*, 5–36.

Fox, E.A., Nutter, J.T., Ahlswede, T., Evens, M., & Markowitz, J. (1988). Building a large thesaurus for information retrieval. In B. Bruce (Ed.), *Proceedings of the ACL Conference on Applied Natural Language Processing* (pp. 101–108).

Frege, G. (1960). Trans. by P. Geach & M. Black. Oxford, UK: Blackwell.

Garey, M.R., & Johnson, D.S. (1979). *Computers and intractability: A guide to the theory of NP-completeness*. New York: W.H. Freeman.

Gazdar, G., Klein E., Pullum, G., & Sag, I. (1985). *Generalized phrase structure grammar*. Oxford: Basil Blackwell.

Gazdar, G., & Mellish, C.S. (1989). *Natural language processing in POP11/LISP/PROLOG: An introduction to computational linguistics*. Reading, MA: Addison-Wesley.

Gonnet, G., & Tompa, F. (1987). Mind your grammar: A new approach to modelling text. *Proceedings of the 13th International Conference on Very Large Data Bases* (pp. 339–346). Brighton, UK.

Grimshaw, J. (1979). Complement selection and the lexicon. *Linguistic Inquiry*.

Guo, C-M. (1991). Interactive vocabulary acquisition in XTRA. In D. Partridge (Ed.), *Artificial intelligence and software engineering* (Vol. 1). Norwood, NJ: Ablex.

Guthrie, L., Slator, B., Wilks, Y., & Bruce, R. (1990, August). Is there content in empty heads? Paper presented at the *13th International Conference on Computational Linguistics*, Helsinki, Finland.

Hanson, S.J., & Burr, D.J. (1990). What connectionist models learn: Learning and representation in connectionist networks. *Behavioral and Brain Sciences*, 13(3).

Hayes, P. (1976). Semantic markers and selectional restrictions. In Y. Wilks & E. Charniak (Eds.), *Computational semantics* (pp. 41–54). Amsterdam: North-Holland.

Hayes-Roth, F., Klahr, P., & Mostow, D. (1981). Advice-taking and knowledge refinement: An iterative view of skill acquisition. In J.R. Anderson (Ed.), *Cognitive skills and their acquisition* (pp. 231–253) Hillsdale, NJ: Erlbaum.

Hinton, G.E. (1981). Implementing semantic networks in parallel hardware. In G.E. Hinton & J.R. Anderson (Eds.), *Parallel models of associative memory*. Hillsdale, NJ: Erlbaum.

Hinton, G.E. (1989). Connectionist learning procedures. *Artificial Intelligence, 40*, 184–235.

Hinton, G.E., McClelland, J.L., & Rumelhart, D.E. (1986). Distributed representations. In D.E. Rumelhart & J.L. McClelland (Eds.), *Parallel distributed processing* (Vol. 1). Cambridge, MA: MIT Press.

Hull, C.L. (1937). Mind, mechanism, and adaptive behavior. *Psychological Review*, 44, 1–32.

Hull, C.L. (1943). *Principles of behavior*. New York: Appleton-Century-Crofts.

Klavans, J.L. (1988). *COMPLEX: A computational lexicon for natural language* systems. Paper presented at *COLING-12*, Budapest, Hungary.

Koskenniemi, K. (1984). A general two-level computational model for word-form recognition and production. Paper presented at *COLING-84*, Stanford, CA.

Kucera, H., & Francis, W.N. (1967). *Computational analysis of present-day American English*. Providence, RI: Brown University Press.

Lado, R. (1957). *Linguistics across cultures: Applied linguistics for language teachers*. Ann Arbor: University of Michigan Press.

Langacker, R.H. (1974). Movement rules in functional perspective. *Language, 50*, 630–664.

Langacker, R.H. (1975). Functional stratigraphy. *Papers from the parasession on functionalism* (pp. 351–397). Chicago: CLS.

Langacker, R.H. (1976). Semantic representations and the linguistic relativity hypothesis. *Foundations of Language*, 14, 307–357.

Langacker, R.H. (1978). The form and meaning of English auxiliary. *Language, 54*, 853–882.

Langacker, R.H. (1979). Grammar as image. *Linguistic Notes from La Jolla*, 6, 88–126.

Langacker, R.H. (1982). Space grammar, analyzability, and the English passive. *Language*, 58, 22–80.

Langacker, R.H., & Munro, P. (1975). Passives and their meaning. *Language*, 51, 789–830.

Lehnert, W.G. (1987). Learning to integrate syntax and semantics. Paper presented at the *Fourth International Workshop on Machine Learning*, Irvine, CA.

Levi, J.N. (1978). *The syntax and semantics of complex nominals*. New York: Academic Press.

Levin, B. (1991). Building a lexicon: the contribution of linguistics. In R. Weischdel & L. Bates (Eds.), *Challenges in natural language processing*. Cambridge, UK: Cambridge University Press.

Levin, B. (in press). *Towards a lexical organization of English verb*. Chicago: University of Chicago Press.

Litkowski, K.C. (1978). Models of the semantic structure of dictionaries. *American Journal of Computational Linguistics*, 81, 25–74.

Litkowski, K.C. (1980). Requirements of text processing lexicons. Paper presented at the *18th Annual Conference of the Association for Computational Linguistics*, Philadelphia, PA.

Litkowski, K.C. (1988). On the search for semantic primitives. *Computational Linguistics*, 14, 52.

Markowitz, J., Ahlswede, T., & Evens, M. (1986). Semantically significant patterns in dictionary definitions. In B. Alan (Ed.), *Proceedings of the 24th Annual Meeting of the ACL* (pp. 112–119). New York.

McCarthy, J. (1958). Programs with commonsense. In *Proceedings of the Symposium on the Mechanization of Thought Processes* (pp. 77–84). National Physical Laboratory.

McDonald, J., Plate, T., & Schvaneveldt, R. (1989). Using pathfinder to extract semantic information from text. In R. Schvaneveldt (Ed.), *Pathfinder associative networks*. Norwood, NJ: Ablex.

McNaught, J. (1990). Reusability of lexical and terminological resources: Steps towards independence. *Proceedings of the International Workshop on Electronic Dictionaries*. Kanagawa, Japan: EDR.

Meyer, I., Onyshkevich, B., & Carlson, L. (1990). Lexicographic principles and design for KBMT (CMT Tech. Rep. 118). Pittsburgh, PA: Carnegie-Mellon University.

Michalski, R.S. (1983). A theory and methodology of inductive learning. In R.S. Michalski, J.G. Carbonell, & T.M. Mitchell (Eds.), *Machine learning* (Vol. 1, pp. 83–134). Palo Alto, CA: Tioga.

Michalski, R.S., Carbonell, J.G., & Mitchell, T.M. (Eds.). (1986). *Machine learning: An artificial intelligence approach* (Vol. 2). Los Altos, CA: Morgan Kaufmann.

Nagao, M. (1984). A framework of a mechanical translation between Japanese and English by analogy principle. In A. Elithorn & R. Banerji (Eds.), *Artificial and human intelligence*. Amsterdam: Elsevier.

Nirenburg, S., & Goodman, K. (1990, June). Treatment of meaning in MT systems. Paper presented at the *Third International* Conference on Theoretical and M*ethodological Issues in Machine Translation*, Austin, TX.

Nirenburg, S., & Raskin, V. (1987). The subworld concep
t lexicon and the lexicon management system. *Computational Linguistics*, 13(3–4), 276–289.

Nutter, J.T. (1989). *A lexical relation hierarchy* (Tech. Rep. 89-6). Blacksburg, VA: Virginia Polytechnic Institute and State University, Department of Computer Science.

Nutter, J.T., Fox, E., & Evens, M. (1990). Building a lexicon from machine-readable dictionaries for improved information retrieval. *Literary and Linguistic Computing*, 5, 129–137.

Nyberg, E. (1988). *The framekit user's guide* (CMU CMT memo). Pittsburgh, PA: Carnegie Mellon University.

Ogden, C.K. (1942). *The general basic English dictionary*. New York: Norton.

Olney, J. (1968). *To all interested in the Merriam-Webster transcripts and data derived from them* (Tech. Rep. L-13579). Santa Monica, CA: Systems Development Corporation.

Olney, J., et al. (1967). *Toward the development of computational aids for obtaining a formal semantic description of English*. Paper presented at COLING-67.

Patten T. (1985). A problem solving approach to generating text from systemic grammars. *Proceedings of 2nd European Conference on Computational Linguistics* (pp. 251–257). Geneva.

Pereira, F. (1987). Grammars and logics of partial information. *Proceedings of the 4th International Conference on Logic Programming* (pp. 989–1013). Cambridge, MA: MIT Press.

Pollack, J.B. (1990). Recursive distributed representations. *Artificial Intelligence*, 46, 77–106.

Pustejovsky, J. (1990). The generative lexicon. *Computational Linguistics*.

Pustejovsky, J., & Anick, P. (1988). On the semantic interpretation of nominals. Paper presented at the *12th International Conference on Computational Linguistics*, Budapest, Hungary.

Quillian, R. (1962). A revised design for an understanding machine. *Machine Translation*, 7, 17–29.

Quillian, M.R. (1968). Semantic memory. In M. Minsky (Ed.), *Semantic information processing*. Cambridge, MA: MIT Press.

Quine, W.v.O (1960). *Word and object*. Cambridge, MA: MIT Press.

Ramsay, A.M. (1990). *The logical structure of English: Computing semantic content*. London: Pitman.

Reifler, E. (1955). The mechanical determination of meaning. In W.N. Locke & A.D. Booth (Eds.), *Machine translation of language* (pp.136–164). Cambridge, MA: The Technology Press of M.I.T.

Rosenblatt, F. (1957). *The perceptron: A perceiving and recognizing automation* (Rep. No. 85–460-1, Project Para). Ithaca, NY: Cornell Aeronautical Laboratory.

Rumelhart, D.E., Hinton, G.E., & Williams, R.J. (1986). Learning internal representations by error propagation. In D.E. Rumelhart & J. L. McClelland (Eds.), *Parallel distributed processing* (Vol. 1). Cambridge, MA: MIT Press.

Sag, I., Kaplan, R., Karttunen, L., Kay, M., Pollard, C., Shieber, S., & Zaenen, A. (1986). Unification and grammatical theory. Paper presented at *the Fifth West Coast Conference on Formal Linguistics*.

Sager, N. (1981). *Natural language information processing*. Reading, MA: Addison-Wesley.

Sampson, G.E. (1973). *The form of language*. London: Weidenfield and Nicholson.

Sato, S., & Nagao, M. (1990). Toward memory-based translation. In*Proceedings of the 13th International Conference on Computational Linguistics* (Vol. 3, pp.247–252). Helsinki.

Schank, R.C. (1972). Conceptual dependency: A theory of natural language understanding. *Cognitive Psychology* , 3(4), 552–631.

Servan-Schreiber, D., Cleeremans, A., & McClelland, J.L.(1988). *Encoding sequential structure in simple recurrent nets* (Tech. Rep. TR CMU-CS-88–183). Pittsburgh, PA: Carnegie-Mellon University.

Sharkey, N.E., & Reilly, R. (1990). *Connectionism and natural language*. In Parallel Update, Newsletter of BSCS Parallel Processing Specialist Group.

Sharkey, N.E. (in press). Connectionist representation techniques. *AI Review*.

Slator, B. (1988). *Lexical semantics and preference semantics analysis* (PhD thesis). Las Cruces: New Mexico State University.

Slator, B. (1989). Extracting lexical knowledge from dictionary text. *Knowledge Acquisition*, 1, 89–112.

Slocum, J., & Morgan, M.G. (1987). The role of dictionaries and machine-readable lexicons in translation. In D. Walker, A. Zampolli, & N. Calzolari (Eds.), Proceedings of the Linguistics Summer Institute Lexicon Workshop. Morristown, NJ: Bell Communications Research.

Smith, R. (1981). On defining adjectives, Part lll. *Dictionary: Journal of the Dictionary Society of North America*, 3, 28–38.

Smolensky, P. (1988). On the proper treatment of connectionism. *Behavioral and Brain Sciences*, 11, 1–74.

Smolensky, P. (1990). Tensor product variable binding and the representation of symbolic structures in connectionist systems. *Artificial Intelligence*, 46, 159–216.

Sparck Jones, K. (1964). *Synonymy and semantic classification* (PhD thesis). Cambridge, UK: University of Cambridge.

Sparck Jones, K. (1965). Experiments in semantic classification. *Mechanical Translation, 8*, 97–112.

Sparck Jones, K. (1967). *Dictionary circles* (Tech. memo TM-3304). Santa Monica, CA: System Development Corporation.

St. John, M.F., & McClelland, J.L. (in press). Learning and applying contextual constraints in sentence comprehension. In R. Reilly & N.E. Sharkey (Eds.), *Connectionist approaches to natural language processing*. Hove, UK: Erlbaum.

Sumita, E., Iida, H., & Kohyama, H. (1990). Translating with examples: A new *approach to machine translation*. Paper presented at *the third international conference on theoretical and methodological issues in machine translation of natural language*, Austin, TX.

Tolman, E.C. (1932). *Purposive behavior in animals and men*. New York: Appleton-Century.

Ullman, J.D. (1988). *Principles of database and knowledge-base systems* . Computer Science Press.

Van Gelder, T. (1990). Compositionality: a connectionist variation on a classical theme. *Cognitive Science*, 14.

Vermeir, D., Geerts, P., & Nute, D. (1989). *A logic for defeasible perspectives*. Unpublished manuscript, University of Antwerp.

Vossen, P. (1991). Comparing noun-taxonomies cross-linguistically (ESPRIT BRA-3030 ACQUILEX WP NO. 014). Amsterdam: University of Amsterdam.

Wang, Y-C, Vandendorpe, J., & Evens, M. (1985). Relational thesauri in information retrieval. *Journal of the American Society for Information Science, 36*(1), 15–27.

Weaver, W. (1949). Translation. In W.N. Locke & A.D. Booth (Eds.), *Machine Translation of Language*. Cambridge, MA: The Technology Press of MIT.

Werner, O. (1978). The synthetic informant model: The simulation of large lexical/semantic fields. In M. Loflin & J. Silverberg (Eds.), *Discourse and difference in cognitive anthropology* (pp. 45–83). The Hague: Mouton.

Wilks, Y. (1968). Online semantic analysis of English text. *Mechanical Translation*, 11, 59–72.

Wilks, Y. (1972). *Grammar, meaning, and machine analysis of language*. London: Routledge.

Wilks, Y. (1975a). A preferential pattern seeking semantics for natural language inferences. *Artificial Intelligence*, 6, 53–74.

Wilks, Y. (1975b). An intelligent analyzer and understander for English. *Communications of the ACM*, 18, 264–274

Wilks, Y. (1977). Good and bad arguments about semantic primitives. *Communication and Cognition*, 10, 182–221.

Wilks, Y. (1978). Making preference more active. *Artificial Intelligence*, 10, 1–11.

Wilks, Y., Fass, D., Guo, C-M, McDonald, J. E., Plate, T., & Slator, B. M. (1988). Machine tractable dictionaries as tools and resources for natural language processing. In *Proceedings of the 12th International Conference on Computational Linguistics* (pp. 750–755). Budapest, Hungary.

Wilks, Y., Fass, D., Guo, C-M., MacDonald, J., Plate, T., & Slator, B. (1989). A tractable machine dictionary as a resource for computational semantics. In B. Boguraev & T.

Briscoe (Eds.), *Computational lexicography for natural language processing.* London: Longman.

Winston, P.H. (1975). Learning structural descriptions from examples. In P.H. Winston (Ed.), *The psychology of computer vision* . New York: McGraw-Hill.

Yngve, V. (1955). Syntax and the problem of multiple meaning. In W.N. Locke & A.D. Booth (Eds.), *Machine translation of language* (pp. 208–226). Cambridge, MA: The Technology Press of MIT.

Zajac, R. (1990). A relational approach to translation. Paper presented at the *3rd International Conferenc*
e on Theoretical and Methodological Issues in Machine Translation of Natural Language.

Zarechnak, M. (1965). An applied radical semantics. *Mechanical Translation,* 8, 90–96.

Zwicky, A.M. (1973). Linguistic as chemistry: The substance theory of semantic primes. In J.M. Anderson & P. Kiparsky (Eds.), *Festschrift for Morris Halle* (pp. 467-485). New York: Holt, Rinehart and Winston.

BIBLIOGRAPHY

Ackerman, M., Wertheim, S., Hodges, M., & Sasnett, R. (1988). The Athena Muse reference facility. In D. L. Berg (Ed.), *Information in text: Proceedings of the University of Waterloo (UW) Centre for the New Oxford English Dictionary 4th Annual Conference* (pp. 26–28, 47–60). Waterloo, Canada.

Ageno, A., Cardoze, S., Castellon, I., Marti, M.A., Rigau G., Rodriguez, H., Taule, M., & Verdejo M.F. (1991). An interactive environment for the extraction and management of taxonomies from MRDs. *ESPRIT BRA-3030 ACQUILEX WP NO.020.*

Ahlswede, T. (1985a). A tool kit for lexicon building. In M. William (Ed.), *Proceedings of the Association for Computational Linguistics 23rd Annual Meeting* (pp. 268–276). Chicago.

Ahlswede, T. (1985b). A linguistic string grammar for adjective definitions. In W. Stephanie (Ed.), *Humans and machines* (pp. 101–127). Norwood, NJ: Ablex.

Ahlswede, T. (1988). *Syntactic and semantic analysis of definitions in a machine-readable dictionary* (doctoral dissertation). Chicago: Illinois Institute of Technology.

Ahlswede, T., & Evens, M. (1988a). Generating a relational lexicon from a machine-readable dictionary. *International Journal of Lexicography, 1,* 214–237.

Ahlswede, T., & Evens, M. (1988b). Parsing vs. text- processing in the analysis of dictionary definitions. In H. Jerry (Ed.), *Proceedings of the Association for Computational Linguistics (ACL): 26th annual meeting* (pp. 217–224). Morristown, NJ: ACL

Ahlswede, T., & Evens, M. (1988c). A lexicon for a medical expert system. In M. Evens (Ed.), *Relational models of the lexicon* (pp. 97–112). Cambridge, UK: Cambridge University Press.

Ahlswede, T., Anderson, J., Evens, M., Li, S-M., Neises, J., Pin-Ngern, S., & Markowitz, J. (1988). Automatic construction of a phrasal thesaurus for an information retrieval system. *Proceedings of RIAO88 (Recherche d'Information Assistee par Ordinateur;* pp. 597–608). Cambridge, MA.

Ahlswede, T., Evens, M., Rossi, K., & Markowitz, J. (1986). Building a lexical database by parsing Webster's Seventh New Collegiate Dictionary. In G. Johannesen (Ed.), *Advances in lexicology: Proceedings of the University of Waterloo (UW) Centre for the New Oxford English Dictionary 2nd Annual Conference* (pp. 65–78). Waterloo, Canada.

Akkerman, E. (1989). An independent analysis of the LDOCE grammar coding system. In

B. Boguraev, & T. Briscoe (Eds.), *Computational lexicography for natural language processing*. London: Longman.

Alexander, D., & Kunz, W.J. (1964). *Some classes of verbs in English*. Bloomington: Indiana University, Linguistics Club.

Allen, S. (1982). *Text processing: Text analysis and generation; text typology and attribution*. Stockholm: Almqvist & Wiksell.

Allen, S. (1986). *Word list of the Swedish academy*. Stockholm: Norstedts Forlag.

Alonge, A. (1991, May). Extraction of information on aktionsart from verb definitions in *machine-readable dictionaries*. Paper presented at the Conference on Natural Language Processing and its Applications, 11th International Workshop on Expert Systems and their Applications, Avignon, France.

Alshawi, H. (1987). Processing dictionary definitions with phrasal pattern hierarchies. *Computational Linguistics, 13,* 195–203.

Alshawi, H. (1989). Analyzing the dictionary definitions. In B. Boguraev & T. Briscoe (Eds.), *Computational lexicography for natural language processing*. London: Longman.

Alshawi, H., Boguraev, B., & Carter, D. (1989). Placing the dictionary online. In B. Boguraev & T. Briscoe (Eds.), *Computational lexicography for natural language processing* (pp. 41–64). Longman: London.

Amsler, R. (1980). *The structure of the Merriam-Webster pocket dictionary* (PhD dissertation). Austin, TX: University of Texas, Department of Computer Science.

Amsler, R. (1981). A taxonomy for English nouns and verbs. *Proceedings of the 19th Annual Meeting of the ACL* (pp. 133–138). Stanford, CA.

Amsler, R. (1982). Computational lexicology: A research program. In M.H. Lee (Ed.), *Proceedings of the American Federation of Information Processing Societies (AFIPS) national computer conference* (pp. 657–663). Reston, VA: AFIPS Press.

Amsler, R. (1984). Machine-readable dictionaries. In M.E. Williams (Ed.), *Annual review of information science and technology* (Vol.19, pp. 161–209). White Plains, NY: Knowledge Industry Publications for the American Society for Information Science.

Amsler, R. (1986). *Deriving lexical knowledge base entries from existing machine-readable information sources*. Paper presented at the Workshop on Automating the Lexicon, Grosseto, Italy.

Amsler, R. (1987a). Words and worlds. In Y. Wilks (Ed.), *Proceedings of the Theoretical Issues in Natural Language Processing 3rd Conference*. Las Cruces, NM.

Amsler, R. (1987b). Deriving lexical knowledge base entries from existing machine-readable information sources. In D. Walker, A. Zampolli, & N. Calzolari (Eds.), *Proceedings of the Linguistics Summer Institute Lexicon Workshop* (pp. 186–205). Morristown, NJ: Linguistics Summer Institute.

Amsler, R. (1987c). How do I turn this book on? Preparing text for access as a computational medium. In D. L. Berg (Ed.), *The uses of large text databases: Proceedings of the University of Waterloo (UW) Centre for the New Oxford English Dictionary 3rd Annual Conference* (pp. 75–88). Waterloo, Canada.

Amsler, R., & Tompa, F. (1988). An SGML-based standard for English monolingual dictionaries. In D. L. Berg (Ed.), *Information in text: Proceedings of the University of Waterloo (UW) Centre for the New Oxford English Dictionary 4th Annual Conference* (pp. 61–79). Waterloo, Canada.

Amsler, R., & White, J.S. (1979). *Development of a computational methodology for deriving natural language semantic structures via analysis of machine-readable dictionaries* (Tech. Rep. No. TR MCS77-01315). Austin: University of Texas, Linguistics Research Center.

Apresyan, Y.D., Mel'cuk, I.A., & Zolkovsky, A.K. (1970). Semantics and lexicography: Towards a new type of unilingual dictionary. In F. Kiefer (Ed.), *Studies in syntax and semantics* (pp. 1–33). Dordrecht, Holland: Reidel.

Arens, Y., Granacki, J., & Parker, A.C. (1987). Phrasal analysis of long noun sequences.

In C. Sidner (Ed.), *Proceedings of the Association for Computational Linguistics (ACL) 25th annual meeting* (pp. 59–64). Stanford, CA.

Atkins, B. (1987). Semantic ID tags: Corpus evidence for dictionary senses. In D. L. Berg (Ed.), *The uses of large text databases: Proceedings of the University of Waterloo (UW) Centre for the New Oxford English dictionary 3rd annual conference* (pp. 17–36). Waterloo, Canada.

Atkins, B.T.S. (1990). The dynamic database. *Proceedings of the International Workshop on Electronic Dictionaries*. Kanagawa, Japan: EDR.

Atkins, B.T. (1991). Building a lexicon: Beware of the dictionary. In L. Bates & R. Weischedel (Eds.), *Challenges of natural language processing*. Cambridge, UK: Cambridge University Press.

Atkins, B.T., Kegl, J., & Levin, B. (1987). *Anatomy of a verb entry: From linguistic theory to lexicographic practice*. Paper presented at the Workshop on the Lexicon, Stanford, CA.

Atkins, B., Kegl, J., & Levin, B. (1986). Explicit and implicit information in dictionaries. In G. Johannesen (Ed.), *Advances in lexicology: Proceedings of the University of Waterloo (UW) Centre for the New Oxford English Dictionary 2nd Annual Conference* (pp. 45–64). Waterloo, Canada.

Atkins, B., Kegl, J., & Levin, B. (1988). Anatomy of a verb entry. *Journal of Lexicographic Research*, 1.

Atkins, B., & Levin, B. (1988). Admitting impediments. In D.L. Berg (Ed.), *Information in text: Proceedings of the University of Waterloo (UW) Centre for the new Oxford English Dictionary 4th Annual Conference* (pp. 97–113). Waterloo, Canada.

Atkins, B., & Levin, B. (1991). Admitting impediments. In U. Zernik (Ed.), *Lexical acquisition: exploiting online resources to build a lexicon*. Hillsdale, NJ: Erlbaum.

Baeza-Yates, R. (1989). *Efficient text searching*. (Rep. CS-89-17). Waterloo, Canada: University of Waterloo, *Department of Computer Science*.

Baeza-Yates, R., & Gonnet, G.H. (1989a). *Boyer-Moore automata* (Report CS-89-29). Waterloo, Canada: Univeristy of Waterloo, *Department of Computer Science*.

Baeza-Yates, R.A., & Gonnet, G.H. (1989b). *Efficient text searching of regular expressions* (Tech. Rep. OED-89-01). Waterloo, Canada: University of Waterloo, *Centre for the New Oxford English Dictionary and Text Research*.

Barnett, B., Lehmann, H., & Zoeppritz, M. (1986). A word database for natural language parsing. *COLING86: Proceedings of the 11th International Conference on Computational Linguistics* (pp. 435–440). Bonn, Germany.

Beale, A.D. (1985). Grammatical analysis by computer of the Lancaster-Oslo/Bergen (LOB) Corpus of British English texts. In M. William (Ed.), *Proceedings of the Association for Computational Linguistics 23rd Annual Meeting* (pp. 293–298). Morristown, NJ: ACL.

Becker, J.D. (1975). The phrasal lexicon. In R.C. Schank & B. Nash-Webber (Eds.), *Theoretical issues in natural language processing, ACL annual meeting* (pp. 38–41). Cambridge, MA.

Beckwith, R., Fellbaum, C., Gross, D., & Miller, G. (1991). WordNet: A lexical database organized on psycholinguistic principles. In U. Zernik (Ed.), *Lexical acquisition: Exploiting online resources to build a lexicon*. Hillsdale NJ: Erlbaum.

Benbow, T.J., et al. (1987). *Report on the New Oxford English Dictionary user survey* (Tech. Rep. OED-87-05). Waterloo, Canada: University of Waterloo, *Centre for the New Oxford English Dictionary and Text Research*.

Benson, M., Benson, E., & Ilson, R. (1987). *The BBI combinatory dictionary of English: A guide to word combinations*. Amsterdam: John Benjamins.

Berg, D.L. (1989). *The research potential of the electronic OED2 database at the University of Waterloo: A guide for scholars* (Tech. Rep. OED-89-02). Waterloo, Canada: Universiy of Waterloo, *Centre for the New Oxford English Dictionary and Text Research*.

Berg, D.L., Gonnet, G., & Tompa, F. (1988). *The New Oxford English Dictionary project at the*

University of Waterloo (Tech. Rep. OED-88–01). Waterloo, Canada: University of Waterloo, Centre for the New Oxford English Dictionary.

Besemer, D., & Jacobs, P.S. (1987). FLUSH: A flexible lexicon design. In C. Sidner (Ed.), *Proceedings of the Association for Computational Linguistics (ACL) 25th Annual Meeting* (pp. 186–192). Stanford, CA.

Bienkowski, M. (1987). *Tools for lexicon construction* (CSL Tech. Rep. No. 10). Princeton, NJ: Princeton University.

Bierwisch, M., & Ferenc, K. (1970). Remarks on definitions in natural language. In F. Kiefer (Ed.), *Studies in syntax and semantics* (pp. 55–79). Dordrecht, Netherlands: Reidel.

Blake, G.E., Bray, T., & Tompa, F.W. (1991). *Shortening the OED: Experience with a grammar-defined database* (Tech. Rep. OED-91-02). Waterloo, Canada: University of Waterloo, *Centre for the New Oxford English Dictionary and Text Research.*

Boguraev, B. (1986). *Machine-readable dictionaries and research in computational linguistics.* Paper presented at the Workshop on Automating the Lexicon, Grosseto, Italy.

Boguraev, B. (1987a). Machine-readable dictionaries and computational linguistics research. In D. Walker, A. Zampolli, & N. Calzolari (Eds.), *Proceedings of the Linguistics Summer Institute Lexicon Workshop* (pp. 279–303). Morristown, NJ: Bell Communications Research.

Boguraev, B. (1987b). Experiences with a machine-readable dictionary. In D.L. Berg (Ed.), *The uses of large text databases: Proceedings of the University of Waterloo (UW) Centre for the New Oxford English Dictionary 3rd Annual Conference* (pp. 37–50). Waterloo, Canada: University of Waterloo, *Centre for the New Oxford English Dictionary and Text Research.*

Boguraev, B. (1990*a*). The defining power of words. In Y. Wilks (Ed.), *Proceedings of 3rd International Conference: Theoretical issues of natural language processing.* Hillsdale, NJ: Erlbaum.

Boguraev, B. (1990b). Data models for lexicon acquisition. *Proceedings of the International Workshop on Electronic Dictionaries.* Kanagawa, Japan: EDR.

Boguraev, B. (in press). Machine-readable dictionaries and research in computational linguistics. In D. Walker, A. Zampolli, & N. Calzolari (Eds.), *Automating the lexicon.* Oxford, UK: Oxford University Press.

Boguraev, B., & Briscoe, T. (1987). Large lexicons for natural language processing: Utilizing the grammar coding system of LDOCE. *Computational Linguistics, 13,* 203–218.

Boguraev, B., & Briscoe, T. (1989). Utilising the LDOCE grammar codes. In B. Boguraev & T. Briscoe (Eds.), *Computational lexicography for natural language processing.* London: Longman.

Boguraev, B., Briscoe, T., & Copestake, A. (1990). Enjoy the paper: Lexical semantics via lexicology. *ESPRIT BRA-3030 ACQUILEX WP NO.011.*

Boguraev, B., Briscoe, T., Carroll, J., Carter, D., & Grover, C. (1987). The derivation of a grammatically indexed lexicon from the Longman Dictionary of Contemporary English. In C. Sidner (Ed.), *Proceedings of the Association for Computational Linguistics (ACL) 25th Annual Meeting* (pp. 193–200). Stanford, CA.

Boguraev, B., Carroll, J., Pulman, S., Russell, G., Ritchie, G., Black, A., Briscoe, T., & Grover, C. (1987). The lexical component of a natural language tool kit. In D. Walker, A. Zampolli, & N. Calzolari (Eds.), *Proceedings of the Linguistics Summer Institute Lexicon Workshop.* Morristown, NJ: Linguistic Summer Institute.

Boguraev, B., Carter, D., & Briscoe, T. (1987c). A multipurpose interface to an online dictionary. *Proceedings of an association for computational linguistics European chapter meeting* (pp. 63–69). Copenhagen, Denmark.

Boguraev, B., & Pustejovsky, J. (1990). A richer characterization of lexical entries. *Proceedings of the 13th International Conference for Computational Linguistics.* Helsinki, Finland.

Boyer, M., & LaPalme, G. (1985). Generating paraphrases from meaning-text semantic networks. *Computer Intelligence, 1* 103–117.

Braden-Harder, L., & Zadrozny, W. (1991). Lexicons for broad coverage semantics. In U. Zernik (Ed.), *Lexical acquisition: Exploiting online resources to build a lexicon*. Hillsdale NJ: Erlbaum.

Brazil, D. (1987). Representing pronunciation. In J.M. Sinclair (Ed.), *Looking up: An account of the COBUILD project in lexical computing* (pp. 160–166). London: William Collins.

Brent, M.R. (1991). Automatic acquisition of subcategorization frames from untagged text. *Proceedings of the 29th ACL* (pp. 209–214). Berkeley, CA.

Bridgeman, L. (1965). *Nouns before that clauses in English*. Bloomington: Indiana University, Linguistics Club.

Bridgeman, L., Dillinger, D., Higgins, C., Seaman, P.D., & Shank, F. (1965). *More classes of verbs in English*. Bloomington: Indiana University, Linguistics Club.

Briscoe, T., & Carroll, J. (1991). Generalised probabilistic LR parsing of natural language (corpora) with unification-based grammars (Tech. Rep. No. 224). Cambridge, UK: University of Cambridge, Computer Laboratory.

Briscoe, T., & Copestake, A. (1991). Sense extensions as lexical rules. *ESPRIT BRA-3030 ACQUILEX WP NO.022.*

Briscoe, T., Copestake, A., & de Paiva, V. (1991). ACQUILEX workshop on default inheritance in the lexicon (Tech. Rep. No 234). Cambridge, UK: University of Cambridge, Computer Laboratory.

Byrd, R.J. (1987). Dictionary systems for office practice. In D. Walker, A. Zampolli, & N. Calzolari (Eds.), *Proceedings of the Linguistics Summer Institute Lexicon Workshop*. Morristown, NJ: Linguistics Summer Institute.

Byrd, R.J., Calzolari, N., Chodorow, M., Klavans, J., Neff, M., & Rizk, O. (1987). Tools and methods for computational lexicology. *Computational Linguistics, 13*, 219–240.

Byrd, R.J., & Chodorow, M. (1985). Using an online dictionary to find rhyming words and pronunciations for unknown words. In M. William (Ed.), *Proceedings of the Association for Computational Linguistics (ACL) 23rd Annual Meeting* (pp. 277–283). Chicago.

Byrd, R.J., Klavans, J., Aronoff, M., & Anshen, F. (1986). Computer methods for morphological analysis. In B. Alan (Ed.), *Proceedings of the Association for Computational Linguistics (ACL) 24th Annual Meeting* (pp. 120–127). New York.

Byrd, R.J., & Rizk, O.A. (1987). *LQL: A lexical query language for querying and maintaining lexical data bases*, Unpublished manuscript.

Byrd, R.J., & Tzoukermann, E. (1988). Adapting an English morphological analyzer for French. In J. Hobbs (Ed.), *Proceedings of the Association for Computational Linguistics (ACL) 26th Annual Meeting* (pp. 1–6). Buffalo, NY.

Calzolari, N. (1984). Detecting patterns in a lexical data base. *COLING84. Proceedings of the 10th international conference on computational linguistics* (p. 173). Stanford, CA.

Calzolari, N. (1987). Structure and access in an automated lexicon and related issues. In D. Walker, A. Zampolli, & N. Calzolari (Eds.), *Proceedings of the Linguistics Summer Institute Lexicon Workshop*. Morristown, NJ: Linguistics Summer Institute.

Calzolari, N. (1988). The dictionary and the thesaurus can be combined. In E. Martha (Ed.), *Relational models of the lexicon* (pp. 75–96). Cambridge, UK: Cambridge University Press.

Calzolari, N. (1990). Lexical databases and textual corpora: Perspectives of integration for a lexical knowledge base. *ESPRIT BRA-3030 ACQUILEX WP NO.006.*

Calzolari, N. (1991a). Acquiring and representing semantic information in a lexical knowledge base. *ESPRIT BRA-3030 ACQUILEX WP NO.016.*

Calzolari, N. (1991b). Lexical databases and textual corpora: Perspectives of integration for a lexical knowledge-base. In U. Zernik (Ed.), *Lexical acquisition: Exploiting online resources to build a lexicon*. Hillsdale NJ: Erlbaum.

Calzolari, N., Peters, C., & Roventini, A. (1990). Computational model of the dictionary entry. *ACQUILEX Deliverable,* 1.

Calzolari, N., & Picchi, E. (1986). A project for a bilingual lexical database system. In G. Johannesen (Ed.), *Advances in lexicology: Proceedings of the University of Waterloo (UW) Centre for the New Oxford English Dictionary 2nd Annual Conference* (pp. 79–92). Waterloo, Canada.

Calzolari, N., & Zampolli, A. (1990). Lexical databases and textual corpora: a trend of convergence between computational linguistics and literary and linguistic computing. *ESPRIT BRA-3030 ACQUILEX WP NO.005.*

Carpenter, R. (1990). Typed feature structures: Inheritance, (in)equality and extensionality. *Proceedings of Workshop on Inheritance in Natural Language Processing*. Tilburg, Netherlands.

Carpenter, R. (in press). *The logic of typed feature structures.* Cambridge, UK: Cambridge University Press.

Carroll, J. (1990). Lexical database system: User manual. *Esprit BRA-3030 ACQUILEX deliverable,* 2.3.3(c).

Carroll, J., & Grover, C. (1989). The derivation of a large computational lexicon for English from LDOCE. In B. Boguraev & T. Briscoe (Eds.), *Computational lexicography for natural language processing* (pp. 117–134). London: Longman.

Carter, D. (1989a). Lexical acquisition in the core language engine. *Proceedings of the 4th European. ACL* (pp. 137–144). Manchester, UK.

Carter, D. (1989b). LDOCE and speech recognition. In B. Boguraev & T. Briscoe (Eds.), *Computational lexicography for natural language processing* (pp. 135–152). London: Longman.

Carver, D.J. (1974). *Collins English Dictionary*. Birmingham, UK: Collins.

Casagrande, J.B., & Kenneth, L.H. (1967). Semantic relationships in Papago folkdefinitions. In D. Hymes & W. E.Bittle (Eds.), *Studies in southwestern ethnolinguistics* (pp. 165–196). The Hague: Mouton.

Cassidy, F. (1987). The Dictionary of American regional English. In D.L. Berg (Ed.), *The uses of large text databases: Proceedings of the University of Waterloo (UW) Centre for the New Oxford English Dictionary 3rd Annual Conference* (pp. 1–8) Waterloo, Canada.

Castellon, I., & Marti, M.A. (1990). Gramatica del diccionario Vox. ESPRIT *BRA-3030 ACQUILEX WP NO.018.*

Castellon, I., Rigau, G., Rodriguez, H., Marti, M.A., & Verdejo, M.F. (1991). Loading the MRD into the LDB: Characteristics of the Vox dictionary. *ESPRIT BRA-3030 ACQUILEX WP NO.019.*

Chanod J.P., Harriehausen, B., & Montemagni, S. (1991, May). Processing multilingual argument structures. Paper presented at the Conference on Natural Language Processing and its Applications, 11th International Workshop on Expert Systems and their Applications. Avignon, France.

Chodorow, M., Byrd, R.J., & Heidorn, G. (1985). Extracting semantic hierarchies from a large online dictionary. In M. William (Ed.), *Proceedings of the Association for Computational Linguistics 23rd Annual Meeting* (pp. 299–304) Chicago.

Christodoulakis, S., & Ford, D.A. (1988). File organizations and access methods for CLV optical disks (Research Rep. CS-88-21). Waterloo, Canada: University of Waterloo, Department of Computer Science.

Christodoulakis, S., & Ford, D.A. (1988). Performance analysis and fundamental performance trade offs for CLV optical disks (Research Rep. CS-88-06). Waterloo, Canada: University of Waterloo, Department of Computer Science.

Christodoulakis, S., et al (1988). Optical mass storage systems and their performance (Research Rep. CS-88-05). Waterloo, Canada: University of Waterloo, Department of Computer Science.

Church, K. (1985). Stress assignment in letter-to-sound rules for speech synthesis. In M. William (Ed.), *Proceedings of the Association for Computational Linguistics (ACL) 23rd Annual Meeting*. Chicago.

Church, K. (1986). Morphological decomposition and stress assignment for speech synthesis. In B. Alan (Ed.), *Proceedings of the Association for Computational Linguistics (ACL) 24th Annual Meeting* (pp. 156–164) New York.

Church, K., Gale, W., Hanks, P., & Hindle, D. (1991). Using statistics in lexical analysis. In U. Zernik (Ed.), *Lexical acquisition: Exploiting online resources to build a lexicon.* Hillsdale, NJ: Erlbaum.

Church, K., & Hanks, P. (1990). Word association norms, mutual information and lexicography. *Computational Linguistics,* 16, 1.

Clark, D. (1991). Finite state text transduction tools. (Tech. Rep. OED-91-03). Waterloo, Canada: University of Waterloo, *Centre for the New Oxford English Dictionary and Text Research.*

Clear, J. (1987). Computing. In J.M. Sinclair (Ed.), *Looking up: An account of the COBUILD project in lexical computing* (pp. 41–61). London: William Collins.

Collier, G., & Fellbaum, C. (1988). Exploring the verb lexicon with the Sensus electronic thesaurus. In D.L. Berg (Ed.),*Information in text: Proceedings of the University of Waterloo (UW) Centre for the New Oxford English Dictionary 4th Annual Conference* (pp. 11–28) Waterloo, Canada.

Condoravdi, C. (1990). Symmetric predicates, verbal classes & diathesis alternations. *ESPRIT BRA-3030 ACQUILEX WP NO.003.*

Condoravdi, C., & Sanfilippo, A. (1990). Notes on psychological predicates. *ESPRIT BRA-3030 ACQUILEX WP NO.007.*

Copestake, A. (1990a). A system for building disambiguated taxonomies. *ESPRIT BRA-3030 ACQUILEX WP NO.012.*

Copestake, A. (1990b, August). An approach to building the hierarchical element of a lexical knowledge base from a machine-readable dictionary. *ESPRIT BRA-3030 ACQUILEX WP NO.008.*

Copestake, A. (1991). The LKB: A system for representing lexical information extracted from machine-readable dictionaries. Paper presented at the *ACQUILEX Workshop on Default Inheritance in the Lexicon.* Cambridge, UK.

Copestake, A., & Briscoe, T. (1991). Lexical operations in a unification based framework. *ESPRIT BRA-3030 ACQUILEX WP NO.021.*

Copestake, A., & Jones, B. (1991). Support for multilingual lexicons in the LKB system. Unpublished manuscript. Cambridge, UK: University of Cambridge, Computer Laboratory.

Corwin, D. (1988). *The lexikon.* North Andover, MA: Lexikos Corporation.

Cowie, A.P., & Mackin, R. (1975). *Oxford dictionary of current idiomatic English, Vol.1: Verbs with prepositions and particles.* London: Oxford University Press.

Cowie, A.P., Mackin, R., & McCaig, I.R. (1983). *Oxford dictionary of current idiomatic English, Vol. 2: Phrase, clause, and sentence idioms.* London: Oxford University Press.

Cumming, S. (1986). *Design of a master lexicon* (Tech. Rep. No. ISI/RR-85-163). Los Angeles: University of Southern California, Information Sciences Institute.

Cumming, S. (1987). The lexicon in text generation. In D. Walker, A. Zampolli, & N. Calzolari (Eds.), *Proceedings of the Linguistics Summer Institute Lexicon Workshop.* Morristown, NJ: Linguistics Summer Institute.

Cumming, S., & Albano, R. (1986). *A guide to lexical acquisition in the JANUS system* (Tech. Rep. No. ISI/RR-85-162). Los Angeles: University of Southern California, Information Sciences Institute.

Daelemans, W. (1987). A tool for automatic creation, extension, and updating of lexical knowledge bases. *Proceedings of an Association for Computational Linguistics European chapter meeting* (pp. 70–74). Copenhagen, Denmark.

Dahl, D., Palmer, M., & Passonneau, R. (1987). In C. Sidner (Ed.), *Proceedings of the Association for Computational Linguistics (ACL) 25th Annual Meeting* (pp. 131–139). Stanford, CA.

de Paiva, V. (1991). Types and constraints in the LKB. *Paper presented at the ACQUILEX Workshop on Default Inheritance in the Lexicon.* Cambrige, UK.

Dorr, B. (1991). Conceptual basis of the lexicon in machine translation. In U. Zernik (Ed.), *Lexical acquisition: Exploiting online resources to build a lexicon.* Hillsdale NJ: Erlbaum.

Doyle, L.B. (1962). Indexing and abstracting by association. *American Documentation, 13,* 4.

Dyer, M. (1991). Lexical acquisition through symbol recirculation. In U. Zernik (Ed.), *Lexical acquisition: Exploiting online resources to build a lexicon.* Hillsdale NJ: Erlbaum.

EDR. (1990a). An overview of the EDR electronic dictionaries (TR-024). Tokyo, Japan: EDR.

EDR. (1990b). Bilingual dictionary (TR-029). Tokyo, Japan: EDR.

EDR. (1990c). Concept dictionary (TR-027). Tokyo, Japan: EDR.

EDR. (1990d). English word dictionary (TR-026). Tokyo, Japan: EDR.

EDR. (1990e). Japanese word dictionary (TR-025). Tokyo, Japan: EDR.

Evans, R., & Gazdar, G. (1990). The DATR papers (Cog. Sci. Research Paper, 139) Sussex, UK: University of Sussex, School of Cognitive and Computing Sciences.

Evens, M. (1988). *Relational models of the lexicon.* Cambridge, UK: Cambridge University Press.

Evens, M., & Smith, R.N. (1978). A lexicon for a computer question-answering system. *American Journal of Computational Linguistics, 4,* 1–96.

Evens, M., Litowitz, B., Markowitz, J., Smith, R.N., & Werner, O. (1980). *Lexical-semantic relations: A comparative survey.* Edmonton, Canada: Linguistic Research, Inc.

Evens, M., Markowitz, J., Ahlswede, T., & Rossi, K. (1987). Digging in the dictionary: Building a relational lexicon to support natural language processing applications. *IDEAL (Issues and Developments in English and Applied Linguistics)* 2, 33–44.

Evens, M., Pin-Ngern, S., Ahlswede, T.M., & Markowitz, J. (1989). *Acquiring information from informants for a lexical database.* Paper presented at the First International Lexical Acquisition Workshop, Detroit, MI.

Evens, M., Vandendorpe, J., & Wang, Y.C. (1985). Lexical-semantic relations in information retrieval. In W. Stephanie (Ed.), *Humans and machines* (pp. 73–100). Norwood, NJ: Ablex.

Ezawa, K. (1990, November). Japanese-German dictionary project. *Proceedings of the International Workshop on Electronic Dictionaries.* Kanagawa, Japan: EDR.

Fawcett, H.J. (1989a). *Adopting SGML: The implications for writers.* (Tech. Rep. OED-89–03). *Waterloo, Canada:* University of Waterloo, *Centre for the New Oxford English Dictionary and Text Research.*

Fawcett, H.J. (1989b). Using tagged text to support online views. (Tech. Rep. OED-89–04). *Waterloo, Canada:* University of Waterloo, *Centre for the New Oxford English Dictionary and Text Research.*

Fillmore, C.J., & Atkins, B.T. (1992). Risk: the challenge of corpus lexicography. In A. Zampolli and B.T. Atkins (Eds.), *Automating the lexicon II.* Oxford, UK: Oxford University Press.

Flickinger, D., Pollard, C., & Wasow, T. (1985). Structure-sharing in lexical representation. In M. William (Ed.), *Proceedings of the Association for Computational Linguistics.(ACL) 23rd Annual Meeting* (pp. 262–267). Chicago.

Fox, E. (1987). Development of the coder system: A testbed for artificial intelligence methods in information retrieval. *Information Processing & Management, 23,* 341–366.

Fox, E., Nutter, J.T., Ahlswede, T., & Markowitz, J. (1988). Building a large thesaurus for information retrieval. In B. Bruce (Ed.), *Proceedings of the ACL 2nd conference on applied natural language processing* (pp. 101–108). Dallas, TX.

Fox, E.A., Robert, C.W., Phyllis, R.S., Qi Fan, C., & Robert, K.F. (1986). *Building the CODER lexicon: The Collins English dictionary and its adverb definitions* (Tech. Rep. No. 86–23). Blacksburg: VirginiaPolytechnic Institute, Computer Science Department.

Fox, G. (1987). The case for examples. In J.M. Sinclair (Ed.), *Looking up: An account of the COBUILD project in lexical computing* (pp. 137–149). London: William Collins.

Frank, R., & Cameron, A. (1973). *A plan for the dictionary of old English*. Toronto, Canada: University of Toronto Press.

Frawley, W. (1988). Relational models and metascience. In E. Martha (Ed.), *Relational models of the lexicon* (pp. 335–372). Cambridge, UK: Cambridge University Press,

Gehrke, M., & Block, H.U. (1986). Morpheme-based lexical analysis. In G. Johannesen (Ed.), *Advances in lexicology: Proceedings of the University of Waterloo (UW) Centre for the New Oxford English Dictionary 2nd Annual Conference* (pp. 1–15). Waterloo, Canada.

Gellerstam, M. (1988). *Studies in computer-aided lexicology*. Stockholm: Almqvist & Wiksell.

Goldfarb, C. (1990). *The SGML Handbook*. Oxford, UK: Oxford University Press.

Gonnet, G.H. (1987). *Examples of PAT applied to the Oxford English Dictionary* (Tech. Rep. OED-87-02). *Waterloo, Canada:* University of Waterloo, *Centre for the New Oxford English Dictionary and Text Research.*

Gonnet, G.H. (1988). *Efficient searching of text and pictures* (Tech. Rep. OED-88-02). *Waterloo, Canada:* University of Waterloo, *Centre for the New Oxford English Dictionary and Text Research.*

Gonnet, G.H., Baeza-Yates, R.A., & Snider, T. (1991). *Lexicographical indices for text: Inverted files vs. PAT trees* (Tech. Rep. OED-91-01). *Waterloo, Canada:* University of Waterloo, *Centre for the New Oxford English Dictionary and Text Research.*

Gonnet, G., & Tompa, F. (1987). Mind your grammar: A new approach to modelling text. *Proceedings of the 13th Very Large Database Conference* (pp. 339–346). Brighton, UK.

Gove, P. (1963). *Webster's seventh new collegiate dictionary*. Springfield, MA: G & C Merriam Co.

Gove, P.B. (1968). On defining adjectives: Part I. *American Speech, 45,* 5–32.

Granville, R. (1984). *Controlling lexical substitution in computer text generation. Proceedings of COLING84* (pp. 381–384). Stanford, CA.

Grimes, J. (1984). *Denormalization and cross referencing in theoretical lexicography. Proceedings of COLING84* (pp. 38–41). Stanford, CA.

Grimes, J. (1988). Information dependencies in lexical subentries. In E. Martha (Ed.), *Relational models of the lexicon* (pp. 167–181). Cambridge, UK: Cambridge University Press.

Grimshaw, J. (1979). Complement selection and the lexicon. *Linguistic Inquiry*.

Grimshaw, J., & Jackendoff, R. (1985). *Brandeis verb lexicon in machine-readable form* (NSF Grant, Tech. Rep. No. IST-81-20403). Waltham, MA: Brandeis University, Department of Linguistics.

Gross, M. (1984). *Lexicon grammar and the syntactic analysis of French. Proceedings of COLING84* (pp. 275–282). Stanford, CA.

Guthrie, L., Slator, B., Wilks, Y., & Bruce, R. (1990). Is there content in empty heads? *Proceedings of the 13th International Conference on Computational Linguistics*. Helsinki.

Hanks, P. (1979). *Collins English dictionary*. London: William Collins.

Hanks, P. (1987). Definitions and explanations. In J.M. Sinclair (Ed.), *Looking up: An account of the COBUILD project in lexical computing* (pp. 116–136). William Collins.

Hindle, D., & Rooth, M. (1991) Structural ambiguity and lexical relations. *Proceedings of the 29th ACL* (pp. 229–236). Berkeley, CA.

Hirst, G. (1986). Why dictionaries should list case structure. In G. Johannesen (Ed.), *Advances in lexicology: Proceedings of the University of Waterloo centre for the New Oxford English Dictionary 2nd Annual Conference* (pp. 147–163). Waterloo, Canada.

Hobbs, J. (1984). *Building a large knowledge base for a natural language system. Proceedings of COLING84* (pp. 283–286). Stanford, CA.

Hobbs, J., Croft, W., Daview, T., Edwards, D., & Laws, K. (1987). Commonsense metaphysics and lexical semantics. *Computational Linguistics, 13,* 241–250.

Hodgkin, A. (1987). The uses of large text databases. In D.L. Berg (Ed.), *The uses of large text databases: Proceedings of the University of Waterloo centre for the new Oxford English dictionary 3rd annual conference* (pp. 9–16).Waterloo, Canada.

Hornby, A.S. (1980). *Oxford advanced learner's dictionary of current English (11th ed.)*. Oxford, UK: Oxford University Press.

Householder, F., Alexander, D., & Matthews; P.H. (1964). *Adjectives before that-*clauses in English. Bloomington: Indiana University, Linguistics Club.

Householder, F., Wolck, W., Matthews, P.H., Tone, J., & Wilson, J. (1965). *Preliminary classification of adverbs in English*. Bloomington: Indiana University, Linguistics Club.

Hovy, E. (1988). Generating language with a phrasal lexicon. In D. McDonald & L. Bolc (Eds.), *Natural language generation systems* (pp. 353–384). New York: Springer-Verlag.

Huber, D. (1990). An electronic dictionary for computer speech applications. *Proceedings of the International Workshop on Electronic Dictionaries*. Kanagawa, Japan: EDR.

Hudson, R. (1987). Identifying the linguistic foundations for lexical research and dictionary design. In D. Walker, A. Zampolli, & N. Calzolari (Eds.), *Proceedings of the Linguistics Summer Institute Lexicon Workshop*. Morristown, NJ: Linguistic Summer Institute.

Ikegami, Y. (1990). Recent development in linguistic semantics and some of its implications for lexicographical description. *Proceedings of the International Workshop on Electronic Dictionaries*. Kanagawa, Japan: EDR.

Ingria, R. (1987a). Lexical information for parsing systems: Points of convergence and divergence. In D. Walker, A. Zampolli, & N. Calzolari (Eds.), *Proceedings of the Linguistics Summer Institute Lexicon Workshop*. Morristown, NJ: Linguistic Summer Institute.

Ingria, R. (1987b). *Survey of verb complement types in English*. Paper presented at Linguistics Summer Institute, Workshop on the Lexicon in Theoretical and Computational Perspective, Stanford, CA.

Iris, M., Bonnie L., & Martha, E. (1988). The part-whole relation in the lexicon: An investigation of semantic primitives. In M. Evens (Ed.), *Relational models of the lexicon* (pp. 261–268). Cambrdige, UK: Cambridge University Press.

Isoda, M., Aiso, H., Kamibayashi, N., & Matsunaga, Y. (1986, August). *Model for lexical knowledge base*. Paper presented at COLING86, The 11th International Conference on Computational Linguistics, Bonn, Germany.

Jacobs, P. (1991). Making sense of lexical acquisition. In U. Zernik (Ed.), *Lexical acquisition: Exploiting online resources to build a lexicon*. Hillsdale NJ: Erlbaum.

Jacobson, S. (1964). *Adverbial positions in English dissertation*. Stockholm: AB Studentbok.

Jacobson, S. (1978). *On the use, meaning, and syntax of English preverbial adverbs*. Stockholm: Almqvist & Wilksell.

Jensen, K., & Binot, J.L. (1987). Disambiguating prepositional phrase attachments by using online dictionary definitions. *Computational Linguistics, 13*, 251–260.

Johnson, J.H. (1986a). Rational equivalence relations (Research Rep. CS-86–16). Waterloo, Canada: University of Waterloo, *Department of Computer Science*.

Johnson, J. H. (1986b). Single-valued finite transduction (Research Rep. CS-86–59). Waterloo, Canada: University of Waterloo, *Department of Computer Science.*

Kameda, H. (1990). A discussion on the criterion of words registration. *Proceedings of the International Workshop on Electronic Dictionaries*. Kanagawa, Japan: EDR.

Kay, M. (1983). The dictionary of the future and the future of the dictionary. *Linguistica Computazionale, 3*,161–174.

Kazman, R. (1986). Structuring the text of the Oxford English Dictionary through finite state transduction (Research Rep. CS-86–20). University of Waterloo, *Department of Computer Science.*

Kegl, J. (1987). Machine-readable dictionaries and education. In D. Walker, A. Zampolli, & N. Calzolari (Eds.), *Proceedings of the Linguistics Summer Institute lexicon workshop*. Morristown, NJ: Linguistics Summer Institute.

Kipfer, B.A. (1983a). *Bibliography of writings on computer applications in lexicography*. Paper presented at the Workshop on Machine Readable Dictionaries, SRI, Menlo Park, CA.

Kipfer, B.A. (1983b). *Usage ordering of thirty words in dictionaries vs. Kucera & Francis*. Presented at the Workshop on Machine Readable Dictionaries, SRI, Menlo Park, CA.

Klavans, J. (1987, July). *Extracting selectional restrictions from online dictionaries*. Paper presented at Linguistics Summer Institute Workshop on the Lexicon in Theoretical and Computational Perspective, Stanford, CA.

Klavans, J., & Wacholder, N. (1990). From dictionary to knowledge base via taxonomy. *Proceedings of the 6th Annual Conference of the Waterloo Centre for the New OED*. Waterloo, Canada.

Koskenniemi, K. (1984, July). *A general computational model for word-form recognition and production*. Paper presented at COLING84, The 10th International Conference on Computational Linguistics, Stanford, CA.

Krieger, H., & Nerbonne, J. (1991). Feature-based inheritance networks for computational lexicons. *Proceedings of the ACQUILEX Workshop on Default Inheritance in the Lexicon*. Cambridge, UK: University of Cambridge.

Krishnamurthy, R. (1987). The process of compilation. In J.M. Sinclair (Ed.), *Looking up: An account of the COBUILD project in lexical computing* (pp. 62–85). London: William Collins.

Krovetz, R. (1991). Lexical acquisition and information retrieval. In U. Zernik (Ed.), *Lexical acquisition: Exploiting online resources to build a lexicon*. Hillsdale NJ: Erlbaum.

Kucera, H. (1985, November). The uses of online lexicons. In G. Johannesen (Ed.), *Information in data: Proceedings of the University of Waterloo (UW) Centre for the New Oxford English dictionary 1st Annual Conference* (pp. 6–10). Waterloo, Canada.

Kucera, H., & Francis, W.N. (1967). *Computational analysis of present-day American English*. Providence, RI: Brown University Press.

Lancashire, I. (1987). Using a textbase for English language research. In D.L. Berg (Ed.), *The uses of large text databases: Proceedings of the University of Waterloo (UW) Centre for the New Oxford English Dictionary 3rd Annual Conference* (pp. 51–64). Waterloo, Canada.

Lemmens, M., & Wekker, H. (1986). *Grammar in English learner's dictionaries*. Tubingen, Germany: Niemeyer.

Lesk, M. (1987). Can machine-readable dictionaries replace a thesaurus for searches in online catalogs?. In D.L. Berg (Ed.), *Proceedings of the University of Waterloo (UW) centre for the New Oxford English Dictionary 3rd Annual Conference* (pp. 65–74). Waterloo, Canada.

Lesk, M. (1988). "They said true things, but called them by wrong names" - Vocabulary problems over time in retrieval. In D.L. Berg (Ed.), *Information in text: Proceedings of the University of Waterloo (UW) Centre for the New Oxford English Dictionary 4th Annual Conference* (pp. 1–10). Waterloo, Canada.

Levin, B. (1985). Lexical semantics in review (*Lexicon Working Papers*, No. 1). Cambridge, MA: MIT.

Levin, B. (1987). The representation of semantic information in the lexicon. In D. Walker, A. Zampolli, & N. Calzolari (Eds.), *Proceedings of the Linguistics Summer Institute Lexicon Workshop*. Morristown, NJ: Linguistics Summer Institute.

Levin, B. (1992). Approaches to lexical semantic representation. In D. Walker, A. Zampolli, & N. Calzolari (Eds.) *Automating the lexicon: Research and practice in a multilingual environment*. Oxford, UK: Oxford University Press.

Levin, B (in press). *Towards a lexical organisation of English verbs*. Chicago: University of Chicago Press.

Liberman, M. (1991). *The ACL data collection initiative*. Unpublished manuscript, University of Pennsylvania.

Logan, H.M., & Logan, G. (1988). An inquiry into inquiry systems: A discussion of some applications of data retrieval to the new OED database. In D.L. Berg (Ed.), *Information in text: Proceedings of the University of Waterloo (UW) Centre for the New Oxford English Dictionary 4th Annual Conference* (pp. 81–95). Waterloo, Canada.

Mamrak, S., Kaelbling, M., Nicholas, C., & Share, M. (1987). A software architecture for supporting the exchange of electronic manuscripts. *Communications of the Association for Computing Machinery, 30,* 408–414.

Marinai, E., & Peters, C., & Picchi, E. (in press). A prototype system for the semi-automatic sense linking and merging of mono- and bilingual LDBs. In N. Ide & S. Hockey (Eds.), *Research in humanities computing*. Oxford, UK: Oxford University Press.

Marita, H. (1990). The architecture of an electronic dictionary. *Proceedings of the International Workshop on Electronic Dictionaries*. Kanagawa, Japan: EDR.

Markowitz, J., Ahlswede, T., & Evens, M. (1986). Semantically significant patterns in dictionary definitions. In B. Alan (Ed.), *Proceedings of the Association for Computational Linguistics (ACL) 24th annual meeting* (pp. 112–119). New York.

Markowitz, J., Pin-Ngern, S., Evens, M., Anderson, J., & Li, S.M. (1988). Generating lexical database entries for phrases. In D.L. Berg (Ed.), *Information in text: proceedings of the University of Waterloo (UW) Centre for the New Oxford English Dictionary 4th Annual Conference.* Waterloo, Canada.

Martin, J. (1991). Representing and acquiring metaphor-based polysemy. In U. Zernik (Ed.), *Lexical acquisition: Exploiting online resources to build a lexicon.* Hillsdale NJ: Erlbaum.

Maxwell, E., & Raoul N.S. (1974). A computerized lexicon of English. In Mitchell (Ed.), *Computers in the humanities* (pp. 124–131). Edinburgh, Scotland: Edinburgh University Press.

McCawley, J. (1979). *Adverbs, vowels, and other objects of wonder.* Chicago: University of Chicago Press.

McCawley, J. (1986). What linguists might contribute to dictionary making if they could get their act together. *The real-world linguist* (pp. 3–18). Norwood, NJ: Ablex.

Melby, A. (1985). *MERCURY user's guide*. Provo, UT: LinguaTech.

Mel'cuk, I. (1984). *Dictionnaire explicatif et combinatoire du Francais contemporain*. Montreal: University of Montreal Press.

Mel'cuk, I., & Polguere, A. (1987). A formal lexicon in the meaning-text theory (or How to do lexica with words). *Computational Linguistics,* 13, 261–275.

Mel'cuk, I., & Zholkovsky, A. (1988). The explanatory-combinatory dictionary. In E. Martha (Ed.), *Relational models of the lexicon* (pp. 41–73). Cambridge, UK: Cambridge University Press.

Miike, S. (199). How to define concepts for electronic dictionaries. *Proceedings of the International Workshop on Electronic Dictionaries.* Kanagawa, Japan: EDR.

Miller, G.A. (1985a). Dictionaries of the mind. In M. William (Ed.), *Proceedings of the Association for Computational Linguistics (ACL) 23rd annual meeting* (pp. 305–314). Chicago.

Miller, G.A. (1985b). Wordnet: A dictionary browser. In G. Johannesen (Ed.), *Information in data: Proceedings of the University of Waterloo (UW) Centre for the New Oxford English Dictionary 1st Annual Conference* (pp. 25–28). Waterloo, Canada.

Miller, G.A., & Gildea, P. (1987). How children learn words. *Scientific American 257*(3), 94–99.

Mish, F. (Ed.). (1985). *Webster's ninth new collegiate dictionary*. Springfield, MA: Merriam-Webster.

Moon, R. (1987). The analysis of meaning. In J.M. Sinclair (Ed.), *Looking up: An account of the COBUILD project in lexical computing* (pp. 86–103). London: William Collins.

Moortgat, M., Hoekstra, T., & van der Hulst, H. (1980). *Lexical grammar*. Dordrecht, Germany: Foris.

Muraki, K. (1990). Machine translation systems and large-scale electronic dictionaries. *Proceedings of the International Workshop on Electronic Dictionaries*. Kanagawa, Japan: EDR.

Murray, J.A.H, Bradley, H., Craigie, W.A., Onion, C.T., & Burchfield, R.W. (Eds.). (1933). *The Oxford English dictionary*. Oxford, UK: Oxford University Press.

Nagao, M. (1990). Some dictionary information for machine translation. *Proceedings of the International Workshop on Electronic Dictionaries*. Kanagawa, Japan: EDR.

Nakao, Y. (1990). How to extract dictionary data from the EDR corpus. *Proceedings of the International Workshop on Electronic Dictionaries*. Kanagawa, Japan: EDR.

Neff, M., Byrd, R.J., & Rizk, O. (1988). Creating and querying hierarchical lexical databases. In B. Bruce (Ed.), *Proceedings of the Association for Computational Linguistics (ACL) 2nd Conference on Applied Natural Language Processing* (pp. 84–93). Dallas, TX.

Neuhaus, H.J. (1986). Lexical database design: The Shakespeare dictionary model. *COLING86: Proceedings of the 11th International Conference on Computational Linguistics* (pp.411–444). Bonn, Germany.

Nirenberg, S., Carlson, L., Meyer, I., & Onyshkevych, B. (1990). Lexicons for KBMT. *Proceedings of the International Workshop on Electronic Dictionaries. Kanagawa,* Japan: EDR.

Nirenburg, S., & Raskin, V. (1987). The subworld concept lexicon and the lexicon management system. *Computational Linguistics, 13,* 276-289.

Normier, B., & Nossin, M. (199). Genelex project: EUREKA for linguistic engineering. *Proceedings of the International Workshop on Electronic Dictionaries*. Kanagawa, Japan: EDR.

Nutter, J.T., Fox, E., & Evens, M. (1990). Building a lexicon from machine-readable dictionaries for improved information retrieval. *Literary and Linguistic Computing, 5.*

Olney, J. (1968). *To: All interested in the Merriam-Webster transcripts and data derived from them* (Tech. Rep. L-13579). Santa Monica, CA: System Development Corp.

Ostler, N., & Atkins, B.T.S. (1991) Predictable meaning shift: some linguistic properties of lexical implication rules. *ACL SIGLEX Workshop on Lexical Semantics and Knowledge Representation* (pp. 76–87). Berkeley, CA.

Palmer, M., Dahl, D., Schiffman, R., Hirschman, L., Linebarger, M., & Dowding, J. (1986). Recovering implicit information. In B. Alan (Ed.), *Proceedings of the Association for Computational Linguistics (ACL) 24th Annual Meeting* (pp. 10–19). New York.

Papegaaij, B.C., Sadler, V., & Witkam, A.P.M. (1986). Experiments with an MT-directed lexical knowledge bank. *COLING86: Proceedings of the 11th International Conference on Computational Linguistics*, Bonn, Germany.

Peterson, J.L. (1982). Use of Webster's seventh new collegiate dictionary to construct a master hyphenation list. *Proceedings of NCC* (pp. 665–670). Houston, TX.

Peterson, J.L. (1986a). *Webster's seventh new collegiate dictionary* (Tech. Rep. No. TR-196). Austin: University of Texas.

Peterson, J.L. (1986b). A note on undetected typing errors. *Communications of the Association for Computing Machinery, 7,* 633–637.

Pin-Ngern, S., Evens, M., & Ahlswede, T. (1990). Generating a lexical database for adverbs. *Proceedings of the Waterloo Conference on Electronic Text Research*. Waterloo, Canada.

Pin-Ngern, S., Strutz, R., & Evens, M. (1989). Lexical acquisition for lexical databases. *Proceedings of the First Great Lakes Computer Science Conference.* New York: Springer.

Procter, P. (1983). *Beyond the dictionary in lexicography*. Paper presented at the Workshop on Machine-Readable Dictionaries, SRI, Menlo Park, CA.

Procter, P. (Ed.). (1978). *Longman dictionary of contemporary English*. London: Longman Group.

Proud, J.K. (1989). *The Oxford text archive* (*British Library R&D Rep.* No. 5985). London: British Library.

Pustejovsky, J. (1989). Current issues in computational lexical semantics. *Proceedings of the 4th European ACL*. Manchester, UK.

Pustejovsky, J., & Anick, P. (1988). On the semantic interpretation of nominals. *Proceedings of the 12th International Conference for Computational Linguistics*. Budapest, Hungary.

Pustejovsky, J., & Nirenburg, S. (1987). Lexical selection in the process of language generation. In C. Sidner (Ed.), *Proceedings of the Association for Computational Linguistics (ACL) 25th Annual Meeting* (pp. 201–206). Stanford, CA.

Raymond, D.R. (1987). *Dispatches from the front: the prefaces to the Oxford English Dictionary* (Tech. Rep. OED-87–04). Waterloo, Canada: University of Waterloo, *Centre for the New Oxford English Dictionary and Text Research.*

Raymond, D.R.(1990). *Lector : An interactive formatter for tagged text* (Tech. Rep. OED-90–02). Waterloo, Canada: University of Waterloo, *Centre for the New Oxford English Dictionary and Text Research.*

Raymond, D.R., et al. (1990). A potpourri of prototypes. (Tech. Rep. OED-90–01). Waterloo, Canada: University of Waterloo, *Centre for the New Oxford English* Dictionary and Text Research.

Raymond, D.R., & Fawcett, H.J. (1990). *Playing detective with full text searching software* (Tech. Rep. OED-90–03). Waterloo, Canada: University of Waterloo, *Centre for the New Oxford English Dictionary and Text Research.*

Raymond, D.R., & Warburton, Y.L. (1987). Computerization of lexicographical activity on the Oxford English Dictionary (Tech. Rep. OED-87–03). Waterloo, Canada: University of Waterloo, *Centre for the New Oxford English Dictionary and Text Research.*

Raymond, D.R., & Tompa, F.W. (1987). *Hypertext and the New Oxford English Dictionary* (Tech. Rep. OED-87–06). Waterloo, Canada: University of Waterloo, *Centre for the New Oxford English Dictionary and Text Research.*

Raymond, D., & Tompa, F. (1988). Hypertext and the New Oxford English Dictionary. *Communications of the Association for Computing Machinery, 31(7),* 971–879.

Renouf, A. (1987). Corpus development. In J.M. Sinclair (Ed.), *Looking up: An account of the COBUILD project in lexical computing.* London: William Collins.

Ritchie, G., Pulman, S., Black, A., & Russell, G. (1987). A computational framework for lexical description. *Computational Linguistics, 13*(3–4), 290–307.

Rodriguez, H., et al. (1991). Guide to the extraction and conversion of taxonomies (*ACQUILEX project draft user manual*). Barcelona, Spain: Universitat Politechnica de Catalunya.

Roget, P.M. (1958). *Thesaurus of words and phrases.* New York: Harper and Row.

Roventini, A., & Antelmi, D. (1990). Semantic relationships within a set of verbal entries in the Italian lexical database. *ESPRIT BRA-3030 ACQUILEX WP NO.13.*

Russell, G., Carroll, J., & Warwick-Armstrong, S. (1991). Multiple default inheritance in a unification based lexicon. *Proceedings of the 29th ACL* (pp. 215–221). Berkeley, CA.

Russell, G., Pulman, S., Ritchie, G., & Black, A. (1986). A dictionary and morphological analyzer for English. *COLING86: Proceedings of the 11th International Conference on Computational Linguistics,* Bonn, Germany.

Sager, N. (1981). *Natural language information processing.* Reading, MA: Addison-Wesley.

Sager, N., Friedman, C, & Lyman, M. (1987). *Medical language processing: Computer management of narrative data.* Reading, MA: Addison-Wesley.

Sager, N., Lynette H., Carolyn W., Carol F., Susanne W., Robert G., & Eileen F. (1980). *Research into methods for automatic classification and fact retrieval in science subfields* (String Rep. No. 13). New York: New York University.

Sakamoto, Y., Ishikawa, T., & Satoh, M. (1986). Concept and structure of semantic markers for machine translation in Mu-Project. *COLING86: Proceedings of the 11th International Conference on Computational Linguistics,* Bonn, Germany.

Sakamoto, Y., Satoh, M., & Ishikawa, T. (1984). Lexicon features for Japanese syntactic analysis in Mu-Project-JE. *COLING84. Proceedings of the 10th International Conference on Computational Linguistics,* Stanford, CA.

Sanfilippo, A. (1990a). A morphological analyser for English & Italian. *ESPRIT BRA-3030 ACQUILEX WP NO.004.*

Sanfilippo, A. (1990b). *Grammatical relations, thematic roles and verb semantics* (PhD dissertation). Edinburgh, Scotland: University of Edinburgh.

Sanfilippo, A. (1991). LKB encoding of lexical knowledge from machine-readable dictionaries. Paper presented at the *ACQUILEX Workshop on Default Inheritance in the Lexicon.* Cambridge, UK: University of Cambridge.

Schreuder, R. (1985). *Using lexical databases in psycholinguistic research.* Paper presented at Workshop on Machine-Readable Dictionaries, Grosseto, Italy.

Schwind, C., & Janas, J. (1977). Automatic thesaurus construction from natural language definitions. *SIGART Newsletter, 61,* 49–50.

Scott, D.S. (1987). What should we demand of electronic dictionaries? In D.L. Berg (Ed.), *The uses of large text databases: Proceedings of the University of Waterloo (UW) Centre for the New Oxford English Dictionary 3rd Annual Conference* (pp. 97–111). Waterloo, Canada.

Sebastiani, F., Ferrari, G., & Prodanof, I. (1986). A conceptual dictionary for contextually based structure selection. In G. Johannesen (Ed.), *Advances in lexicology: Proceedings of the University of Waterloo Centre for the New Oxford English Dictionary 2nd Annual Conference* (pp. 127–146). Waterloo, Canada.

Sedelow, S.Y. (1985). Computational lexicography. *Computers and the Humanities, 19,* 97–101.

Sedelow, S.Y., & Sedelow, W.A., Jr. (1986a). The lexicon in the background. *Computers and Translation, 1,* 73–81.

Sedelow, S.Y., & Sedelow, W.A., Jr. (1986b). Thesaural knowledge representation. In G. Johannesen (Ed.), *Advances in lexicology: Proceedings of the University of Waterloo Centre for the New Oxford English Dictionary 2nd Annual Conference* (pp. 29–43). Waterloo, Canada.

Simpson, J. (1985). The new OED project. In G. Johannesen (Ed.), *Information in data: Proceedings of the University of Waterloo Centre for the New Oxford English Dictionary 1st Annual Conference* (pp. 1–6). Waterloo, Canada.

Simpson, J., & Nash, D. (Eds.). (1989). *Australian Bicentennial dictionary of Aboriginal languages.*

Sinclair, J.M. (1987a). Grammar in the dictionary. In J.M. Sinclair (Ed.), *Looking up: An account of the COBUILD project in lexical computing* (pp. 104–115). London: William Collins.

Sinclair, J.M. (Ed.). (1987b). *Looking up: An account of the COBUILD project in lexical computing.* London: William Collins.

Sinclair, J.M. (1987c). The nature of the evidence. In J.M. Sinclair (Ed.), *Looking up: An account of the COBUILD project in lexical computing.* London: William Collins.

Sinclair, J.M. (Ed.). (1987d). *The Collins COBUILD English language dictionary.* London: William Collins.

Slator, B. (1991). Using context for sense preference. In U. Zernik (Ed.), *Lexical acquisition: Exploiting online resources to build a lexicon.* Hillsdale NJ: Erlbaum.

Slocum, J., & Morgan, M. (1987). The role of dictionaries and machine-readable lexicons in translation. In D. Walker, A. Zampolli, & N. Calzolari. (Eds.), *Proceedings of the Linguistics Summer Institute Lexicon Workshop.* Morristown, NJ: Linguistics Summer Institute.

Smadja, F. (1991). Macrocoding the lexicon with co-occurrence knowledge. In U. Zernik (Ed.), *Lexical acquisition: Exploiting online resources to build a lexicon.* Hillsdale NJ: Erlbaum.

Smith, R.N. (1981). On defining adjectives, Part III. *Dictionaries: Journal of the Dictionary Society of North America, 3,* 28–38.

Smith, R.N. (1984). *Collocational relations.* Paper presented at the Workshop on Relational Models, COLING '84, Stanford, CA.

Smith, R.N. (1985). Conceptual primitives in the English lexicon. *Linguistics, 18,* 99–137.

Smith, R., & Edward, M. (1977). An English dictionary for computerized syntactic and semantic processing. In A. Zampolli & N. Calzolari (Eds.), *Computational and mathematical linguistics* (pp. 303–322). Florence, Italy: Olschki.

Sowa, J. (1985). Using a lexicon of canonical graphs in a semantic interpreter. In G. Johannesen (Ed.), *Information in data: Proceedings of the University of Waterloo Centre for the New Oxford English Dictionary 1st Annual Conference* (pp. 63–82). Waterloo, Canada.

Sowa, J. (1988). Relations in a lexicon of canonical graphs. In E. Martha (Ed.), *Relational models of the lexicon* (pp. 113–138). Cambridge, UK: Cambridge University Press.

Sparck Jones, K., & Tait, J.I. (1984). Linguistically motivated descriptive term selection. *COLING84: Proceedings of the 10th International Conference on Computational Linguistics*, Stanford, CA.

Sperberg-McQueen, C.M., & Bumard, L. (Eds.). (1990, July). *Guidelines for the encoding and interchange of machine-readable texts* (Version 1.0).

Stallard, D. (1987). The logical analysis of lexical ambiguity. In C. Sidner (Ed.), *Proceedings of the Association for Computational Linguistics 25th Annual Meeting* (pp. 179–185). Stanford, CA.

Stubbs, J., & Tompa, F. (1984). Waterloo and the new Oxford English dictionary. *Proceedings of the 20th Annual Conference on Editorial Problems* (pp. 19–44). New York: AMS Press.

Suematsu, H. (1990). A simutaneous selection algorithm for English sentence patterns. *Proceedings of the International Workshop on Electronic Dictionaries*. Kanagawa, Japan: EDR.

Summers, D. (1990). Longm

an computerization initiatives, corpus building, semantic analysis and Prolog version of LDOCE by Cheng-ming Guo. *Proceedings of the International Workshop on Electronic Dictionaries*. Kanagawa, Japan: EDR.

Teubert, W. (1984). Applications of a lexicographical data base for German. COLING84. *Proceedings of the 10th International Conference on Computational Linguistics* (pp. 34–37). Stanford, CA.

Tompa, F.W., & Raymond, D.R. (1989). Database design for a dynamic dictionary. (Tech. Rep. OED-89-05). Waterloo, Canada: University of Waterloo, *Centre for the New Oxford English Dictionary and Text Research.*

Townsend, G.V.J. (1989). Citation matching in the Oxford English Dictionary. (Tech. Rep. OED-89-06). Waterloo, Canada: University of Waterloo, *Centre for the New Oxford English Dictionary and Text Research.*

Trowsdale, G.G.(1988). Efficient implementation of subsequential transducers (Research Rep. CS-88-20). Waterloo, Canada: University of Waterloo, *Department of Computer Science.*

Tsurumaru, H. (1990). Extraction of semantic hierarchical relations from a Japanese language dictionary. *Proceedings of the International Workshop on Electronic Dictionaries*. Kanagawa, Japan: EDR.

Tsurumaru, H., Hitaka, T., & Yoshida, S. (1986). An attempt at automatic thesaurus construction from an ordinary Japanese dictionary. *COLING86: Proceedings of the 11th International Conference on Computational Linguistics*, Bonn, Germany.

Tuttle, M., Bolis, M., Nelson, S., & Sherertz, D. (1988). Towards a biomedical thesaurus: Building the foundation of the UMLS. *Symposium on Computer Applications in Medical Care (SCAMC)*, Washington, DC.

Uchida, H. (1990). Electronic dictionaries. *Proceedings of the International Workshop on Electronic Dictionaries*. Kanagawa, Japan: EDR.

UW Centre for the New OED. (1985, November). *Information in Data: Proceedings of the First Annual Conference of the UW Centre for the New OED*. Waterloo, Ontario.

UW Centre for the New OED. (1986, November). *Advances in Lexicology: Proceedings of the Second Annual Conference of the UW Centre for the New OED*. Waterloo, Canada.

UW Centre for the New OED. (1987, November). *The Uses of Large Text Databases:*

Proceedings of the Third Annual Conference of the UW Centre for the New OED. Waterloo, Canada.

UW Centre for the New OED. (1988, October). *Information in Text: Proceedings of the Fourth Annual Conference of the UW Centre for the New OED.* Waterloo, Canada.

UW Centre for the New OED. (1989, September). *Dictionaries in The Electronic Age: Proceedings of the Fifth Annual Conference of the UW Centre for the New OED.* Oxford, UK.

UW Centre for the New OED. (1990, October). *Electronic Text Research: Proceedings of the Sixth Annual Conference of UW Centre for the New OED.* Waterloo, Canada.

UW Centre for the New OED. (1991, September). *Using Corpora: Proceedings of the Seventh Annual Conference of UW Centre for the New OED.* Oxford, UK.

van Herwijnen, E. (1990). *Practical SGML.* Dordrecht, Germany: Kluwer.

Velardi, P. (1991). Acquiring a semantic lexicon for natural language processing. In U. Zernik (Ed.), *Lexical acquisition: Exploiting online resources to build a lexicon.* Hillsdale NJ: Erlbaum.

Venezky, R. (1987). Unseen users, unknown systems: Computer design for a scholar's dictionary. In D.L. Berg (Ed.), *The Uses of Large Text Databases: Proceedings of the University of Waterloo Centre for the New Oxford English Dictionary 3rd Annual Conference* (pp. 113–121). Waterloo, Canada.

Vossen, P. (1989a). Getting to grips with the structure of the VanDale Dictionary. *ESPRIT BRA-3030 ACQUILEX WP NO.002* .

Vossen, P. (1989b). Polysemy and vagueness of meaning: descriptions in the Longman dictionary of contemporary English. *ESPRIT BRA-3030 ACQUILEX WP NO.001.*

Vossen, P. (1990). The end of the chain: Where does decomposition of lexical knowledge lead us eventually? *ESPRIT BRA-3030 ACQUILEX WP NO.010.*

Vossen, P. (1991). Comparing noun-taxonomies cross-linguistically. *ESPRIT BRA-3030 ACQUILEX WP NO.014.*

Vossen, P., Meijs, W., & Den Broeder, M. (1989). Meaning and structure in dictionary definitions. In B. Boguraev & T. Briscoe (Eds.), *Computational lexicography for natural language processing* (pp. 171–190) London: Longman.

Vossen, P., & Serail, I. (1990). Word-Devil: A taxonomy-browser for decomposition via the lexicon. *ESPRIT BRA-3030 ACQUILEX WP NO.009.*

Walker, D. (1984). Machine-readable dictionaries. *COLING84: Proceedings of the 10th International Conference on Computational Linguistics,* Stanford, CA.

Walker, D. (1985). Knowledge resource tools for accessing large text files. In G. Johannesen (Ed.), *Information in Data: Proceedings of the University of Waterloo Centre for the New Oxford English Dictionary 1st Annual Conference* (pp. 11–24). Waterloo, Canada.

Walker, D.E. (1986a). Knowledge resource tools for accessing large text files. In G. Johannesen. (Ed.), *Information in data: Proceedings of the First Conference of the University of Waterloo Center for the New Oxford English Dictionary* (pp. 11–24). Waterloo, Canada.

Walker, D. E. (1986b). Knowledge resource tools for information access. *Future Generations Computer Systems,* 2, 161–171.

Walker, D.E. (1987). Knowledge resource tools for accessing large text files. In S. Nirenberg (Ed.), *Machine translation: Theoretical and methodological issues.* Cambridge, UK: Cambridge University Press.

Walker, D.E. (1989a). Developing lexical resources. In L.M. Jones, (Ed.), *Dictionaries in the Electronic Age: Proceedings of the 5th Conference of the University of Waterloo Center for the New Oxford English Dictionary* (pp. 1–22). Waterloo, Canada.

Walker, D.E. (1989b). The world of words. In Y. Wilks (Ed.), *Theoretical issues in natural language processing* (pp. 2–6). Hillsdale, NJ: Erlbaum.

Walker, D.E. (1990a). Collecting texts, tagging texts, and putting texts in context. In P.S. Jacobs (Ed.), *Text-based intelligent systems: Current research in text analysis, information extraction, and retrieval.* Schenectady, NY.

Walker, D.E. (1990b, March). Prerequisites for research on electronic document delivery. In C. Egido (Ed.), *First Bellcore/BCC Conference on Electronic Document Delivery* (pp. 37–41). Piscataway, NJ: Bellcore.

Walker, D.E. (1990c). The ecology of language. *Proceedings of the International Workshop on Electronic Dictionaries.* Kanagawa, Japan: EDR.

Walker, D.E. (1991). Developing resources for natural language research. Bulletin du CID. Paris, France: Centre de Hautes Etudes Internationales d'Informatique Documentaire.

Walker, D.E. (1992a). Developing computational lexical resources. In E.F. Kittay and A. Lehrer (Eds.), *Frames, fields, and contrasts: New essays in lexical and semantic organization.* Hillsdale, NJ: Erlbaum.

Walker, D.E. (1992b). Introduction. In D.E. Walker, A. Zampolli, & N. Calzolari (Eds.), *Automating the lexicon: Research and practice in a multilingual environment.* Oxford, UK: Oxford University Press.

Walker, D.E., & Amsler, R. (1986). The use of machine-readable dictionaries in sublanguage analysis. In G. Ralph & K. Richard (Eds.), *Analyzing language in restricted domains: Sublanguage description and processing* (pp. 69–83). Hillsdale, NJ: Erlbaum.

Walker, D.E., & Hockey, S. (1991). The text encoding initiative. Bulletin du CID. Paris, France: Centre de Hautes Etudes Internationales d'Informatique Documentaire.

Walker, D.E., Zampolli, A., & Calzolari, N. (1992). *Automating the lexicon: Research and practice in a multilingual environment.* Oxford, UK: Oxford University Press.

Walker, D.E., Zampolli, A., & Calzolari, N. (Eds.). (1987). Automating the lexicon: Research and practice in a multilingual environment. *Proceedings of the Linguistics Summer Institute Lexicon Workshop.* Morristown, NJ: Linguistics Summer Institute.

Wang, Y.C., Vandendorpe, J., & Evens, M. (1985). Relational thesauri in information retrieval. *Journal of the American Society for Information Science, 1,* 15–27.

Warwick, S. (1987). Automated lexical resources in Europe: A survey. In D. Walker, A. Zampolli, & N. Calzolari (Eds.), *Proceedings of the Linguistics Summer Institute Lexicon Workshop.* Morristown, NJ: Linguistics Summer Institu te.

Wehrli, E. (1985). Design and implementation of a lexical database. *Proceedings of the Conference of the European Chapter of the Association for Computational Linguistics (ACL)* (pp. 146–153). Geneva.

Werner, O. (1988). How to teach a network. In E. Martha (Ed.), *Relational models of the lexicon* (pp. 141–166). Cambridge, UK: Cambridge University Press.

White, C. (1983). *The linguistic string project dictionary for automatic text analysis.* Paper presented at the Workshop on Machine-Readable Dictionaries, SRI, Menlo Park, CA.

White, J. (1988). Determination of lexical-semantic relations for multilingual terminology structures. In E. Martha (Ed.), *Relational models of the lexicon* (pp. 183–198). Cambridge, UK: Cambridge University Press.

Wilks, Y., Fass, D., Guo, C-M., MacDonald, J., Plate, T., & Slator, B. (1989). A tractable machine dictionary as a resource for computational semantics. In B. Boguraev & T. Briscoe (Eds.), *Computational lexicography for natural language processing.* London: Longmans.

Wilks, Y., Fass, D., Guo, C-M., MacDonald, J., Plate, T., & Slator, B. (1990). Providing machine tractable dictionary tools. *Journal of Machine Translation,* 5, 99–151.

Wilks, Y., Fass, D., Guo, C-M., MacDonald, J., Plate, T., & Slator, B. (in press). Providing machine-tractable dictionary tools. In J. Pustejovsky (Ed.), *Lexical semantics.* Amsterdam: Kluwer Academic.

Wilks, Y., Guthrie, J., Guthrie, L., & Aidenejad, H. (1991). Subject-dependent co-occurrence and word-sense disambiguation. *Proceedings of the Confernece of the Association for Computational Linguistics.* Berkeley, CA.

Wilks, Y., & Guthrie, L. (1990). The consortium for lexical research. *Proceedings of the International Workshop on Electronic Dictionaries.* Kanagawa, Japan: EDR.

Wilks, Y., & Slator, B. (1987). Towards semantic structure from dictionary entries. *Proceedings of the Second Annual Rocky Mountain Conference on AI*. Boulder, CO.

Wilson, E. (1988). Electronic books: The automatic production of hypertext documents from existing printed books. In D.L. Berg (Ed.), *Information in text: Proceedings of the University of Waterloo Centre for the New Oxford English Dictionary 4th Annual Conference* (pp. 29–45). Waterloo, Canada.

Wolff, S. (1985). The use of morphosemantic regularities in the medical vocabulary for automatic lexical coding. *Methods of Information in Medicine, 23*, 195–203.

Yokoi, T. (1990). Collaboration and cooperation for development of electronic dictionaries. *Proceedings of the International Workshop on Electronic Dictionaries*. Kanagawa, Japan: EDR.

Yokoyama, S., & Ogino, T. (1990). A step toward a computer-assisted bilingual dictionary for learning Japanese. *Proceedings of the International Workshop on Electronic Dictionaries*. Kanagawa, Japan: EDR.

Zernik, U. (1991). Tagging word sense in corpus. In U. Zernik (Ed.), *Lexical acquisition: Exploiting online resources to build a lexicon*. Hillsdale NJ: Erlbaum.

Zernik, U., & Dyer, M. (1985). Towards a self-extending lexicon. *Proceedings of the 23rd Annual Meeting of the ACL* (pp. 284–292). Chicago.

Zernik, U., & Dyer, M. (1987). The self-extending phrasal lexicon. *Computational Linguistics, 3/4*, 308–327.

GLOSSARY

Bootstrapping schedule: The bootstrapping schedule is concerned with which word senses are to be processed first, and which later. The need for the bootstrapping schedule stems from the fact that both lexical and world-knowledge information concerning the words used in the definition text of a word sense have to be present in the MTD before the definition text of that particular word sense can be analyzed and new lexical and world knowledge acquired.

Controlled senses: All the word senses of the controlled words defined in LDOCE are controlled senses.

Controlled words: Controlled words are words from the list of the controlled vocabulary given at the back of the LDOCE dictionary.

Defining cycle: A defining cycle refers to the process of one group of words defining another group of words, resulting in the second group of words being defined.

Defining senses: Defining senses are individual word senses of the defining words that are used in the definitions of the meanings of the controlled words.

Defining words: Defining words are words that are used to define the meanings of all the controlled words in their sense definitions.

Entry: An entry is defined as a collection of one or more sense definitions that ends at the next head.

FF: An FF, or Fregean Formula, is a MTD definition of a word sense. It is a two-place predicate where the first argument is a word sense being defined and the second a parse tree of its sense definition.

Hanging at each terminal symbol of the parse tree is a primitive or another FF in the case of a nonprimitive leaf.

Head: A head is the word, phrase, or hyphenated word defined by an entry. A single word can be the head of more than one entry if homographs or different parts of speech exist for that word.

LDOCE sense: Any word sense of any LDOCE word is a LDOCE sense.

LDOCE word: Any word contained in LDOCE is a LDOCE word.

Hunch set: A hunch set is a hypothesized set of seed words of LDOCE. The initial hunch set of seed words contains all defining words with multiple defining senses and a subset of defining words with single defining senses.

Seed senses: Seed senses are natural semantic primitives derived from this work on LDOCE.

Seed words: The words that the seed senses are senses of are called the seed words.

Semantic preference: Semantic preference (Wilks, 1972) refers to the behavioral tendency of words where more semantically related word senses prefer to stay with each other. For example, it is of common knowledge that "a doctor in the hospital" probably refers to a medical doctor. In other words, the sense of *doctor* as a medical doctor "prefers," so to speak, the sense of *hospital* as "a place where ill people stay and have treatment that should cure them."

Sense definition: A sense definition is a set of definitions, examples, and other text associated with one sense of a head.

APPENDIX A

SAMPLE DEFINITION TEXTS OF MINI-LDOCE

Mini-LDOCE belongs to a new type of machine-tractable dictionary being published by Longmans. It explores the research results of the present author while he was a doctoral student at New Mexico State University under Professor Yorick Wilks. Mini-LDOCE consists of about 4,000 word-sense entries, each of which was found to define the meanings of the 2,000 words in the controlled vocabulary of LDOCE. What is shown below is a simplified version of part of the C-sample submitted to Longmans for technical verifications. The so-called "Extended Form" paraphrases, in normal English, the definition texts given in Section A of the appendix. Word senses in the definition texts that are not Mini-LDOCE entries are further defined in terms of Mini-LDOCE entries up to three levels of embedding. A computer disk version of the Mini-LDOCE C-sample is available on request through Longman Dictionaries at Longman House, Burnt Mill, Harlow, England.

A.1. SIMPLIFIED FORM

mini_ldoce(cement, n, 517, 1, [a1, grey1, powder1, make1, from6, a1, burn2, mixture1, of2, lime1, and1, clay1, which2b, become1, hard1, like15, stone1, after2, 'have1a', be2, mix1, with4, water1, and1, allow1, to29, dry18]).

mini_ldoce(cent, n, 518, 1, ['0.01', of1, any12, of1, certain9, money1, standard2, such2, as25, the10, dollar1]).

mini_ldoce(centre, n, 519, 1, [a1, middle1, part2, or2, point7,;, point7, [equally1, [as1, much12b, to4, an1, equal1, degree1]], distant1, from2, all6, side6,;, the10, exact2, middle2, esp,., the1, point7, around12, which2b, a1, circle2, be2, draw22a]).

mini_ldoce(centre, n, 520, 2, [a1, point7, area1, person1, or2, thing1, that16, be7c, the1, most4, important1, [in_relation_to1, [relation5, [concerning1, [with_regard_to1, [regard5, [regarding1]]]]]], an1, interest3, activity3, or2, condition1]).

mini_ldoce(ceremony, n, 521, 1, [a1, special1, formal1, solemn1, and1, [well_established1,['have1a', exist1, for25, a2, 'long1b', time4]], action2, or2, set27, of1, action2, use11, for11, mark25, an1, important1, private1, or2, public1, social1, or2, religious1, event1]).

mini_ldoce(certain, adj, 522, 1, [sure1,;, establish5, beyond4, all5, doubt4, or2, question3,;, know1]).

mini_ldoce(certain, determiner, 523, 9, [name14, but2, not1, well7, know1]).

mini_ldoce(certainty, n, 524, 1, [the1, state1, of9, be7c, certain1,;, [freedom4, [the1, condition1, of9, be7e, without1a, something1, harmful, or2, [unpleasant1, [cause2, [dislike2], not1, [enjoyable1], [displease1]]]]], from14, doubt4]).

mini_ldoce(chain, n, 525, 1, ['(', a1, length4, of2, ')', usu,., metal1, ring2, connect1, to6, or2, fit14, into2, [one_another1, ['each_other1', ['(', mean7, that15, each2, 'of5a', 2, or2, more1, do18, something1, to25, the1, 'other1b', '(', s, ')', ')']]], use11, for1, fasten1, support1, ornament4, etc,.]).

mini_ldoce(chain, n, 526, 2, [a1, number3, of5a, connect1, thing1, such2, as25, event1, shop1, restaurant1, mountain1, etc,.]).

mini_ldoce(chair, n, 527, 1, [a1, 'piece1b', of1, furniture1, on1, which2b, one1, person1, may1, sit1, which2b, 'have4c', [typically3, [in17, a1, typical1, case1, or2, example1,;, if1, true1, to10, type1]], a1, back6, seat1, usu,., 4, leg6, and1, sometimes1, arm2]).

mini_ldoce(chairman, n, 528, '1a', [a1, person1, in18, charge9, of8, a1, meeting1]).

mini_ldoce(chairman, n, 529, '1b', [a1, person1, who2, direct2, the1, work1, of1, a1, committee1, department1, etc]).

mini_ldoce(chalk, n, 530, 2, ['(', a1, 'piece1b', of1, ')', this1, material4, white1a, or2, [coloured1, ['(', esp, in18, comb, ')', the1, state7, colour2]], use11, for1, write2, or2, draw21]).

mini_ldoce(chance, n, 531, 1, [the1, force1, that16, seem1, to29, make5, thing6, happen1, without1a, cause1, or2, reason1,;, luck1,;, good1, or2, bad1, fortune1]).

mini_ldoce(chance, n, 532, 3, ['(', a1, ')', possibility1,;, [likelihood1, [the1, fact1, or2, degree1, of1, be7c, likely1]], that15, something1, will1, happen1]).
mini_ldoce(chance, n, 533, 4, [a1, favourable2, occasion1,;, [opportunity1, [a1, favourable2, [opportune1, ['(', of1, time15, ')', right9, for1, a1, purpose1]], moment2, or2, occasion1, for1, do18, something1]]]).
mini_ldoce(chance, n, 534, 5, [a1, risk1]).
mini_ldoce(change, v, 535, 1, [to29, '(', cause7, to29, ')', become1, different1]).
mini_ldoce(change, n, 536, 15, ['(', an1, example1, of1, ')', the1, act8, or2, result2, of1, change1]).
mini_ldoce(character, n, 537, 2, [the1, [combination2, [the1, state1, of9, be2, combine1]], of8, quality2, which2b, make3, a1, thing1, event1, place1, etc,., different1, from14, another6]).
mini_ldoce(character, n, 538, 3, [the1, quality2, which2b, make3, a1, person1, different1, from14, another6,;, moral1, nature1a]).
mini_ldoce(character, n, 539, 6, [a1, person1, 'in1', a1, book1, play3a, etc,.]).
mini_ldoce(charge, v, 540, 1, [to29, ask3, in19, [payment2, [an1, amount1, of1, money1, to29, be2, pay1]]]).
mini_ldoce(charge, n, 541, 9, [care3,;, control5,;, [responsibility1, [the1, condition1, of9, be7c, responsible1]]]).
mini_ldoce(charge, n, 542, 12, [a1, speak5, or2, write2, [statement1, [something1, that16, be2, state7, a1, write2, or2, speak5, [declaration2, [a1, [statement1], give5, information1, in1, a1, court1, of1, law2]], esp, of1, a1, formal1, kind1]], blame1, a1, person1, for11, a1, crime1, for11, break6, the10, law1, or2, for11, do18, something1, [morally2, [[with_regard_to1, [regard5, [regarding1]]], right7, or2, good3, behaviour1]], wrong6]).

A.2. EXTENDED FORM

% 517 **cement** n 1 %

£ ldoce definition £

a grey powder, made from a burned mixture of lime and clay, which becomes hard like stone after having been mixed with water and allowed to dry

$ Mini ldoce definition in normal English $

a grey powder, made from a burned mixture of lime and clay, which becomes hard like stone after having been mixed with water and allowed to dry

& Mini ldoce extended definition text &

a1 — one

grey1 — of the colour like black mixed with white; the colour of lead, ashes, rain clouds, etc.

powder1 — (often in comb.) (a kind of) substance in the form of very fine dry grains

make1 — to produce by work or action

from6 — based on; using; out of

a1 — one

burn2 — to be on fire

mixture1 — (esp. of chemicals in a liquid) a set of substances mixed together, which keep their separate qualities while combined in one mass

of2 — made from

lime1 — also quicklime - a white substance obtained by burning limestone, used in making cement

and1 — (used to show connection or addition, esp. of words of the same type or sentences of the same importance) as well as; together with; with; also; besides

clay1 — heavy firm earth, soft when wet, becoming hard when baked at a high temperature, and from which bricks, pots, earthenware, etc., are made

which2b — (used for showing relationship between things) being the one (s) that

become1 — to come to be

hard1 — firm and stiff; which cannot easily be broken, or pressed down, or bent, etc.

like15 — in the same way as

stone1 — a piece of rock, esp. not very large, either of natural shape or cut out specially for building

after2 — following in time or order; later than; next

have1a — (the auxiliary verb used to form perfect forms)

be2 — (forms the pass. voice of verbs)

mix1 — to (cause to) be combined so as to form a whole, of which the parts have no longer a separate shape, appearance, etc., or cannot easily be separated one from another

with4 — having as material or contents

water1 — the most common liquid, without colour, taste, or smell, which falls from the sky as rain, forms rivers, lakes, and seas, and is drunk by people and animals

and1 — (used to show connection or addition, esp. of words of the same type or sentences of the same importance) as well as; together with; with; also; besides

allow1 — to let (somebody) do something; let (something) be done; permit to29—(used before a verb to show it is the infinitive, but not before can, could, may, might, will, would, shall, should, must, ought to; sometimes left out when the verb is understood. note the following patterns)

dry18-to (cause to) become dry

%518 **cent** n 1 %

£ ldoce definition £

0.01 of any of certain money standards, such as the dollar

$ Mini ldoce definition in normal English $

0.01 of any of certain money standards, such as the dollar

cent grammatical code - label - abbrev. for

& Mini ldoce extended definition text &

0.01@

of1—(of qualities, possessions, etc.) belonging to x; that x has

any12—any thing or things; any quantity or number

of1—(of qualities, possessions, etc.) belonging to x; that x has

certain9—named, but not well known

money1—pieces of metal made into coins, or paper notes with their value printed on them, given and taken in buying and selling

standard2—something fixed as a rule for measuring weight, value, purity, etc.

such2—(sometimes with as) of the same kind; like

as25—like

the10—(used with a singular noun to make it general followed by a singular verb)

dollar1—any of various standards of money, as used in the us, canada, australia, new zealand, hong kong, etc. it is worth 1 cents and its sign is

%519 **centre** n 1 %

£ ldoce definition £

a middle part or point; point equally distant from all sides; the exact middle esp. the point around which a circle is drawn:@I Although London is Britain's capital it is not at the centre of the country@R—see picture at@S GEOMETRY

$ Mini ldoce definition in normal English $

a middle part or point; point equally distant from all sides; the exact middle esp. the point around which a circle is drawn

& Mini ldoce extended definition text &

a1—one

middle1—in or nearly in the centre; at the same distance from 2 or more points, or from the beginning and end of something

part2—any of the divisions into which something is or may be considered as being divided (whether separated from a whole or connected with it) and which is therefore less than the whole

or2—(often with either; used before the last of a set of possibilities)

point7—a place; particular real or imaginary place exactly stated

equally1*

as1—to the same degree or amount; equally

much12b—[usu, nonassertive] to a great degree

to4—towards; reaching the state of

an1—(used when the following word begins with a vowel sound) a

equal1—(of 2 or more) the same in size, number, value, rank, etc.

degree1—(the size of) a step or stage in a set of steps or stages rising in order from lowest to highest

distant1—separate in space or time; far off; away

from2—(showing a starting point in place) having left; beginning at (the) (often in the phr. from (a [c] noun used as a [u] noun) to (a [c] noun used as a [u] noun))

all6—(includes every member or separate part of a group of countable nouns)

side6—(often in comb.) an edge or border

the10—(used with a singular noun to make it general followed by a singular verb)

exact2—(esp. of things that can be measured) correct and without mistakes

middle2—the central part, point, or position

the1—(used when it is clearly understood who or what is meant)

point7—a place; particular real or imaginary place exactly stated

around12—on all sides of; all round; surrounding

which2b—(used for showing relationship between things) being the one (s) that

a1—one

circle2—something having the general shape of this line; ring

be2—(forms the pass. voice of verbs)

draw22a—to make with a pencil or pen

%520 **centre** n 2 %
£ ldoce definition £
a point, area, person, or thing that is the most important in relation to an interest, activity, or condition:@l a shopping centre | She likes to be the centre of attention all the time
$ Mini ldoce definition in normal English $
a point, area, person, or thing that is the most important in relation to an interest, activity, or condition
& Mini ldoce extended definition text &
a1 – one
point7 – a place; particular real or imaginary place exactly stated
area1 – a particular space or surface
person1 – a human being considered as having a character of his or her own, or as being different from all others
or2 – (often with either; used before the last of a set of possibilities)
thing1 – any material object; an object that need not or cannot be named
that16 – not fml (used as the subject of a defining relative clause, to mean) who or which
be7c – (as a connecting verb with adjectives)
the1 – (used when it is clearly understood who or what is meant)
most4 – (forming the superl. of the greater number of adjectives and adverbs with more than one syllable)
important1 – which matters a lot
in_relation_to1*
relation5*
concerning1
with_regard_to1*
regard5 – in / with regard to regarding - see as for (usage)
regarding1*
an1 – (used when the following word begins with a vowel sound) a
interest3 – an activity, subject, etc., which one gives time and attention to
activity3 – action; deed
or2 – (often with either; used before the last of a set of possibilities)
condition1 – a state of being or existence

%521 **ceremony** n 1 %
£ ldoce definition £
a special formal, solemn, and well_established action or set of actions used for marking an important private or public, social or religious event:@l The wedding ceremony was beautiful
$ Mini ldoce definition in normal English $
a special formal, solemn, and well - established action or set of actions used for marking an important private or publik, social or religious event
& Mini ldoce extended definition text &
a1 – one
special1 – of a particular kind; not ordinary or usual
formal1 – ceremonial; according to accepted rules or customs
solemn1 – done, made, etc., seriously, having a sense of religious - like importance
and1 – (used to show connection or addition, esp. of words of the same type or sentences of the same importance) as well as; together with; with; also; besides
well_established1*
have1a – (the auxiliary verb used to form perfect forms)
exist1 – to live or be real; to have being
for25 – (sometimes left out if it follows directly after the verb) during; till the end of (a period of time)
a2 – (before certain determiners of quantity)
long1b – covering a great distance or time
time4 – a limited period as between 2 events, for the completion of an action, etc.
action2 – something done; deed
or2 – (often with either; used before the last of a set of possibilities)
set27 – a group of naturally connected things; group forming a whole
of1 – (of qualities, possessions, etc.) belonging to x; that x has
action2 – something done; deed
use11 – to employ; put to use
for1 – that is / are intended to belong to, be given to, or used for the purpose of
mark25 – to be a sign of
an1 – (used when the following word begins with a vowel sound) a
important1 – which matters a lot

private1 – personal; one's own; not shared with others
or2 – (often with either; used before the last of a set of possibilities)
public1 – of, to, by, for, or concerning people in general
social1 – of or concerning human society, its organization, or quality of life
or2 – (often with either; used before the last of a set of possibilities)
religious1 – of or concerning religion
event1 – a happening, usu. an important one

%522 **certain** adj 1 %
£ ldoce definition £
sure; established beyond all doubt or question; known:@I There's no certain cure for this illness
$ Mini ldoce definition in normal English $
sure; established beyond all doubt or question; known
& Mini ldoce extended definition text &
sure1 – having no doubt
establish5 – to cause people to believe in or recognize (a claim, fact, etc.)
beyond4 – out of reach of; much more than; outside the limits of
all5 – (shows the complete amount or quantity of, or the whole of, an uncountable noun)
doubt4 – (a feeling of) uncertainty of belief or opinion
or2 – (often with either; used before the last of a set of possibilities)
question3 – a doubt
know1 – to have (information) in the mind

%523 **certain** determiner 9 %
£ ldoce definition £
named, but not well known:@I A certain Mrs Jones rang me up today but she'd got the wrong number
$ Mini ldoce definition in normal English $
named, but not well known
& Mini ldoce extended definition text &
name14 – to give a name to (someone or something)
but2 – yet; in spite of this
not1 – (used for changing a word or expression to one with the opposite meaning)
well7 – in the right manner; satisfactorily

know1 – to have (information) in the mind

%524 **certainty** n 1 %
£ ldoce definition £
the state of being certain; freedom from doubt:@I I can't say with certainty what my plans are
$ Mini ldoce definition in normal English $
the state of being certain; freedom from doubt
& Mini ldoce extended definition text &
the1 – (used when it is clearly understood who or what is meant)
state1 – a condition in which a person or thing is; way of being
of9 – that is (equal to)
be7c – (as a connecting verb with adjectives)
certain1 – sure; established beyond all doubt or question; known
freedom4*
the1 – (used when it is clearly understood who or what is meant)
condition1 – a state of being or existence
of9 – that is (equal to)
be7e – (as a connecting verb with prepositional phrases)
without1a – not having; lacking
something1 – some unstated or unknown thing
harmful1*
or2 – (often with either; used before the last of a set of possibilities)
unpleasant1*
cause7-to lead to; be the cause of
dislike2*
not1-(used for changing a word or expression to one with the opposite meaning)
enjoyable1*
displease1*
from14 – (in a state of protection, prevention, or separation) with regard to
doubt4 – (a feeling of) uncertainty of belief or opinion

%525 **chain** n 1 %
£ ldoce definition £
(a length of) usu. metal rings, connected to or fitted into one another, used for fastening, supporting, ornamenting, etc.:@I

The bridge was supported by heavy iron chains hanging from 2 towers. | The head of the council wore her chain of office. | a lot of chain@R-see picture at@S TOOL@P^1

$ Mini ldoce definition in normal English $

(a length of) usu. metal rings, connected to or fitted into one another, used for fastening, supporting, ornamenting, etc.

& Mini ldoce extended definition text &

a1 — one

length4 — a piece of something, esp. of a certain length or for a particular purpose

of2 — made from

metal1 — any usu. solid shiny mineral substance of a group which can all be shaped by pressure and used for passing an electric current, and which share other properties

ring2 — a circular band (esp. of the stated substance or for the stated purpose)

connect1 — to join; unite; link

to6 — in a touching position with

or2 — (often with either; used before the last of a set of possibilities)

fit14 — to provide, and put correctly into place

into2-so as to be in

one_another1*

each_other1*

mean7 — to represent (a meaning)

that15 — (used for introducing various kinds of clause)

each2 — every one (of 2 or more) separately

of5a — (used for picking out in a group) from among (after nouns and numbers)

2@

or2 — (often with either; used before the last of a set of possibilities)

more1 — a greater number, quantity, or part of

do18 — (with actions and nonmaterial things)

something1 — some unstated or unknown thing

to25 — in connection with

the1 — (used when it is clearly understood who or what is meant)

other1b — (with the, one ' s both, all, every) the remaining (one or ones) of a set; what is / are left as well as that / those mentioned

s@

use11 — to employ; put to use

for1 — that is / are intended to belong to, be given to, or used for the purpose of

fasten1 — to make or become firmly fixed or closed

support1 — to bear the weight of, esp. preventing from falling

ornament4 — to add ornament to - see decorate (usage)

%526 **chain** n 2 %

£ ldoce definition £

a number of connected things, such as events, shops, restaurants, mountains, etc.

$ Mini ldoce definition in normal English $

a number of connected things, such as events, shops, restaurants, mountains, etc.

& Mini ldoce extended definition text &

a1 — one

number3 — (a) quantity or amount

of5a — (used for picking out in a group) from among (after nouns and numbers)

connect1 — to join; unite; link

thing1 — any material object; an object that need not or cannot be named

such2 — (sometimes with as) of the same kind; like

as25 — like

event1 — a happening, usu. an important one

shop1 — (ame store) - a room or building where goods are regularly kept and sold

restaurant1 — a place where food is sold and eaten

mountain1 — a very high hill, usu. of bare or snow - covered rock

%527 **chair** n 1 %

£ ldoce definition £

a piece of furniture on which one person may sit, which has typically a back, seat, usu. 4 legs, and sometimes arms-see picture at@S LIVING ROOM

$ Mini ldoce definition in normal English $

a piece of furniture on which one person may sit, which has typically a back, seat, usu. 4 legs, and sometimes arms - see picture at living room

& Mini ldoce extended definition text &

a1 — one

piece1b – a bit, such as a single object that is an example of a kind or class, or that forms part of a set

of1 – (of qualities, possessions, etc.) belonging to x; that x has

furniture1 – all large or quite large movable articles that are placed in a house, room, or other area, in order to make it convenient, comfortable, and / or pleasant as a space for living in, such as beds, chairs, tables, etc

on1 – (so as to be) touching (a surface)

which2b – (used for showing relationship between things) being the one (s) that

one1 – (the number) 1

person1 – a human being considered as having a character of his or her own, or as being different from all others

may1 – to be in some degree likely to

sit1 – to rest in a position with the upper body upright and supported at the bottom of the back, as on a chair or other seat

which2b – (used for showing relationship between things) being the one (s) that

have4a – to possess; own

typically3*

in17-as to; as regards

a1-one

typical1 – combining and showing the main signs of a particular kind, group, or class

case1 – an example

or2 – (often with either; used before the last of a set of possibilities)

example1 – something taken from a number of things of the same kind, which shows the usual quality of the rest or shows a general rule

if1 – (not usu. followed by the future tense) supposing that; on condition that

true1 – in accordance with fact or reality; actual

to10 – for; of

type1 – a particular kind, class, or group; group or class of people or things very like each other and different from those outside the group or class

a1 – one

back6 – (of a chair) the part that one leans against when sitting - see picture at living room

seat1 – a place for sitting

4@

legs—6omething like a leg in use or appearance

and1—(used to show connection or addition, esp. of words of the same type or sentences of the same importance) as well as; together with; with; also; besides

sometimes1—at times; now and then; occasionally

arm2—something that is shaped like or moves like an arm

%528 **chairman** n 1a %

£ ldoce definition £

a person@b a@R in charge of a meeting:@l She's one of our best and most experienced chairmen@b b@R who directs the work of a committee, department, etc.:@l He was elected (the) chairman of the education committee

$ Mini ldoce definition in normal English $

a person in charge of a meeting

& Mini ldoce extended definition text &

a1—one

person1—a human being considered as having a character of his or her own, or as being different from all others

in18—having or so as to have (a condition)

charge9—care; control; responsibility

of8—(before a phr. that is like an object in grammar) directed towards or done to

a1—one

meeting1—the coming together of 2 or more people, by chance or arrangement

%529 **chairman** n 1b %

£ ldoce definition £

a person@b a@R in charge of a meeting:@l She's one of our best and most experienced chairmen@b b@R who directs the work of a committee, department, etc.:@l He was elected (the) chairman of the education committee

$ Mini ldoce definition in normal English $

a person who directs the work of a committee, department, etc

& Mini ldoce extended definition text &

a1—one

person1—a human being considered as having a character of his or her own, or as being different from all others

who2—(showing relationship) that one (person) / those ones direct2 – to control and be in charge of (the way something is done)

the1 – (used when it is clearly understood who or what is meant)

work1 – activity which uses effort, esp. with a special purpose, not for amusement

of1 – (of qualities, possessions, etc.) belonging to x; that x has

a1 – one

committee1 – a group of people chosen to do a particular job or for special duties

department1 – any of the important divisions or branches of a government, business, school or college, etc.

%530 **chalk** n 2 %

£ ldoce definition £

(a piece of) this material, white or coloured, used for writing or drawing:@l The teacher wrote with a stick/piece of chalk. | Do you need some more chalk? | coloured chalks

$ Mini ldoce definition in normal English $

(a piece of) this material, white or coloured, used for writing or drawing

& Mini ldoce extended definition text &

a1 – one

piece1b – a bit, such as a single object that is an example of a kind or class, or that forms part of a set

of1 – (of qualities, possessions, etc.) belonging to x; that x has

this1 – being the one or amount stated, going to be stated, shown, or understood

material4 – anything from which something is or may be made

white1a – of a colour which is like that of a clean cloud in a sunny sky; of the colour of milk; of the colour which contains all the colours

or2 – (often with either; used before the last of a set of possibilities)

coloured1*

in18 – having or so as to have (a condition)

comb@

the1 – (used when it is clearly understood who or what is meant)

state7 – to say, express, or put into words, esp. formally

colour2—red, blue, green, black, brown, yellow, white, etc.

use11—to employ; put to use

for1—that is / are intended to belong to, be given to, or used for the purpose of

write2—to express and record in this way, or sometimes by means of a typewriter

or2—(often with either; used before the last of a set of possibilities)

draw21—to make a picture with a pencil or pen

%531 **chance** n 1 %

£ ldoce definition £

the force that seems to make things happen without cause or reason; luck; good or bad fortune:@I Chance plays an important part in many card games

$ Mini ldoce definition in normal English $

the force that seems to make things happen without cause or reason; luck; good or bad fortune

& Mini ldoce extended definition text &

the1—(used when it is clearly understood who or what is meant)

force1—natural or bodily power; active strength

that16—not fml (used as the subject of a defining relative clause, to mean) who or which

seem1—to give the idea or effect of being; be in appearance; appear

to29—(used before a verb to show it is the infinitive, but not before can, could, may, might, will, would, shall, should, must, ought to; sometimes left out when the verb is understood. note the following patterns)

make5—to force or cause (a person to do something / a thing to happen)

thing6—an act; deed

happen1—to take place

without1a—not having; lacking

cause1—something which produces an effect; a person, thing, or event that makes something happen

or2—(often with either; used before the last of a set of possibilities)

reason1—the cause of an event; the explanation or excuse for an action luck1 – that which happens, either good or bad, to a person in the course of events by, or as if by, chance; fate; fortune

good1-having the right qualities

or2 – (often with either; used before the last of a set of possibilities)

bad1 – not of acceptable quality; poor

fortune1 – fate; chance, esp. as an important influence on one 's life; luck

%532 **chance** n 3 %

£ ldoce definition £

(a) possibility; likelihood that something will happen:@I You'd have more chance of catching the train if you got a bus to the station instead of walking

$ Mini ldoce definition in normal English $

(a) possibility; likelihood that something will happen

& Mini ldoce extended definition text &

a1 – one

possibility1 – the state or fact of being possible

likelihood1*

the1 – (used when it is clearly understood who or what is meant)

fact1 – something that has actual existence or an event that has actually happened or is happening; something true

or2 – (often with either; used before the last of a set of possibilities)

degree1 – (the size of) a step or stage in a set of steps or stages rising in order from lowest to highest

of1 – (of qualities, possessions, etc.) belonging to x; that x has

be7c – (as a connecting verb with adjectives)

likely1 – probable; expected

that15 – (used for introducing various kinds of clause)

something1 – some unstated or unknown thing

will1 – (used for expressing the simple future tense)

happen1 – to take place

%533 **chance** n 4 %

£ ldoce definition £

a favourable occasion;@S OPPORTUNITY@P:@I I never miss a chance of playing football. | If I give you a second chance will you promise to be good?

$ Mini ldoce definition in normal English $
a favourable occasion; opportunity
& Mini ldoce extended definition text &
a1 – one
favourable2 – (of conditions) advantageous; favouring ^2 (3)
occasion1 – a time when something happens
opportunity1*
a1 – one
favourable2 – (of conditions) advantageous; favouring ^2 (3)
opportune1*
of1 – (of qualities, possessions, etc.) belonging to x; that x has
time15 – the particular moment at which something happens
right9 – most suitable; best for a particular purpose
for1 – that is / are intended to belong to, be given to, or used for the purpose of
a1 – one
purpose1 – an intention or plan; reason for an action
moment2 – the time for doing something; occasion
or2 – (often with either; used before the last of a set of possibilities)
occasion1 – a time when something happens
for1 – that is / are intended to belong to, be given to, or used for the purpose of
do18 – (with actions and nonmaterial things)
something1 – some unstated or unknown thing

%534 **chance** n 5 %
£ ldoce definition £
a risk:@I That's a chance I'll have to take!
$Mini ldoce definition in normal English $
a risk
&Mini ldoce extended definition text &
a1 – one
risk1 – a danger (of); something that may have a (stated) bad result

%535 **change** v 1 %
£ ldoce definition £

to (cause to) become different:@I In Autumn the leaves change from green to brown. | You've changed such a lot since I last saw you. | He's been a changed man since his wife died
$ Mini Idoce definition in normal English $
to (cause to) become different
& Mini Idoce extended definition text &
to29 – (used before a verb to show it is the infinitive, but not before can, could, may, might, will, would, shall, should, must, ought to; sometimes left out when the verb is understood. note the following patterns)
cause7 – to lead to; be the cause of
to29 – (used before a verb to show it is the infinitive, but not before can, could, may, might, will, would, shall, should, must, ought to; sometimes left out when the verb is understood. note the following patterns)
become1 – to come to be
different1 – unlike; not of the same kind

%536 **change** n 15 %
£ Idoce definition £
(an example of) the act or result of changing:@I If we are to avoid defeat we need a change of leadership. | The doctor said the girl had taken a change for the better but was still seriously ill
$ Mini Idoce definition in normal English $
(an example of) the act or result of changing
& Mini Idoce extended definition text &
an1 – (used when the following word begins with a vowel sound) a
example1 – something taken from a number of things of the same kind, which shows the usual quality of the rest or shows a general rule
of1 – (of qualities, possessions, etc.) belonging to x; that x has
the1 – (used when it is clearly understood who or what is meant)
act8 – fml a thing done; deed (of the stated type)
or2 – (often with either; used before the last of a set of possibilities)
result2 – what happens because of an action or event
of1 – (of qualities, possessions, etc.) belonging to x; that x has
change1 – to (cause to) become different

%537 **character** n 2 %
£ ldoce definition £
the combination of qualities which makes a thing, event, place, etc., different from another:@l This town isn't interesting let's go somewhere else with more character
$ Mini ldoce definition in normal English $
the combination of qualities which makes a thing, event, place, etc., different from another
& Mini ldoce extended definition text &
the1 – (used when it is clearly understood who or what is meant)
combination2*
the1 – (used when it is clearly understood who or what is meant)
state1 – a condition in which a person or thing is; way of being
of9 – that is (equal to)
be2 – (forms the pass. voice of verbs)
combine1 – to (cause to) come together, unite, act together, or join together
of8 – (before a phr. that is like an object in grammar) directed towards or done to
quality2 – something typical of a person or material
which2b – (used for showing relationship between things) being the one (s) that
make3 – to put into a certain state, position, etc.
a1 – one
thing1 – any material object; an object that need not or cannot be named
event1 – a happening, usu. an important one
place1 – a particular part of space or position in space
different1 – unlike; not of the same kind
from14 – (in a state of protection, prevention, or separation) with regard to
another6 – a different one

%538 **character** n 3 %
£ ldoce definition £
the qualities which make a person different from another; moral nature:@l The king is a man of good and noble character
$ Mini ldoce definition in normal English $
the qualities which make a person different from another; moral nature

& Mini ldoce extended definition text &

the1—(used when it is clearly understood who or what is meant)

quality2—something typical of a person or material

which2b—(used for showing relationship between things) being the one (s) that

make3—to put into a certain state, position, etc.

a1—one

person1—a human being considered as having a character of his or her own, or as being different from all others

different1—unlike; not of the same kind

from14—(in a state of protection, prevention, or separation) with regard to

another6—a different one

moral1—concerning character, behaviour, or actions, considered or judged as being good or evil, right or wrong; ethical

nature1a—the qualities which make someone or something different from others; character

%539 **character** n 6 %

£ ldoce definition £

a person in a book, play, etc.: @lI find all the characters in his new play amusing and interesting

$ Mini ldoce definition in normal English $

a person in a book, play, etc.

& Mini ldoce extended definition text &

a1—one

person1—a human being considered as having a character of his or her own, or as being different from all others

in1—(so as to be) contained by (something with depth, length, and height); within, inside

a1—one

book1—a collection of sheets of paper fastened together as a thing to be read, or to be written in

play3a—a piece of writing to be performed in a theatre

%540 **charge** v 1 %

£ ldoce definition £

to ask in payment:@I How much do you charge for your eggs? | This hotel charged me {pound sterling}5 for a room for the night. | They've always charged a tax on bottles of wine brought into this country@R—see@S COST, ORDER@P (USAGE)

$ Mini ldoce definition in normal English $
to ask in payment
& Mini ldoce extended definition text &
to29 – (used before a verb to show it is the infinitive, but not before can, could, may, might, will, would, shall, should, must, ought to; sometimes left out when the verb is understood. note the following patterns)
ask3 – to demand (something, such as a price); expect
in19 – as a / an; by way of
payment2*
an1
amount1 – quantity or sum
of1 – (of qualities, possessions, etc.) belonging to x; that x has
money1 – pieces of metal made into coins, or paper notes with their value printed on them, given and taken in buying and selling
to29 – (used before a verb to show it is the infinitive, but not before can, could, may, might, will, would, shall, should, must, ought to; sometimes left out when the verb is understood. note the following patterns)
be2 – (forms the pass. voice of verbs)
pay1 – to give (money) for goods bought, work done, etc.

%541 **charge** n 9 %
£ ldoce definition £
care; control; responsibility:@I I've got charge of your class tomorrow so you must do as I tell you
$ Mini ldoce definition in normal English $
care; control; responsibility
& Mini ldoce extended definition text &
care3 – charge; keeping; protection; responsibility
control5 – the power to control, command, influence, or direct
responsibility1*
the1 – (used when it is clearly understood who or what is meant)
condition1 – a state of being or existence
of9 – that is (equal to)
be7c – (as a connecting verb with adjectives)
responsible1 – having the duty of looking after someone or something, so that one can be blamed (by the stated person) if things go wrong

%542 **charge** n 12 %
£ ldoce definition £
a spoken or written statement blaming a person for a crime, for breaking the law, or for doing something morally wrong:@l The charge was murder
$ Mini ldoce definition in normal English $
a spoken or written statement blaming a person for a crime, for breaking the law, or for doing something morally wrong
& Mini ldoce extended definition text &
a1 – one
speak5 – to express or say
or2 – (often with either; used before the last of a set of possibilities)
write2 – to express and record in this way, or sometimes by means of a typewriter
statement1*
something1 – some unstated or unknown thing
that16 – not fml (used as the subject of a defining relative clause, to mean) who or which
be2 – (forms the pass. voice of verbs)
state7 – to say, express, or put into words, esp. formally
a1 – one
write2 – to express and record in this way, or sometimes by means of a typewriter
or2 – (often with either; used before the last of a set of possibilities)
speak5 – to express or say
declaration2*
a1 – one
statment1*
give5 – to produce; supply with
information1 – (something which gives) knowledge in the form of facts
in1 – (so as to be) contained by (something with depth length and height); within; inside
a1 – one
court1 – a room or building in which law cases can be heard and judged
of1 – (of qualities, possessions, etc.) belonging to x; that x has
law2 – the whole body of such rules of a country
of1 – (of qualities, possessions, etc.) belonging to x; that x has

a1 – one
formal1 – ceremonial; according to accepted rules or customs
kind1 – a group, the members of which all have certain qualities; type; sort
blame1 – to consider (someone) responsible for (something bad)
a1 – one
person1 – a human being considered as having a character of his or her own, or as being different from all others
for11 – because of
a1 – one
crime1 – an offence which is punishable by law
for11 – because of
break6 – to disobey; not keep; not act in accordance with
the10 – (used with a singular noun to make it general followed by a singular verb)
law1 – a rule that is supported by the power of government and that governs the behaviour of members of a society
or2 – (often with either; used before the last of a set of possibilities)
for11 – because of
do18 – (with actions and nonmaterial things)
something1 – some unstated or unknown thing
morally2*
with_regard_to1*
regard5 – in / with regard to regarding - see as for (usage)
regarding1*
right7-just; morally good
or2 – (often with either; used before the last of a set of possibilities)
good3 – morally right; in accordance with religious standards
behaviour1 – way of behaving
wrong6 – evil; against moral standards

Author Index

Subject Index